Arne Heise

The Socioeconomics of Economics

Studien zur Staatswissenschaft – Studies in Economic Governance

herausgegeben von
edited by

Prof. Dr. Arne Heise

Band 9

LIT

Arne Heise

The Socioeconomics of Economics

Essays on the Construction of the Economic Discipline and its Critique

LIT

This book is printed on acid-free paper.

Bibliographic information published by the Deutsche Nationalbibliothek
The Deutsche Nationalbibliothek lists this publication in the Deutsche Nationalbibliografie; detailed bibliographic data are available on the Internet at http://dnb.d-nb.de.

ISBN 978-3-643-91127-8 (pb)
ISBN 978-3-643-96127-8 (PDF)

A catalogue record for this book is available from the British Library.

Klosbachstr. 107
CH-8032 Zürich
Tel. +41 (0) 44-251 75 05
E-Mail: zuerich@lit-verlag.ch http://www.lit-verlag.ch
Distribution:
In the UK: Global Book Marketing, e-mail: mo@centralbooks.com
In North America: Independent Publishers Group, e-mail: orders@ipgbook.com
In Germany: LIT Verlag Fresnostr. 2, D-48159 Münster
Tel. +49 (0) 2 51-620 32 22, Fax +49 (0) 2 51-922 60 99, e-mail: vertrieb@lit-verlag.de
e-books are available at www.litwebshop.de

Contents

Preface

The economic discipline has always been an object of investigation. But unlike in former times, when methodological and epistemological developments had been the object of historians of economic thought, recently the focus of inquiry shifted towards the constitution, organisation and performativity of the economic discipline. It was intuatively felt that the economic discipline is different from other social sciences: Unlike sociology or the political sciences, economics has reached a state of 'paradigmatic consolidation' which, in a Kuhnian sense, gives the dominant paradigm a state of 'normal science' within which most academic economists pursue their scientific work without questioning the underlying epistemological and ontological assumptions. Unlike sociology or political science, economics is a very hierarchically structured science with a handfull of (US) university departments and (US) academic journals controlling the field. Economists often consider themselves superior to other social scientists based on stricter methodological limits and higher methodical standards – with the invasion of ever more economic methods into other social sciences (something which has been termed 'economic imperialism'), theses sentiments appear to get some substance. Moreover, with the triumph of neoliberalism over the past three to four decades, orchestrated by a group of economists organised in the (in)famous Mont-Pelerin Society, not only became John Maynard Keynes's dictum of

> *"the ideas of economists and political philosopers, both when they are right and when they are wrong, are more powerfull than is commonly understood. Indeed the world is ruled by little else" (Keynes 1936: 383)*

apparently true, but the performativity of economics became an object of inquiry.

Against this background, it does not come as a surprise that not only sociologists and philosopher of science, but also economists themselves started to replace intuition with facts and theoretical argumentation. And this is where the present book hopes to make a contribution: the articles collected in this volume are not meant as a mere self-reflection of the discipline – how is it organised, who is important, what about networks of collaboration etc. – but adress questions that are mainly posed by outsiders to the economic scientific community. Primarily students but also politicians, practitioners and media folk – as consumers of the output of the economic profession in terms of economic education, advice or transferable kowledge – are increasingly irritated by the state of the discipline: what happened to the various approaches that constituted economics until the second half of the 20th century? Should economics not become more interdisciplinary? Would it not be healthier for the profession if the competition among different economic paradigms were stronger? Do phenomena such as the recent 'World Financial Crisis' - which the profession obviously has neither been able to predict nor helped to prepare ready-made remedies – somehow impact on the organisation and development of the discipline? And if so, how should economics be transformed? Can we expect the economic discipline to be 'self-correcting' or do we need external 'stimulation' or support?

To answer such questions, economic methods may help and economists may contribute to an understanding of the working and failures of the 'market for economic ideas'. Yet, economic methods are not sufficient but must be supplemented by methods of other social sciences and the humanities in order to provide tools to present the embeddedness of the individual scientists and, indeed, the entire scientific community. This kind of multi- or interdisciplinary approach constitutes 'socioeconomics' as proposed by Eduard Heimann (1929) – and is used in most of the essays collected in this volume. The essays have all been published previously – but scattered across a number of different academic journals. By bringing them together under one cover, I wish to make this rather new research area – the socioeconomics of economics – more visible and the essays better accessible.

References

Heimann, E. (1929); Soziale Theorie des Kapitalismus, Leipzig

Keynes, J.M. (1936); General Theory of Employment, Interest and Money, London

Part One

The Construction of a Science

One

'When the facts change, I change my mind...' Some developments in the economic scientific community and the situation in Germany*

1. Introduction

According to Thomas S. Kuhn (1962), scientific progress does not advance straightforwardly but is marked again and again by key breaking points, which can be referred to as scientific revolutions. The trigger for these breaking points in the cognitive process, which is associated with a change in the basic explanatory pattern or paradigm[1], is the deviation of the model predictions from the empirically measurable reality. In the natural sciences, such crisis-laden developments are often due to new and improved measurements based on new technologies. In the humanities and social sciences, it is sudden socio-economic developments that (seem to) bust down the framework of the paradigm.

A "crisis" of this sort, however, is a necessary but insufficient condition for a scientific revolution. The existence of an alternative explanation – a new scientific paradigm – is a further condition that must be met. In this sense, the "Keynesian revolution" after the Great Depression of the 1930s can be interpreted as a paradigm shift from the neoclassical, partial analytical theory of marginal utility to total analytical macroeconomics, just as the return of the microeconomic-based general equilibrium theory in the form of new classical macroeconomics (NCM) can be understood as a

* Originally published in real-world economics review, issue no. 62, 15 December 2012, pp. 83-97

[1] Thomas Kuhn's notion of a 'paradigm' carries many similarities with Imre Lakatos' 'research programmes'(see Lakatos 1978) and they are often used interchangeably. However, Kuhn's approach is more conducive to understanding radical changes, while Lakatos' approach sheds more light on the resilience of (dominating) research programmes (or paradigms). I will refer to each of the concepts in its due context.

"counterrevolution" (or as it is sometimes called, a "rational expectations-revolution") after the stagflation of the 1970s that was so empirically fatal for Keynesianism.

On a politically pragmatic level, the global financial crisis of 2008-2009, which sparked the world's worst depression since the 1930s, swept away the state intervention scepticism that derived from the market euphoria of NCM as abruptly as it did the certainty of academic economists that they had actually found in NCM an analytical instrument that was compatible with reality. For example, Olivier Blanchard (2008), professor at the elite US university MIT and chief economist of the IMF, affirmed in 2008 that macroeconomics was in good condition because after the long debates during the "counterrevolution" in the 1970s, a broader consensus (or what KUHN would describe as a paradigm) had taken hold in economics: the so-called D(ynamic) S(tochastic) G(eneral) E(quilibrium) models, which were, in particular, also seen as empirically saturated once they allow some rigidities in their assumptions.[2]

Barely two years later (Blanchard/Dell'Ariccia/Mauro 2010) – after the global financial crisis – he had to admit that the stability of the economic interactions in the DSGE models and economic policy's single-minded focus on price stability (combined with the simultaneous failure of fiscal policy intervention) had had too much of a "lulling" effect and that economics required a reorientation. The Institute for New Economic Thinking (INET), which was founded in the fall of 2009 by a multimillion dollar

[2] Such rigidities then make New Keynesian macroeconomics (NKM) out of new classical macroeconomics (NCM), but paradigmatically both versions of the DSGE approach make up the neoclassical mainstream benchmark model, as Blanchard (2008:. 5ff) maintains: "The new tools developed by the new classicals came to dominate. The facts emphasised by the new-Keynesians forced imperfections back into the benchmark model. A largely common vision has emerged, ...: It starts from a general equilibrium structure, in which individuals maximise the expected present value of utility, firms maximise their value, and markets clear. Then, it introduces a twist, be it an imperfection or the closing of a particular set of markets, and works out the general equilibrium implications. It then performs a numerical simulation, based on calibration, showing that the model performs well. It ends with a welfare assessment." This "fraternity" between NKM and NCM leaves post-Keynesians doubtful as to whether NKM should actually refer to itself as "Keynesian"; see Rotheim (1998), Davidson (1994).

donation by financial guru George Soros, and whose Advisory Board[3] consists of a number of well-known representatives of the DSGE mainstream, from George Akerlof and Joseph Stiglitz to Kenneth Rogoff and Jeffrey Sachs, supports these reorientation efforts and recognises "problems and inadequacies within our current economic system and the modes of thought used to comprehend recent and past catastrophic developments in the world economy. The Institute embraces the professional responsibility to think beyond these inadequate methods and models and will support the emergence of new paradigms in the understanding of cconomic processes." (INET n.d.)

So is economics about to experience a new scientific revolution? In addition to the "crisis" as a trigger, alternative approaches that could replace the dominant mainstream paradigm are also necessary. In the following discussion, an assessment of heterodox developments as a basis for such a paradigm shift (Section 2) will be provided. Based on developments within mainstream thinking, it will be investigated whether the ground is fertile for an effective reorientation (Section 3). Finally, the design of the German academic economics market will be briefly discussed in order to appraise the specific German conditions for a paradigm shift (Section 4).

2. The neoclassical benchmark model and recent developments in the global community?

"Normal" economic science[4] is undoubtedly represented by the neoclassical paradigm of a market or exchange economy. It consists of various schools within the exchange-theoretical axiomatics – NCM or NKM – and is challenged by alternative paradigms – e.g. postKeynesianism or neo-Ricardianism. Protests by French university students provide evidence that

---

[3] Indeed, of the current 31 members of the Advisory Board, only two - Duncan Foley und Paul Davidson – had vigorously advocated for a "New Economic Thinking" before the world financial crisis.

[4] Occasionally, social science is presented as a pre-paradigmatic science in which no consensus on an axiomatic core has yet emerged. This is certainly not the case for economics, as K.W. Rothschild (2005: 440) corroborated: "More than in any other social science, we have in economics a sharp division between a ruling mainstream and a multitude of 'heterodox' theories which have in common that they diverge in one way or another from the neoclassical mainstream."

dissatisfaction with the self-referentiality and compartmentalisation ("autism") of the highly formalised neoclassical paradigm has transformed into a worldwide attack on neoclassical orthodoxy. Many "critical" economists have joined this movement (see Fullbrook 2003), which received further fuel from the developments of the "real global financial crisis". In the following, the hallmarks of the "neoclassical benchmark model" will be explicated and the burgeoning critiques of the model will be presented. This is followed by a consideration of possible alternatives, which is important because science does not permit any "theory vacuums". If there were no available alternatives that could provide consistent substitute interpretations in addition to mere theory criticism, the dominance of neoclassical economics would remain safe for now.[5]

The objective is not to build a straw man which can then be arbitrarily knocked around but rather to describe the "neoclassical benchmark model" – the exemplar of normal science – as accurately as possible. Only in this manner can we prevent criticism from getting lost in the fog of unclear concepts. And I would like to try to examine this description with the help of the Lakatosian idea of an axiomatic core, the assumptions of the "protective belt" and the resultant postulates. The exchange theoretical core of neoclassical economics can be summarised in three axioms: (1) The gross substitution axiom, (2) the rationality axiom, and (3) the ergodicity axiom.

The gross substitution axiom states that, in principle, all goods (and services) are mutually interchangeable. This ensures that the relative price can function as an allocation tool and guarantees the existence of market equilibria (see Reijnierse/van Gellekom/Potters 2002). The rationality axiom states that all economic activity is goal-oriented and consistent – a

[5] Actually, this appears to be the approach of some mainstream economists: simply to deny any valuable alternative: see Schultz (2012). However, my approach is not the extreme opposite – i.e. to deny mainstream (neoclassical) economics its status as scientific theory (as has been done by Lee (2012) or to reduce it to 'pseudo-knowledge' (as has been done by Latsis 1972) – but normatively to deny a monistic understanding of economics and positivistically to inquire into the likelihood of a paradigmatic shift (or, for that matter, paradigmatic opening).

prerequisite for the benefit-maximising homo economicus. Finally, the ergodicity axiom allows for the idea of the stochastic-deterministic development of all variables that are important for economic decisions and necessary for the formation of rational expectations (see Davidson 1984) – rational expectations being a stochastic extension of the overly simplistic assumption of perfect foresight. Economic agents are only able to do what neoclassical economics demands of them if these axioms are valid: optimal consumption, investment, labour supply and labour demand plans have all been established. Furthermore, portfolio decisions and numerous other decisions must also be optimised. In short, every circumstance must be optimised.

If certain assumptions from the "protective belt" are added to these core axioms – typically assumptions about atomistic market competition, infinite adjustment speeds, complete price flexibility and the absence of transaction and information costs – then the following postulates can be derived:

(1) the postulate of a general market equilibrium in either its classical (Say's Law) or neoclassical garb (Walras's Law); (2) (the monetary neutrality postulate (classical quantity theory) with its implicit dichotomy of real and monetary economic spheres; (3) the policy ineffectiveness postulate (Ricardo-Barro equivalence theorem); and (4) the welfare and harmony postulate.

The critics concentrate on these four extremely strong implications of the neoclassical benchmark model, but first we should highlight their importance again.

The particular strength of the neoclassical benchmark model lies in its deductive rigor and coherence. However, this does not mean anything other than that the aforementioned postulates represent more than just doctrines that can either be accepted or (often intuitively) simply rejected. Rather, when the axioms (core) and basic assumptions (the "protective belt") are ultimately accepted, transcendental logic leads to several logically indisputable results.[6] First, there is one "best of all worlds".[7] Perfect markets always reproduce optimal results, even if they are hit by so-called "exogenous shocks". These results show that the existing supply will always find its corresponding demand and that economic agents are free from monetary or nominal illusions; therefore, neither monetary nor fiscal policy interventions can have any positive influence whatsoever on economic agents, who are oriented toward real variables (real income, relative exchange values, real balance, etc.). Ultimately, this interpretation of reality culminates in the conclusion that this "best of all worlds" not only maximises individual economic agents' welfare under the restriction of finite resources, but also does not even require them to engage in any trite behaviour such as benevolent altruism. Instead, individual, self-interested, "rational" behaviour will lead to this result. Adam Smith's famous "invisible hand" guarantees that the common good does not have to suffer under the (supposedly realistically described) behaviour of self-interested individuals.

I have no intention of suggesting that it requires a denial of reality to accept the predictions of this "Panglossian" model.[8] All too easily, the assumptions of the "protective belt" – especially the assumption of atomistic competition and full price flexibility – can be altered with reference to disruptive institutions and organisations, restrictive (e.g. in the labour market) or missing rules (e.g. for competition) in such a manner that reality is restored

---

[6] To my knowledge, there has thus far been only one successful strike against the deductive rigor of the neoclassical benchmark model: the refutation of the price-driven exchange equilibrium during the socalled Cambridge capital controversy. As fundamental as this criticism was, it failed to yield any consequences. The neoclassical side (U.S. Cambridge) had to admit that the equilibrium postulate could logically be properly sustained only under further restrictive assumptions – the "single capital good world" – but argued that, on the other hand, the anomaly exposed by the classical proponents (UK Cambridge) was empirically insignificant and therefore did not warrant further consideration. This continues to be the modus operandi today. (see Hodgson 1999: 46ff.; Cohen/Harcourt 2003)

[7] Reference is made here to Voltaire's critique of the optimistic world view of Gottfried Wilhelm Leibniz's religious philosophy; see Voltaire (1759/1971).

[8] Dr. Pangloss is Candide's instructor in Voltaire's Candide: or, The Optimist; see Voltaire (1759/1971).

into the explanatory framework of the model. It seems more significant to me that this Panglossian world provides an incredible intellectual stimulus as a reference scale and, more particularly, it strongly advocates some exceedingly clear economic policy implications: of course, the basic assumptions are rarely fulfilled in the real world, but it is imperative to approximate them as closely as possible through market-creating, market-enhancing and market-liberalising measures.

Whenever this is impossible or undesired, for example due to social or sociopolitical reasons, the consequences – namely, declining welfare and market imbalances – must be accepted and legitimised. The "protective belt" creates a buffer against reality but also protects the axiomatic core for it is all too easily forgotten that on the one hand, the postulates are ultimately grounded in the axioms, and on the other, that the retained image of actors rationally optimising their actions is a synthetic one with no analytical epistemological value. In other words, these axioms were established a priori; they did not arise a posteriori from the analysis of economic events.[9]

The most well-known criticism takes aim at the basic assumptions of the "protective belt". The call for "microfoundations" has led to the prominence of numerous theoretical approaches which not only introduce ad hoc deviations from the assumption of full price flexibility, for instance, but which also derive these deviations from the rational behaviour of economic agents. It would not be wrong to see this as the common link among all the models that are labelled or operate under the name "neo-Keynesianism".[10] The Keynesian element is generally limited to describing persistent market imbalances, especially in the labour market in the form of unemployment.[11] Ultimately, this means either that there are contradictions between the axioms of the "core" and the basic assumptions of the "pro-

[9] Although axioms are distinguished by their normativity, economists have always tried to portray exchange as a fundamental anthropological fact of human activity; see e.g. Smith (1776/1977: 16). For criticism, see e.g. Heinsohn (1983) and Heise (1990).
[10] See Gordon (1990); Mankiw/Romer (1991).
[11] Especially in German-speaking countries, this occasionally led to discussions of "critical neoclassicists"; see e.g. Schneider (1988).

tective belt" or that there is room for interpretation within the basic assumptions and thus deductive divergences must exist. In fact, the rationality axiom can enter into conflict with the price flexibility assumptions if a collective (political) rationality (rational choice) is justifiable beyond the individual (economic) rationality. Institutions and regulations which increase the benefits of the collective (to the detriment of the community of individuals) by limiting price flexibility can thus be explained (see Olson 1965). In this case, the attractiveness of the neoclassical benchmark model remains justified, as it continues to explain how such incentives must be designed in order to stop the welfare-impairing rent seeking of the collective (cartels, trade unions, etc.) (see Olson 1982).

The situation looks a little different when the assumption of complete information is put into practical effect, such that all information may indeed be present but not equally available to all economic agents and there are rational reasons to exploit these information asymmetries. Joseph Stiglitz's information economy is certainly the most well-known approach that not only develops the consequences of information asymmetry – i.e. market failure due to moral hazard and adverse selection, resulting in long-lasting supply disequilibria or massive temporary aberrations, as recently experienced – but increasingly emphasises that such market failure is not an occasional anomaly of otherwise optimally functioning markets but rather an extremely widespread and therefore universal, nearly systematic phenomenon of market interaction. Information asymmetries acquire particular significance in futures markets such as the monetary, credit and financial markets. Labour markets are also affected to a great extent. None of the previously mentioned postulates hold up under such conditions. The Panglossian world is thus suddenly rendered completely unrelated to a satisfactory interpretation of reality, although the core axioms remain untouched. Stiglitz sees in this a new economic paradigm (see Stiglitz 2002), because the concept of the "perfect market" is consistently replaced by the concept of the "failing market". In accordance with my proposed distinction between different paradigms on the one hand and different schools within a paradigm on the other hand, the latter would probably apply (see also Davidson 2012: 60). In any case, the "failing market" implies broad regulatory and political interventions and thereby justifies a "strong" and present state, which could not be further removed from the "neoclassical benchmark model".

The criticism aimed at the axioms of the paradigmatic core has a broader scope. On the one hand, the rationality axiom of the neoclassical benchmark model is rejected by the experimental, evolutionary and institutional complexity economics[12]; on the other hand, the ergodicity and the gross substitution axioms are regarded as unacceptable by post-Keynesianism. The former criticism is aimed at the allocative decision logic of economic agents – and is therefore microeconomically oriented – while the latter emphasises primarily the macroeconomic implications, in particular the representation of multiple equilibria in a rejection of the general equilibrium of the neoclassical benchmark model.

The rationality axiom states that the actions of economic agents are target-oriented and consistent. In order for this axiom to be deductively expanded to the above mentioned postulates and to action predictions that are testable, it must be specified: the material utility maximisation (e.g. as income or profit maximisation) is assumed as guidance and consistency is understood as the transitivity of preference orderings. Economics Nobel Laureate Vernon L. Smith labels such a rationality axiom[13] produced by a self-interested and rational Homo economicus "constructivist" and contrasts it against the "ecological" rationality axiom, in which economic agents can act with "bounded rationality" in different environments. Experimental economics shows on the one hand that the "constructivist" rationality axiom clashes with the "harmony postulate" when behaviour interdependencies lead to non-cooperative behaviour (prisoner and other cooperation dilemmas or free rider behaviour) of rational, self-interested individuals

---

[12] In no way are experimental, evolutionary and institutional economics identical. Experimental economics can be understood as a research laboratory of strategic interaction in which the behavioural hypotheses of normal science are tested (see e.g. Amann 2007). Evolutionary and institutional economics, on the other hand, emphasise the importance of norms, conventions, routines, etc. for human behaviour and investigate their formation and variations (see M. Hodgson 1999: 127ff.). In the broadest sense, the neo-Marxist approaches of the French Regulation School and the American Social Structure of Accumulation School are included here (see e.g. Boyer 1990; Kotz/McDonough/Reich 1994).

[13] And he imputes it to his version of the neoclassical benchmark model: the "Standard Socioeconomic Science Model" (SSSM); see Smith (2002).

and thus lead to sub-optimal social welfare; a phenomenon which is sometimes called "rationality with regret". Fortunately, this need not overly worry us, as experimental, evolutionary and institutional economics all describe numerous environments (norms such as reciprocity or institutions such as collective bargaining systems) in which "irrationality without regret" leads to cooperation among economic agents and thus increases social welfare. But of course this is also bad news for the neoclassical benchmark model: people all too rarely behave like the idealised Homo economicus. In Adam Smith's time, the assumption of a rational, self-interested economic agent was merely an attempt to hint at the harmony of utility maximisation for both the individual and society as a whole without recourse to an overly optimistic view of man. But in the neoclassical benchmark model, the individual optimiser has been turned into a necessary building block for a Panglossian world, without whom it could not be consistently sustained.[14]

Post-Keynesianism ultimately rejects the ergodicity and gross substitution axioms. One of the central propositions of John Maynard Keynes' General Theory is that in the neoclassical benchmark model the necessary information for the optimisation of decisions by economic agents is neither equally available to all market participants nor can it be sufficiently processed by all. Above all, in many cases – especially when it comes to information about future developments – it simply does not exist, and thus no probability distributions can be objectively set. The issue is one of fundamental uncertainty, not merely one concerned with risk-carrying situations. In order to take any action in such a situation – any discussion of optimisation in the commonly used sense can be dispensed with – the existence of behavioural norms/routines, instincts and institutions is required. Keynes and post Keynesianism place particular emphasis on one institution – money – and one instinct – the animal spirits – in their considerations. The "animal spirits" are surely the attempt to create a rudimentary and expandable theory of expectation formation – in the face of fundamental uncertainty – where money is the one asset that secures economic agents' reproduction ability and is thus assigned a liquidity premium. Money is by

---

[14] And with whom it is also unsustainable: see "rationality with regrets".

no means being "invented" in this theoretical consideration in order to reduce exchange costs; rather, economic agents project their uncertainty about the future onto those assets whose excess of liquidity premium over carrying costs are greatest.

The disposability of money ultimately determines the neutral position of an economy – thus money is neither a neutral exchange medium (neutrality postulate) nor is the economy's neutral position necessarily or even typically in a state of overall balance (equilibrium postulate). Furthermore, the policy effectiveness postulate can also no longer be maintained under these conditions. In this far-reaching rejection of the Panglossian postulates, the friendly relationship of post-Keynesianism to neo-Keynesianism can no doubt be seen, though as shown above, the basis for the rejections are quite different.

As already noted, criticism alone is insufficient if it fails to offer a constructive and consistent alternative interpretation of reality. And of course it is to be expected that the neoclassical "model tree" is much more thickly covered with leaves than the trees in the gardens of post- or neo-Keynesianism and experimental, evolutionary and institutional economics, considering the imbalance in the number of gardeners cultivating them. However, some quite serious intrinsic problems and shortcomings of the critics have been identified, which may be able to explain why the dominance of the neoclassical benchmark model is still so strong: (1) In spite of all the objections to the constructivist rationality axiom, there is still no replacement construction in sight which could substitute the Homo economicus. And perhaps there is no simple model of action upon which economics can build – but then comprehensive microbased, prescriptive models would be nearly unthinkable. Perhaps this perspective is so worrying that even experimental economists such as Vernon L. Smith refuse to reject the constructivist rationality axiom categorically (cf. Smith 2002: 505), claiming instead that only personal, strategic interaction has been experimentally debunked. For more impersonal, market-based and contractual interaction, however, there is much to be said for stricter selfish-materialistic rational behaviour, though with limited information. (2) To this day, post Keynesian theory has neglected one of its central elements: a comprehensive theory of expectation formation.[15] Without a clearer idea of how expectations are formed in conditions of fundamental uncertainty, the ex ante forecast quality of this construction of reality remains limited, and the ex post forecast test can be passed all too easily via the introduction of ad hoc "animal spirits" (see Heise 1993). On the other hand, post-Keynesianism can be connected to all the evolutionary and institutional "bounded rationality" approaches as well as to a reductionist expectancy theory and to a constructive dialogue with neo-Keynesianism. (3) Neo-Keynesianism is probably the most advanced in its development of a "new neoclassical synthesis" as a substitute for the neoclassical benchmark model[16] – which is certainly also due to the fact that it is not an alternative paradigm but simply an alternative theoretical school within the same paradigm. However, its derivable postulates ("failing markets") are sufficiently removed from the criticised mainstream model so as to appear heuristically as an alternative, although one which can not be epistemologically separated from the mainstream model at all. It might be more consistent here to take the paradigmatic step out of the exchange theoretical basis of the neoclassical benchmark model and seek to close ranks with post-Keynesianism and evolutionary and institutional economics.

3. Dominant mainstream or "new plurality" – where is the journey heading for?

Long before the recent global financial crisis and its consequences for the self-image of the economics profession, Robert Clower (1989) described the state of economics as "hopeless, but not serious". His intention was to criticise the constriction of economics to the reductionism of the formal, axiomatic DSGE mainstream. Economics had grown too far removed from the type of science that could contribute solutions to real problems, and instead was wallowing in the self-referentiality of the unending "footnote discussions" it generated. Robert Solow (1989: 37) rightly points out that

[15] This is particularly surprising, as the concept of "bounded rationality" from Herbert Simon (1968) and George Shakles (1955) was an early attempt to do so, and the neoclassical theory of rational expectations would really have to have been challenge enough.
[16] See e.g. Woodford (2003); Carlin/Soskice (2006).

a science that develops a paradigmatic core will become a "normal science" in which droves of economists will produce scientific results that range "from very bad to excellent, with a median somewhere near O.K." Criticism is thus reserved here not for the sprouting of findings that fail to promise to directly solve major global problems, but rather for the size and dominance of this "knowledge tree" which no longer lets in enough light for the growth of other "knowledge trees". But don't the aforementioned variety of alternative theories and perhaps even alternative paradigms point to a sufficient plurality that can in turn flourish now that the mainstream approach has been beset by skepticism? Is it still true that "When the facts change, I change my mind"?[17]

Before this question can be answered, one must first note that the alternative theories and paradigms have received very little propagation, and in recent decades economics has been increasingly restricted to the DSGE mainstream. Let's take the German case: While in the early 1980s only about half of German academic economists considered neoclassical mainstream monism worthwhile, 20 years later this figure had grown to 80%, and it continues to rise, as the more critical opinions are predominantly held by elderly scientists striving toward retirement (cf. Frey/Humbert/Schneider 2007). Fred Lee (2009) puts the number of heterodox academic economists in Germany at about 30, which is no more than 5% of all economists (at the professorial level) teaching at German universities. The most serious problem, though, is that this vast majority of orthodox mainstream economists – due to their monistic concept of science – simply do not take note of heterodox approaches (in terms of a plurality of economics) (Lee/Harley 1998).

Under these conditions, a new scientific revolution – i.e. a paradigm shift away from the equilibrium-centred harmony postulate of the DSGE models that are optimistically inclined toward the market and sceptical of intervention, away from the methodology of optimisation analysis, away from the notion that monism alone has the right to explain economic phenomena – could be expected only if the older economists were to accept

[17] This saying is attributed to John Maynard Keynes, who was responding to a perceived change in his position; see Malabre (1994: 220).

an extensive loss of identity and a devaluation of their hard-earned qualifications and the younger economists were willing to risk starting almost completely anew. But what incentives do they have to confront all of the associated uncertainties?

If we consider the economist as a non-self-interested individual whose sole desire is to be able to understand and describe the economic interrelations of the real world as accurately as possible, then the imminent arrival of a broad reorientation phase in economics would doubtlessly be expected. If not now, then when? However, if economists were such a species, then it would be incomprehensible for the plurality of methods and paradigms to be so strongly and consistently limited, as described above. This becomes understandable, though, when the career interests of economists – in the face of a limited employment market characterised by great uncertainty regarding the utilisation of human capital investment – are taken into account. Under these conditions, the pursuit of acceptance in the scientific community, i.e. attention and reputation, often replaces the search for objective knowledge. Economists research into topics that can be published, and these topics are limited to a methodological and paradigmatic standard[18] designated as mainstream or normal science.

In the development of this standard[19], an important role is played by certain individuals with distinguished reputations – e.g. Nobel Memorial Prize in Economic Sciences winners or the presidents of major research organisations, in particular the American Economic Association (AEA) – and various journals (also note the correlation of these individuals with the editors of these particularly reputable journals form the "elite" of the scientific community).[20] And because of the English language's status as the inter-

[18] Frey (2004) thus writes about "Publishing as Prostitution".
[19] See Swann (2000) regarding the meaning of standards in the scientific market.
[20] Without Keynes' outstanding reputation as an internationally renowned economist at one of the international centres of economic research in the early 20th century – the University of Cambridge – and as editor of the leading international academic journal of the time for economists – the Economic Journal – the "Keynesian revolution" probably never would have occurred. The same applies to Milton Friedman (a former president of the AEA) and the Chicago-based Journal of Political Economy.

national language of science and the cultural hegemony of the United States since World War II, the US maintains a dominant role in the setting of standards.[21]

So if the "elite of the US-dominated scientific community" – or a number of them with loud voices – were to call for a reorientation or at least for greater openness with regard to the acceptance of reality constructions, the likelihood of a paradigm shift or at minimum a pluralisation of economics would be significantly increased.[22]

In fact, one can make out the beginnings of a trend in the U.S. of critics from within the normal science paradigm (though not necessarily critics of the entire DSGE paradigm) being allowed to achieve prominent roles. Influential figures are also increasingly expressing criticism of the normal science paradigm. Of the last twenty presidents of the AEA, five had a critical attitude toward the DSGE paradigm: George Akerlof, Robert Fogel, Amartya Sen, William Vickrey and Robert Eisner. However, there were at least as many AEA presidents who were distinct representatives of the radical DSGE paradigm, e.g. Avinash Dixit, Thomas Sargent, Robert Lucas, Gerard Debreu and Gary Becker.

The list of Nobel laureates in economics in recent years tells a similar story. Although these prizes generally honour accomplishments which were achieved quite some time ago, the timing of the award can be interpreted as a signal. Thus, it is quite astounding that four of the last ten Nobel prizes went to economists who must be regarded as representatives of complexity economics or neo-Keynesianism, while only three Nobel prizes were awarded to economists from the radical DSGE paradigm.

---

[21] This is shown by the fact that the "scientifically" relevant journals – the so-called A-journals – are published almost exclusively in the U.S., textbooks written by U.S. economists have long been used in universities worldwide as a matter of course and the various international economist rankings are comprised nearly exclusively of U.S.-based economists.

[22] There was in fact a call for the diversification of the discipline in the American Economic Review that was signed by several Nobel laureates in 1992, but it seems that the timing was not optimal, as a "crisis of normal science" triggered by new socio-economic developments was not obvious enough to assure the success of the initiative.

Overall, it can be said that there are developments in the hegemonic U.S. economics market outside or at the margins of the DSGE paradigm – as well as from within its core – that will no doubt increasingly call into question the dominance of at least the radical NCM variant. As the pendulum between the NCM and NKM models had already swung back strongly in the direction of the more realistic NKM models even before the recent global economic crisis – or in the American parlance, owing to the regional distribution of the main protagonists of the two variants of the DSGE paradigm, the "saltwater economists"[23] had begun dominating the "freshwater economists"[24] again – the sharp criticism of well-known economists such as Nobel laureates Paul Krugman (2009) and Joseph Stiglitz (2009a; 2009b) could contribute to making economics a more pluralistic discipline.

4. Institutional incentives of the 'economics market' in Germany

The German university system and with it the study of economics are subject to a significant process of transformation. Firstly, the generational turnover after the founding phase of many (reform) universities at the end of the 1960s and the beginning of the 1970s will soon be completed. Additionally, a profiling process has begun that was created in equal measure by the universities themselves as well as imposed upon them from the outside. The reform of the universities in the '60s and '70s was motivated by the demand for the "democratisation" of higher education institutions both inwardly and outwardly (see, e.g., von der Vring 1975). All stakeholders – professors, scientific and administrative staff, and students – should be entitled to participate in the organisation, just as research should be accessible to all social groups. In addition to tripartite representation on boards and committees, this included an alignment of scientific approaches that was as broadly pluralistic as possible. This applied particularly to economics, which was to be broadened from the narrow scientism and reductionism of neoclassical economics to a more comprehensive understanding of political economy (see, e.g., Vogt 1973; Kade 1973; Nutzinger 1973). Chairs and professorships at many of the newly founded universities were

[23] From universities on the East and West Coasts of the US: e.g. UC Berkeley, Princeton, Harvard, MIT.

[24] From universities near the Great Lakes: e.g. University of Chicago, Carnegie Mellon University, University of Minnesota.

filled with representatives who embraced Marxist and (post-)Keynesian worldviews.

Before the Bologna process started to Europeanise the EU's higher education system, there was yet another university reform process – one regulated not based on input ("democratisation"), but rather on output. As part of the wave of globalisation, universities see themselves in an international competition fuelled by rankings lists (e.g. the international "Shanghai list" or the German rankings of the Centre for Higher Education and the Handelsblatt). The particularly poor rankings of non-American universities in general and German universities in particular ostensibly indicate provincialisation and a loss of international prominence; they also subliminally imply a reduction in the quality of European and German science and higher education. What is true for the university as a whole applies equally to most individual academic disciplines, including economics. The near-universal response throughout Europe has been to adopt "excellence initiatives". In Great Britain, for example, a sizable portion of universities' funding has now been made dependent on an assessment of their research outputs (Research Assessment Exercise – RAE), although the quality of research performance is nearly impossible to measure objectively. Since the measurement of quality almost inevitably conforms to the "international standard", which in economics is set by American journals, which in turn are almost exclusively committed to the DSGE paradigm, the result was (and is) a mainstreaming of academic economics in Great Britain (see Lee/Harley 1998; Lee 2007).

In Germany such formal regulation does not yet exist. However, non-university economic research is increasingly subject to evaluations, the results of which determine whether the major research institutes (the so-called "blue list institutes") continue to receive public funding. The research funding from the German Research Foundation (DFG) and the research rankings carried out by private institutions like the Centre for Higher Education (CHE) can also be viewed as informal forms of regulation.[25] However,

[25] Münch (2006) shows that the allocation of DFG funds occurs for the most part based not upon scientific expertise but rather according to representation in the DFG's statutory bodies, i.e. the distribution of power. It can be assumed, though not yet proved, that this

German universities' shortage of (public) basic founding, which has increased the pressure on them to seek out external funding, mainly through the DFG (making such external funding a prerequisite for the internal allocation of funds according to the so-called "performance and load-dependent allocation of funds" process being recently introduced in most German universities), and the federal government's recent "Excellence Initiative" ought to be quite similar to the RAE in its effects. On the one hand, there are no reliable studies yet on the effectiveness of these regulations, and on the other hand, they are in part still too new (the rankings and the German "Excellence Initiative") for us to expect noticeable impacts on the paradigmatic development of economics. The trend towards an increasingly monistic discipline as described above is thus apparently more a matter of self-referential processes within the scientific community (see, e.g., Pieters/Baumgartner 2002; Lockett/McWilliams 2005; Münch 2007), which are increasingly perpetuated by supposedly thoughtful incentive systems to "assure excellence".

According to Max Planck, "(a) new scientific truth does not triumph by convincing its opponents and making them see the light, but rather because its opponents eventually die, and a new generation grows up that is familiar with it" (Planck 1928:22; own translation). If this is true, then the formal and informal frameworks of the German 'economics market' most likely contributed to the fact that the generational turnover at German universities and the reorientation of the university landscape in East Germany since 1990 could not be used for a pluralisation – let alone a paradigm shift – in economics.

5. A sceptical outlook

"Economics today is a discipline that must either die or undergo a paradigm shift—to make itself both more broadminded, and more modest. It must broaden its horizons to recognise the insights of other social sciences and historical studies and it must return to its roots. Smith, Keynes, Hayek, Schumpeter and all the other truly great economists were interested in economic reality. They studied real human behaviour in markets that actually

---

result can be reproduced if the paradigmatic orientation (rather than the regional distribution of DFG representatives) is taken into consideration.

existed. Their insights came from historical knowledge, psychological intuition and political understanding. Their analytical tools were words, not mathematics. They persuaded with eloquence, not just formal logic. One can see why many of today's academics may fear such a return of economics to its roots. Academic establishments fight hard to resist such paradigm shifts, as Thomas Kuhn, the historian of science who coined the phrase in the 1960s, demonstrated. Such a shift will not be easy, despite the obvious failure of academic economics. But economists now face a clear choice: embrace new ideas or give back your public funding and your Nobel prizes, along with the bankers' bonuses you justified and inspired" (Kaletsky 2009: 156). This appraisal by Anatole Kaletsky, economist and former editor-at-large of the British newspaper Times, is probably shared by many heterodox economists – as well as by those with sufficient confidence that the global financial crisis signalled the end of the neoclassical DSGE doctrine (see, e.g., Bouchaud 2008; Kirman 2009). However, the resistance to this view among the vast majority of academic economists as well as the established institutional structures of the economics market should not be overlooked.

Even the "Keynesian revolution" of the 1950s and 1960s was, on closer inspection, not the paradigm shift[26] that Keynes immodestly envisioned when drafting his General Theory.[27] At most, this initial push to swing the pendulum within the neoclassical real-exchange paradigm succeeded in emphasising short-term disequilibria and market imperfections more than the harmony postulate of "general equilibrium" allowed. As a result, the stabilisation point of view temporarily gained the upper hand over the allocation point of view without shaking the structurally formative function of the equilibrium ideal. However, there was room alongside this view for post-Keynesian, Marxist and institutionalist constructions of reality, which together constituted something approaching pluralism. History shows,

---

[26] See, e.g. Minsky (1975: 18f.); Hutton (1986).

[27] As he wrote to George Bernard Shaw on New Year's Day in 1935: "...I believe myself to be writing a book on economic theory, which will largely revolutionise – not, I suppose, at once but in course of the next ten years – the way the world thinks about economic problems" (Keynes 1935/1973: 492).

though, that this pluralism without regulatory intervention in the economics market did not endure.

The events of the global financial crisis created cracks in major components of the dominant DSGE paradigm – in particular the rational expectations hypothesis and the efficient market hypothesis – that are much too grave for the paradigm to be able to survive in its present form.[28] Furthermore, the number of prominent critics who come from within the DSGE paradigm is too large to be able to continue with "business as usual" economic theories after overcoming the economic crisis. The pendulum has already swung back, and perhaps critical, alternative theoretical approaches will also become more popular again. However, the current "crisis of mainstream economics" – at least in Germany – is running up against a largely saturated market for academic economists, one in which the younger generation of mainstream scientists were only recently granted their professorships and steady incomes. Unless an entirely new form of regulation is created[29], it can hardly be expected that the impetus for a renewal will come from Germany.

[28] For example, Joseph Stiglitz writes (2009b: 294): "The models that have predominated within macro-economics, which assume representative agents with rational expectations, are particularly disturbing. What I find even more striking is that some economists still argue that this crisis has not shaken their belief in rational expectations."

[29] For example, one could envision some sort of a "code of scientific pluralism", which would call for all universities to have at least one professor for "heterodox economics" (or the equivalent), and a substantial line of special grants from the DFG for "heterodox or non-mainstream research".

References

Amann, E.; Entscheidungen im Labor. Experimentelle Wirtschaftsforschung, in: Essener Unikate, Vol. 29, 2007, pp. 123 – 128

Blanchard, O.J.; The State of Macro; NBER working paper series No. 14259, Washington 2008 (published in: Annual Review of Economics, Vol. 1, No.1, 2009)

Blanchard, O., Dell'Ariccia, G., Mauro, P.; Rethinking Macroeconomic Policy, IMF Staff Position Note, Washington 2009

Bouchaud,J.P.; Economics needs a scientific revolution; in: Real-World Economics Review Issue 48, 2008, pp. 48 – 49

Boyer, R.; The Regulation School: a Critical Introduction, New York 1990

Carlin, W., Soskice, D.; Macroeconomics. Imperfections, Institutions and Policies, Oxford 2006

Cohen, A.J., Harcourt, G.C.; Whatever Happened to the Cambridge Capital Theory Controversies, in: Journal of Economic Perspectives, Vol. 17, No. 1, 2003, pp. 199 – 214

Clower, R.W.; The state of economics: hopeless but not serious?; in: Colander, D.C., Coats, A.W. (Hrsg.); The spread of economic ideas, Cambridge 1989, pp. 23 – 29

Davidson, P.; Reviving Keynes' revolution, in: Journal of Post Keynesian Economics, Vol. 6, No.4, 1984, pp. 561 – 575

Davidson, P.; Post Keynesian Macroeconomic Theory: A Foundation for Successful Economic Policies in the Twenty-First Century, Aldershot 1994

Davidson, P.; Is economics a science? Should economics be rigorous?; in: Real-World Economics Review, Issue No. 59, March 2012, pp. 58-66

Frey, B.S.; Publishing as Prostitution? Choosing between one's own ideas and academic failure; in: Public Choice, Vol. 116, 2003, pp. 205 – 223

Frey, B.S., Humbert, S., Schneider, F.; Was denken deutsche Ökonomen? Eine empirische Auswertung einer Internetbefragung unter den Mitgliedern des Vereins für Socialpolitik im Sommer 2006; in:

Perspektiven der Wirtschaftspolitik, Vol. 8, Nr.4, 2007, pp. 359 – 377

Fullbrook, E.; The crisis in economics. The post-autistic economics movement: the first 600 days, London 2003

Gordon, R.J.; What is New-Keynesian Economics?, in: Journal of Economic Literature, Vol. 28, 1990, pp. 1151 – 1171

Heinsohn, G.; Privates Grundeigentum, patriarchalische Monogamie und geldwirtschaftliche Produktion – eine sozialtheoretische Rekonstruktion der Antike, Bremen 1983

Heise, A.; Tauschwirtschaft und Geldökonomie, Frankfurt 1990

Heise, A; Erkenntnisfortschritt, Paradigmenwechsel und die Monetäre Theorie der Produktionsökonomie, in: H.-J. Stadermann, O. Steiger (Hrsg.): Der Stand und die nächste Zukunft der Geldforschung, Berlin 1993, pp. 177 – 183

Hodgson, G.M.; Evolution and Institutions, Cheltenham 1999

Hutton, W.; The Revolution that never was: An assessment of Keynesian economics, London 1986

Institute for New Economic Thinking (INET); About the Institute; New York o.J. (http://ineteconomics.org/about-the-institute)

Kade, G.; Politische Ökonomie – heute; in: Vogt, W.; Seminar: Politische Ökonomie. Zur Kritik der herrschenden Nationalökonomie, Frankfurt 1973, pp. 149 – 167

Kaletsky, A.; Goodbye, homo oeconomicus; in: Real-World Economics Review, Issue No. 50, 2009, pp. 151 – 156

Keynes, J.M.; Letter to George Bernhard Shaw of 01.01.1935; in: Moggridge, D. (Hrsg.); Collected Writings of John Maynard Keynes, Vol. XIII, London 1973, pp. 492 – 493

Keynes, J.M.; General Theory of Employment, Interest and Money, London 1936

Kirman, A.; Economic Theory and the Crisis; in: Real-World Economic Review, Issue 51, 2009, pp. 80 – 83

Kotz, D.M., McDonough, T., Reich, M.; Social Structures of Accumulation. The Political Economy of Growth and Crisis, Cambridge 1994

Krugman, P.; How Did Economists Get It So Wrong?; in: The New York Times v. 02.09.2009

Kuhn, T.S.; The Structure of Scientific Revolutions, Chicago 1962

Lakatos, I.; The Methodology of Scientific Research Programmes: Philosophical Papers, Vol. 1, Cambridge 1978

Latsis, S.J.; Situational Determinism in Economics; in: British Journal for the Philosophy of Science, Vol. 23, 1972, pp. 207 - 245

Lee, F.S.; The Research Assessment Exercise, the state and the dominance of mainstream economics in British universities; in: Cambridge Journal of Economics, Vol. 31, 2007, pp. 309 – 325

Lee, F.S.; Heterodox Economics and its Critics, Department of Economics, University of Missouri 2009 (unveröffentlichtes Manuskript)

Lee, F.S.; Heterodox Economics and its Critics; in: Review of Political Economy, Vol. 24, No.2, 2012, pp. 337 - 351

Lee, F.S., Harley, S.; Peer Review, the Research Assessment Exercise and the Demise of NonMainstream Economics; in: Capital and Class, Nr. 66, 1998, pp. 23 – 51

Lockett, A., McWilliams, A.; The Balance of Trade between Disciplines: Do we effectively manage knowledge?; in: Journal of Management Inquiry, Vol. 14, No.2, 2005, pp. 139 – 150

Malabre, A.L.; Lost Prophets: An Insider's History of Modern Economists, Cambridge (Mass) 1994

Mankiw, G.N., Romer, D.; New Keynesian Economics, 2 Vol., Cambridge 1991

Minsky, H.P.; John Maynard Keynes, New York 1975

Münch, R.; Wissenschaft im Schatten von Kartell, Monopol und Oligarchie. Die latenten Effekte der Exzellenzinitiative; in: Leviathan, Jg. 34, H.4, 2006, pp. 466 – 486

Münch, R.; Die akademische Elite, Frankfurt 2007

Nutzinger, H.G.; Wirtschaftstheorie aus Sicht der Politischen Ökonomie; in: Vogt, W.; Seminar: Politische Ökonomie. Zur Kritik der herrschenden Nationalökonomie, Frankfurt 1973, pp. 205 – 234

Olson, M.; The Logic of Collective Action, Cambridge (MA.) 1965

Olson, M.; The Rise and Decline of Nations, New Haven 1982

Pieters, R., Baumgartner, H.; Who talks to Whom? Intra- and interdisciplinary communication of economic journals; in: Journal of Economic Literature, Vol. 40., No. 2, 2002, pp. 483 – 509

Planck, M.; Wissenschaftliche Autobiographie, Leipzig 1928

Reijnierse, H., van Gellekom, A., Potters, J.A.M.; Verifying gross substitubility, in: Economic Theory, Vol. 20, 2002, pp. 767 – 776

Rotheim, R. (Hrsg.); New Keynesian economics, post Keynesian alternatives, London 1998

Rothschild, K.W.; New Worlds – New Approaches. A Note on Future Research Strategies, in: Kyklos, Vol. 58, Issue 3, 2005

Schneider, J.; Kritische Neoklassik: Ergebnisse und Perspektiven, in: W. Vogt (Hrsg.): Politische Ökonomie heute, Regensburg 1988, pp. 183 – 221

Schultz, T.; Outlaw Economists; in: Playboy, June 2012, pp. 104 - 108

Shackles, G.; Uncertainty in Economics, Cambridge 1955

Simon, H.; The Science of the Artificial, Cambridge (MA.) 1968

Smith, A.; An Inquiry into the Nature and Causes of the Wealth of Nations, Chicago 1977 (originally published: 1776)

Smith, V.L.; Constructivist and Ecological Rationality in Economics, in: T. FRÄNGSMYR (Hrsg.): The Nobel Prizes 2002, Stockholm 2003, pp. 502 – 561

Solow, R.M.; Faith, hope and clarity; in: Colander, D.C., Coats, A.W. (Hrsg.); The spread of economic ideas, Cambridge 1989, pp. 37 – 41

Stiglitz, J.; Information and Change in the Paradigm of Economics, in: T. FÄNGSMYR (Hrsg.): The Nobel Prizes 2001, Stockholm 2002, pp. 472ff

Stiglitz, D.J.; Moving Beyond Market Fubdamentalism To A More Balanced Economy; in: Annals of Public and Cooperative Economics, Vol. 80, No.3, 2009a, pp. 345 – 360

Stiglitz, J.E.; The Current Economic Crisis and Lessons for Economic Theory; in: Eastern Economic Journal, Vol. 35, 2009b, pp. 281 – 296

Swann, G.M.P.; The Economics of Standardization. Final Report for Standards and Technical Regulations Directorate – Department of Trade and Industry, Manchester Business School, Manchester 2000

Vogt, W.; Zur Kritik der herrschenden Wirtschaftstheorie; in: ders.; Seminar: Politische Ökonomie. Zur Kritik der herrschenden Nationalökonomie, Frankfurt 1973, pp. 179 – 204

Voltaire: Candide oder Die bester der Welten, Stuttgart 1971 (originally published: 1759)
Von der Vring, T.; Hochschulreform in Bremen, Frankfurt 1975
Woodford, M.; Interest and Prices: Foundation of a Theory of Monetary Policy, Princeton 2003

Two

The Future of Economics in a Lakatos-Bourdieu framework*

1. The Keynesian Revolution and Pragmatic Pluralism – A Fruitful Competition Between Theories or a Crisis in Economics?

John Maynard Keynes concludes 'The General Theory of Employment, Interest, and Money' (1936: 383-84) with the following, now-famous words:

> *„At the present moment people are unusually expectant of a more fundamental diagnosis; more particularly ready to receive it; eager to try it out, if it should be even possible. But apart from this contemporary mood, the ideas of economists and political philosophers, both when they are right and when they are wrong, are more powerful than is commonly understood. Indeed, the world is ruled by little else. Practical men, who believe themselves to be quite exempt from any intellectual influences, are usually the slaves of some defunct economist. .... I am sure that the power of vested interests is vastly exaggerated compared with the gradual encroachment of ideas. Not, indeed, immediately, but after a certain interval; for in the field of economic and political philosophy there are not many who are influenced by new theories after they are twenty-five of thirty years of age, so that the ideas which civil servants and politicians and even agitators apply to current events are not likely to be the newest. But, soon or late, it is ideas, not vested interests, which are dangerous for good or evil".*

* Originally published in: International Journal of Political Economy, Vol. 43, No. 3, 70-93

Though even Joan Robinson, Keynes's closest student, viewed the transformative power of ideas as naive[30], this passage makes plain the ambition attached to 'The General Theory' by its author. Keynes expected the book to do nothing less than revolutionize the field of economics. This ambition, which Keynes had already formulated one year earlier in a letter to the Cambridge philosopher George Bernard Shaw (Keynes 1935), was founded on three basic beliefs. First, as Keynes stresses at the book's outset, the theoretical axioms of 'The General Theory' diverge from orthodox economic wisdom[31]: „ For if orthodox economics is at fault, the error is to be found not in the superstructure, which has been erected with great care for logical consistency, but in a lack of clearness and of generality in the premises" (Keynes 1936: xxi). Unfortunately, he did not identify the assumptions he judged to be flawed, and failed to disclose any alternatives. These omissions, as he himself was acutely aware, were likely to draw criticism: „Those, who are strongly wedded to what I shall call the ‚classical theory', will fluctuate, I expect, between a belief that I am quite wrong and a belief that I am saying nothing new" (Keynes 1936: xxi). But if it is true that Keynes believed his book would overturn orthodox economics[32], then he also thought he could convince economists who had not yet been steeped in orthodox wisdom. Specifically, he had in mind young economists who could be exposed to his theories early on and established economists who primarily worked from an empirical or historical perspective, leaving them "without any formal theory of economics which was predominant and generally accepted" (Keynes 1936: xxvi). Here he was surely thinking about the supporters of the Historical School, who were

[30] See Joan Robinson (1976).

[31] The orthodox wisdom Keynes was referring to is general equilibrium theory, which was developed at Cambridge University by the political economist Alfred Marshall and his successor, Arthur Cecil Pigou. Today this theory is known as the mainstream view or the benchmark model.

[32] Although Keynes's line of argument ultimately amounts to an alternate theory – an assemblage of deductive arguments based on alternate assumptions – he repeatedly emphasizes that he is merely formulating a general theory that provides room for preserving orthodox economics (general equilibrium theory) as a special case (see Keynes 1936: VI). Keynes didn't appear to be cognizant of the difference.

still numerous, particularly in Germany, despite their defeat in the *Methodenstreit.*[33]

The second belief concerned impact. A lecturer at King's College, Cambridge, Keynes considered himself influential enough to spark a worldwide revolution in economic thought. While this speaks to Keynes's unshakable self-confidence as a member of the English intelligentsia, it is also a testament to the central position Cambridge University and Keynes occupied in contemporary academia. In the late 19th and early 20th centuries, during the reign of Alfred Marshall and Arthur C. Pigou, Cambridge University enjoyed a particularly esteemed status in the eyes of foreign economists.[34] And by 1936 Keynes had become an internationally acclaimed economist, a status he reached in a matter of years thanks to the publication of 'The Economic Consequences of the Peace' (1919) and 'The Economic Consequences of Mr. Churchill' (1925). Moreover, as the editor of 'The Economic Journal' since 1912 – one of the world's most prominent journals for economics – he played a decisive role in determining what economists talked about in the English-speaking world and elsewhere; and he used his influence to generate publicity for his theories and advance the 'Keynesian revolution' (see Moggridge 1990; Aslanbeigni & Oakes 2007).

The third belief had to do with the state of the economy. In 'The General Theory' Keynes makes an oblique reference to 'contemporary mood', vaguely intimating why he thought economics had to be rescued from the

---

33 In the U.S., the 'old institutionalists' were quite strong (Youay 1998), and even Cambridge University – at the time, the stronghold of orthodox economics – nearly fell into the hands of the Historical School when it came time to select a successor to Alfred Marshall. That Arthur Cecil Pigou was appointed chair – and not H.S. Foxwell, who closely associated with members of the Historical School – was most likely attributable to Alfred Marshall's having directly intervened in the hiring process. For more, see Coase (1994:151ff.)

34 A number of prominent economists, including Gerard Debreu, Milton Friedman, and John Kenneth Galbraith, spent time as guest researchers at Cambridge University. Cambridge University also boasted a large number of extremely renowned teachers in economics, including Henry Sidgewick, Inglis Palgrave, Herbert S. Foxwell, John N. Keynes, Alfred Marshall, Arthur C. Pigou, John M. Keynes, Joan Robinson, Dennis Robertson, and Richard Kahn.

fangs of orthodox theory. At least for many non-economists, the depression in the 1930s had exposed the deep flaws in orthodox economics, which held that unregulated markets inherently found a stable equilibrium, and that falling real wages were the solution for mass unemployment.[35] Keynes feared the economic, social, and political effects of misguided economic policy, in addition to the loss of credibility for a profession that did nothing to contribute to solving the problems of the day, and may even have aggravated them.

Keynes's beliefs proved accurate and his book had its intended effect. For at that historical juncture, all the ingredients of what Thomas S. Kuhn (1962) calls a scientific revolution were on hand: empirical reality (the economic crisis) had shown prevailing theory to be false, an alternative theory (Keynesian theory) was available as a replacement, and the cultural dominance needed to install this new paradigm (Keynes and Cambridge) was in place. These conditions allowed the so-called Keynesian revolution to gain steam (Klein 1947), and Keynesian economics soon became the mainstream view in the U.S. and Europe, particularly after the Second World War. Though the true extent of the Keynesian revolution has been disputed[36], one thing can be said for certain: Keynesian economics facilitated the search for alternative paradigms (see e.g. Lee 2000, Lee 2009) and strongly influenced the assumptions of orthodox paradigms – standard Keynesianism, neo-Keynesianism, and neoclassical economics – operating within the 'dynamic-stochatic general equilibrium model' (DSGE).

Should Keynes's work really be conceived as revolutionary? Applying Kuhn's ideas about scientific revolutions to non-experimental sciences such as economic theory has proven very problematic, though a thorough explanation would take us too far afield. It suffices to say that Imre Lakatos's model of 'battle' between 'research programs' (1970) does a better job of capturing dynamic changes to paradigms relative to changing

[35] The most explicit proponent of orthodox theory, Keynes's colleague Arthur C. Pigou, clung tenaciously to the thesis – despite empirical evidence to the contrary – that nominal and real wages merely needed to continue falling in order to bring about full employment (1941).

[36] See Hutton (1986), who speaks of a 'revolution that never was'.

environments, and, in this regard, is more receptive to conceptions of plurality (competing paradigms based on axiomatic variation) and variation (approaches based on varied assumptions within the so-called protective belt).[37] In contrast to Kuhn, Lakatos believes that dominant paradigms are not replaced by alternatives that previously lurked in the shadows; rather, scientific progress is a result of competition between research programs that fluctuate between progressive and degenerative shifts.[38] A research program may eventually fail to prove its scientific value, and may as a consequence be abandoned, when it no longer is expected to be progressive, which is to say, when it no longer allows for the prediction of new facts. This awareness is not triggered by singular events (in the social sciences) or experiments (in the natural sciences); rather, it becomes evident over the course of extensive 'repair work'.[39] Based on Lakatos's model, then, scientific progress, especially in the social sciences,[40] requires paradigmatic competition, and in this regard the Keynesian revolution undoubtedly made a considerable contribution.[41]

---

[37] Though I prefer Lakatos's model to Kuhn's, I continue to use the terms 'paradigm' and 'paradigm shift' because they are more succinct than 'research programme'.

[38] A theory or approach can generate paradigmatic competition if, by positing alternate assumptions or introducing ad hoc assumptions, it is capable of delivering new, falsifiable prognoses (ex ante) or at least explaining existing anomalies within a research paradigm (ex post).

[39] Looking back historically, the economic crisis of the 1930s or even the current global financial crisis may well prove to be *experimenta crucis* for the further development of the field of economics. But they cannot be portrayed as anomalies that necessarily lead to the instant overthrow of orthodox wisdom such as the dynamic-stochastic general equilibrium model.

[40] This is true on the one hand because social reality is also social constructed, i.e. does not exist independent of our perception, which is merely influenced by economic models. And this is true on the other hand because falsification is not possible in non-experimental sciences. *Ceteris paribus* hypotheses can at best be falsified. Ultimately, the Duhem-Quine thesis exposes the methodological limits to the empirical assessment of purely theoretical predictions (see Cross 1982).

[41] If one accepts Feyerabend's critique of Lakatos – namely, that his categorization into progressive and degenerative research programs is not logical, and that, accordingly, a 'rational' selection of research programs cannot deliver an acceptable basis for investigation – then the calls for pluralism become all the more important. As Feyerabend once stated: 'anything goes' (Feyerabend 1975: 27-28). This view is particularly prevalent

Yet science is not just a 'battle'. It is also what Pierre Bourdieu calls a 'power struggle' (Bourdieu 1990; 1991), for actors in the domain of science are outfitted with varying degrees of social, cultural, and economic capital, making for a very uneven playing field when it comes to competition between paradigms. Under the dominance of a monistic understanding of science (as part of the cultural capital)[42] – in which, taking a cue from Kuhn, the rise of a dominant mainstream in scientific thought is seen as a desirable state of affairs and the mark of a mature (or 'true') body of thought (see Middleton 1998, Schultze 1996, Williamson 1997) – the process of standardization, or agreement on a common paradigm (what Lakatos calls a positive heuristic), reduces lack of certainty about the usability of one's specific human capital by securing career opportunities. It is reasonable to assume that the degree to which various paradigms (or, rather, their proponents) are outfitted with economic capital (material resources) and social capital (cooperative ties to other actors within and outside the academic filed such as influencial journal editors, economic policymakers, business leaders, sponsors and, not to be forgotten, the media) plays a large role in determining who gets to define orthodox economic thought, and how much heterodox paradigms are marginalized (particularly in terms of professorial positions at universities).

Using a Lakatos-Bourdieu framework, it becomes apparent why the relative plurality of economic paradigms that prevailed following the Keynesian revolution was interpreted as a crisis in economics (see Kazmierski 1993), as well as why the DSGE mainstream – as a result of the monetarist counterrevolution – underwent a wave of standardization that primarily

---

among constructivists who study the sociology of scientific knowledge (see Yonay 1998: 218f.).

[42] Feyerabend describes this monistic understanding as follows: "More than one social scientist has pointed out to me that at last he has learned to turn his field into a 'science' – by which of course he meant that he had learned how to improve it. The recipe, according to these people, is to restrict criticism, to reduce the numer of comprehensive theories to one, and to create a normal science with this one theory as its paradigm. Students must be prevented from speculating along different lines and the more restless colleagues must be made to conform and 'to do serious work'" (1970: 198).

emanated[43] from a handful of elite American universities[44] instead of witnessing a 'scientific revolution' as has been argued using a Kuhnian approach (see Peabody 1971, Worland 1972). By the outbreak of the 2007 global financial crisis, the ascendancy of DSGE at universities, research institutes, central banks, and international organizations (such as the IMF and Worldbank) was so complete that economists began speaking of a consensus model, which was viewed positively (see Blanchard 2008) insofar as it seemed to have largely laid to rest the disputes within the DSGE mainstream between freshwater and sweetwater economists (see Goodfriend 2004).[45]

2. On Classifying Plurality and Variation

How the field of economics will develop in the wake of the global financial crisis is an important question, but before speculating on an answer we need to categorize the current landscape of economic thought in order to clarify the mainstream/non-mainstream divide necessary to understand the difference between variation (among paradigms) and plurality (between paradigms). Despite the criticism leveled from many quarters at the dualistic division between 'mainstream' and 'non-mainstream' (see Mearman

[43] Here, as well, we find the three necessary conditions for a 'counterrevolution': Milton Friedman as a driving force and influential personality; the University of Chicago as an institutional vehicle; and the stagflation of the 1970s, which triggered the crisis in Keynesian economics.

[44] The hegemonial ability of elite U.S. universities similarily to advance a scientific discipline and to enforce standardized views in various fields of research is rarely contested (see Rosser, Holt & Colander 2010; Lebaron 2006: 92ff; Graham & Diamond 1997) and has been put forward as early as the 1970s (see Deutsch, Platt & Senghaas 1971). Mata (2009) points out the importance of US elite universities (namely Harvard) in promoting heterodox issues on the one hand and the efforts of the mainstream community to hold these strongholds.

[45] The terms 'saltwater' and 'freshwater' refer to the intellectual divide in the field of economics between universities on the East and West Coasts of the United States (Columbia, Harvard, Princeton, Berkeley, Stanford, and Yale) and those around the Great Lakes (particularly the University of Chicago and Carnegie Melon University). These two geographic poles reflect the lines of tension between the Keynesian and neoclassical perspectives much better than the terms 'revolution' and 'counterrevolution'.

2012)[46], I want to retain these terms for two reasons: (1) to show that this dualism sometimes hides a wide range of competing paradigms; and (2) to clarify that the establishment of an alternative paradigm requires more than critical engagement with a few underlying assumptions.

Using Lakatos's concept of research programs as a framework, we can identify the dimensions that constitute a scientific model[47]: (1) the methodical dimension, i.e. a methodology considered acceptable, or 'scientific'; (2) the epistemological dimension, i.e. a series of core assumptions (axioms) that underlie the model; and (3) the heuristic dimensions, i.e. postulates that are derived from these core assumptions and that must be accepted ('positive heuristics') or, at least, may not be called into question ('negative heuristics'). The DSGE mainstream – an amalgam of new classical economics and neo-Keynesianism – is based on the core assumptions of rationality, ergodicity, and substitutionality (the hallmarks of social exchange theory; see e.g. Davidson 1984, Davidson 2005). In addition, the DSGE relies exclusively on a formal, mathematical, positivist deductivism (see Lawson 2006). Over the course of the so-called empirical turn of the past three decades, this constellation of elements has been combined with sophisticated systems of micro- and macroeconometrics, as well as experimental designs that harness approaches used in the natural sciences, such as physics and chemistry (see Schmidt & aus dem Moore 2010). The postulate of stability and optimality (Walras's Law), which is operational *a priori* in the core assumptions of DSGE theory, guides 'ideal solution' (*Musterlösungen*), thus functioning as metric for negative heuristics, i.e. the research methods and approaches not to be called into question. The ostensibly large differences in forecasts delivered by the hyperstable equilibrium models of New Classical Economics compared with the non-equilibrium-based models of Keynesianism and neo-Keynesianism are at-

[46] In addition to the criticism directed at such dualism, the static nature of classificational categories is also regularly reproached, as they fail to capture the complex variation inevitably manifest in field of intellectual endeavor (see Colander, Holt & Rosser 2009). Yet this accusation cannot be leveled against the classification scheme proposed here.

[47] For the problems surrounding the application of Lakatos's method to economics, see Cross (1982).

tributable to modified assumptions within the 'protective belt' (e.g. concerning adjustment speeds, price and quantity rigidities, expectation formation, etc.), yet these differences are not evidence of divergent paradigmatic origins.[48]

When criticism is raised against the core assumptions of the DSGE mainstream, we often hear the explanation that while these assumptions are an element of formal training in DSGE theory, they do not inform the work of today's professional economists, who have long since availed themselves of new approaches native to behavioral economics, neuroeconomics, and complexity economics (see e.g Davis 2006: 4 – 5). Researchers in these subfields who accept the methodological limitations imposed by the mainstream but refrain from attacking its foundations[49] are accepted by the mainstream, and sometimes even lauded as the vanguard of mainstream research, even as they continue to be thought of as nonconformists or dissenters (see Colander, Holt & Rosser 2009).[50] The same does not apply to people within the mainstream who accept the core axioms of DSGE theory along with its faith in stability and optimality, but who reject the methodological requirements of its rigorously formal deductivism. Accordingly, fields such as *Ordnungsökonomie* or Hayek's Austrian School are recognized for their contributions but are marginalized as outdated and methodologically weak (see Schmidt & aus dem Moore 2010: 170ff.).[51]

---

[48] Accordingly, both approaches are found in modern textbooks, where a distinction is made between short-term forecasts (the neo-Keynesian model) and long-term forecasts (the neoclassical model). For more, see Abel & Bernanke (2005); and Blanchard (2006).

[49] When certain assumptions are shown to be invalid (rationality, say), economists confirm their loyalty to the mainstream by asserting that contradictory findings are not universally applicable (see Smith 2003: 505), or by explicitly stating that such findings are intended as a supplement to the mainstream, not an alternative: "The objective (of behavioral economics, A.H.) is definitely not to critizise the standard economic model, or accentuate the negatives,..." (Cartwright 2011: 4).

[50] On the relationship between the mainstream and their dissenters see Vernengo (2010: 392).

[51] Critical neoclassicism has a special status in this connection. Heuristically and axiomatically identical to DSGE, critical neoclassicism abandons positivism in favor of normativity (particularly with a view to distribution and the ownership of production factors)

Heterodoxy is characterized by the rejection of some (or all) mainstream axioms; by methodological receptiveness to less formal, narrative deduction as well as inductive techniques; and by a rejection of the stability and optimality of market-based coordination mechanisms (which is to say, by the rejection of Walras's Law[52]). The schools of thought that qualify as heterodox in this sense are post-Keynesianism, neo-Marxist regulation theory and the radical school, socio-economic theories, and, provided it still exists, the Historical School. The neo-Ricardianism advanced by Piero Sraffa also saw itself as heterodox, for it rejected the stability and optimality postulate of the mainstream, even though it accepts the mainstream's research methods and core axioms. This apparent inconsistency can be explained by the outcome of the Cambridge Capital Controversy (CCC), during which the neo-Ricardians provided evidence that the stable equilibrium solutions founded on the core assumptions of the DSGE mainstream are only valid under very specific conditions.[53] This controversy rocked the entire deductive apparatus of the mainstream to the core, but it failed to furnish a plausible alternative.

(see Vogt 1986). Due to the heuristic, axiomatic, and at least partial methodological proximity to DSGE, this theoretical school is generally not considered a 'heterodoxy' (see Hickel 1986). In certain cases, 'critical neoclassicism' is so broadly defined that it is difficult to distinguish it from neo-Keynesianism (see Schneider 1988).

[52] The idea that the establishment of a true paradigmatic alternative implies a rejection of Walras's Law was first put forward by Robert Clower (1965). Yet long before, 'heterodox' economists such as Karl Marx and Thomas Robert Malthus had questioned the predecessor to Walras's Law, Say's Theory of Markets. See Mishan (1963) for more on the relationship between Walras's Law and Say's Theory.

[53] Namely, we'd have to have a one-good world (such as Ricardo's corn economy) or make special assumptions about the capital intensity of the subsistence good industry and all of its input producers. But neither of these scenarios is particularly realistic.

Table 1: Classification of Economic Paradigms

Epistemology (Core Assumptions)	Methodology	Heuristics	Paradigm	Theoretical school
- Rationality assumption - Ergodicity assumption - Substitutionality assumption	Deductive, positivist reductionism based on formal mathematics + highly developed empiricism/experimentalism	Acceptance of the stability of market clearing as an 'ideal solution'	DSGE	- New classical macroeconomics - Neo-Keynesianism - Standard Keynesianism
Questioning Some Core Assumptions	Deductive, positivist reductionism based on formal mathematics + highly developed empiricism/experimentalism	Acceptance of the stability of market clearing as an 'ideal solution'	DSGE dissenters	- Behavioral economics - Neuroeconomics - Complexity economics - Evolutionary economics
- Rationality assumption - Ergodicity assumption - Substitutionality assumption	Rejection of deductive, positivist reductionism based on formal mathematics	Acceptance of the stability of market clearing as an "ideal solution"	DSGE dissenters	- *Ordnungsökonomie* - The Austrian School - Critical Neoclassicism
- Rationality assumption - Ergodicity assumption - Substitutionality assumption - Asymmetric information assumption	Deductive reductionism based on formal mathematics + highly developed empiricism/experimenta-lism	Rejection of the stability of market clearing as an 'ideal solution'	Dissenters/Heterodoxy	- Information economics
Questioning Some Core Assumptions	Acceptance of deduction based on formal mathematics + narrative analysis	Rejection of the stability of market clearing as an 'ideal solution'	Heterodoxy	- Post-Keynesianism - Social economics/Social economic institutionalism - Regulation theory/ SSA/Radicals - The Historical School
- Rationality assumption - Ergodicity assumption - Substitutionality assumption	Deductive reductionism based on formal mathematics + highly developed empiricism/experimenta-lism	Rejection of the stability of market clearing as an 'ideal solution'	Heterodoxy	- Neo-Ricardianism

Finally we come to information economics, which shares the core assumptions and methodology of the mainstream, but which rejects the stability and optimality ideal. This apparent inconsistency is not based on a demonstration of the deductive weaknesses in the theoretical derivation of the stability and optimality postulate, but rather, on highlighting how information is distributed among economic subjects (who can no longer be viewed as representative agents). The focus on informational aspects amounts to an alternate – and divergent – core assumption. The unclear classification of this school is revealed in the uncertain role played by the distribution of information – is it an alternate core axiom, or merely the modification of an assumption within the protective belt? Drawing attention to the asymmetric distribution of information as a cause for various forms of market failure is a core argument of neo-Keynesianism, yet most proponents of neo-Keynesianism do not view asymmetric information as a defining feature of market activity that must be incorporated into the core axioms of mainstream thought. Rather, they see it solely as a phenomenon that manifests itself in partial markets. Obviously, the inclusion of asymmetric information as a core axiom only appears logical if it is a pandemic feature of market-based coordination; the 'ideal solution' of stable market equilibrium can hardly serve as a reasonable negative heuristic under such circumstances. The status of information economics in our classification is sure to remain a point of deliberation for some time to come.

3. Joseph Stiglitz and Paul Krugman – Mainstream Dissenter or Paradigm Warriors?

The trajectory of an academic field cannot be determined by a single person. This is certainly even more true today than it was during the time of John Maynard Keynes or Milton Friedman. Yet we should be cognizant of the fact that particularly in the social sciences, the victor on the battlefield of ideas is not the one who makes the better argument or who develops the more incisive model or paradigm. What is crucial is acceptance and circulation within the epistemic community. And in this connection, the status of the actors – the economists participating in the struggle – plays a determinant role.

Criticism of the current state of economics has grown louder since the outbreak of the global financial crisis in 2007. Outsiders ask why a crisis of this magnitude was not anticipated, and why it has not been possible to overcome the effects of the crisis in most industrial nations (see Besley & Hennesey 2009). Yet there are also many critical voices from within the field of economics. Some of these critics attribute the current helplessness of the profession to a lack of intellectual diversity, as well as to an autistic focus on formal elegance that overlooks the problems of the real world. Still others charge that mainstream economists, with their singular fixation on equilibrium, are one of the problems besetting the real economy (see Blanchflower 2009, Caballero 2010, Kirman 2010, Pesaran & Smith 2011, Koppl & Luther 2012).[54] It should thus come as little surprise that heterodox economists view the current situation as an *experimentum crucis*.[55] Indeed, in many respects the current environment resembles the era in which Keynes sought to spark an intellectual revolution. Insofar as the above considerations are valid, the mere existence of paradigmatic alternatives that could potentially supplant the DSGE mainstream is not sufficient. Rather, support is required from influential personalities within the ranks of the elite who promulgate the current orthodoxy (see Cronin 2010: 1477)[56]. In the following sections we ask whether Joseph Stiglitz and Paul Krugman could contribute to a reorientation of the economics profession[57]

[54] On the other hand, some attempt to explain the global financial crisis using the mainstream paradigm; naturally they reject the notion that economics is experiencing an existential crisis. See, for example, Lucas (2009), Cochrane (2011), Minford (2010), and Bernanke (2010).

[55] See in this regard the numerous contributions published since 2007 in heterodox journals such as the *Real-World Economics Review*, the *Cambridge Journal of Economics*, the *Review of Radical Political Economics*, the *Journal of Post Keynesian Economics* and the *Journal of Economic Issues*.

[56] This covers influential converts from the mainstream to the heterodoxy as well as 'prestigious members of the economics profession' who actively support plurality and diversity – without such support, the University of Massachusetts/Amherst could not have become a hub of heterodoxy in the 1970s; see Katzner (2011: 108 – 21).

[57] This will be done by a brief overview of their lifes and achievements in order to account for their position in the field of academic economics. Of course, a deeper Bourdieuian analysis would have to provide much more information in order to descibe more appropriatly their habitus and doxa as in Bourdieu (1990).

– if not by initiating a paradigm shift, then at least by making the field receptive to greater plurality. Stiglitz and Krugman have been selected because, as Nobel laureates, they qualify as members of the elite in economics[58]. At the same time, they have been particularly vocal in their criticism of mainstream dogma (see Krugman 2009, Stiglitz 2008a, 2008b, 2008c, 2009a).

3.1 Joseph Stiglitz

Joseph Stiglitz was born in Gary, Indiana, in 1943. He was educated at Amherst and MIT, earning his doctorate under the tutelage of the later Noble laureates Paul Samuelson, Franco Modigliani, and Robert Solow. Stiglitz has held positions at Yale, Standford, Oxford, Princeton, and Columbia – a veritable who's who of elite universities. When Stiglitz was awarded the Noble prize in 2001 the decision had an air of inevitability about it (see Pressman 1999): Stiglitz was one of the most influential neo-Keynesians, a school of thought that had yet to be distinguished with a Noble prize, as opposed to 'New Classical Macroeconomics', which had received the award in the 1990s. Yet Stiglitz was not content to be a recluse in the ivory tower. He was a member of the Council of Economic Advisors under Clinton from 1993 to 1997, was chief economist at the World Bank from 1997 to 2000, and has written a number of bestselling books (see Stiglitz 2002a, 2003, 2006). According to bibliometric rankings (e.g. IDEAS), Joseph Stiglitz is one of the five most renowned economists in the world. He was formerly the Vice President of the American Economic Association (AEA), as well as editor of the AEA's 'Journal of Economic Perspectives'. In 1979, he received the John Bates Clark Medal, granted to influential economists under 40 years old. In 2008–09 Stiglitz was the president of the Eastern Economic Association (EEA), and has been president of the International Economic Association (IEA) since 2011.

In the first phase of his academic career (1966–97), Stiglitz's research centered on the effects of information asymmetries on macroeconomic development. He demonstrated that under conditions of limited information,

[58] On the symbolic capital associated with the Nobel Prize in Economics, see Lebaron (2006).

rational actors tend to adopt behaviors that at least temporarily lead to market imbalances, thus delivering "Keynesian" results on a microeconomic basis. Examples of such behaviors include the rationing of credit on credit markets, or the payment of real wages on labor markets above the equilibrium level as so-called efficiency wages. On the basis of this microfoundational analysis, he satisfied the methodological expectations of the growing mainstream, and by limiting his assessment of informational asymmetries to deviations from market clearing he also fulfilled the mainstream's 'negative heuristic'. In this way, he was able – in collaboration with many other colleagues, such as George Akerlof, Greg Mankiw, David Romer, and David Soskice – to reformulate Keynesianism within the mainstream paradigm.

After working outside of academia between 1994 and 2000 – and perhaps due to the experience he gathered in the 'real world' – Stiglitz's view of the profession of economics became more radical. With the outbreak of the global financial crisis, Stiglitz's calls for a new economic paradigm – both within academia and publicly, in newspaper columns, books, and interviews – have grown louder:

> *"Changing paradigms is not easy. Too many have invested too much in the wrong models. Like the Ptolemaic attempts to preserve earth-centric views of the universe, there will be heroic efforts to add complexities and refinements to the standard paradigm. The resulting models will be an improvement and policies based on them may do better, but they too are likely to fail. Nothing less than a paradigm shift will do"* (Stiglitz 2010).

Stiglitz clearly lays out the stakes, calling for a veritable revolution in the field of economics, and not just for the use of alternate assumptions within the 'protective belt', or for greater room for dissenting views within the mainstream paradigm. But the path to be taken to achieve this revolution remains unclear. In recent articles (Stiglitz 2009b, 2011) intended for an academic audience, he sharply attacks the mainstream paradigm for its empirical anomalies, *ad hoc* parameter settings, and, in particular, the inappropriateness of its assumptions about representative agents. Yet he notes that these points of criticism have been raised many times before in the past, and that this is precisely the reason why theoretical variations exist within the mainstream paradigm. Nevertheless, he sees a burgeoning paradigm shift, from a 'competition paradigm' to an 'information paradigm', and not just a state of variation with the mainstream (like most neo-Keynesians), because he views informational asymmetries as ubiquitous, and the associated phenomenon of market failure as systematic and inevitable:

> *"In the aftermath of the Great Depression, a peculiar doctrine came to be accepted, called the neo-classical synthesis. It argued that once markets were restored to full employment, neoclassical principles would apply – the economy would be efficient. ... The irony, of course, was that other strands of modern economic theory, including the theory of imperfect information to which I have contributed, were simultaneously explaining why markets often do not work so well. Bruce Greenwald and I, for instance, showed that the reason that Adam Smith's invisible hand often appeared invisible was that it was not actually there: market equilibria were not constrained Pareto efficient whenever there were information imperfections and asymmetries and imperfect risk markets -* ***that is always"*** (Stiglitz 2009b: 293; my emphasis).

Under these conditions, using the optimal market outcome as an 'ideal solution' and as a negative heuristic of the paradigm is deeply flawed. Furthermore, a fundamental skepticism toward government intervention is untenable as an economic policy stance. Elsewhere, however, Stiglitz had to acknowledge the limitations of his critique (in particular with respect to the neo-Keynesian pole of the mainstream):

> *"My research over the past thirty years has focused, however, on only one aspect of my dissatisfaction with that paradigm. It is not easy to change views of the world, and it seemed to me the most effective way of attacking the paradigm was to keep within the standard framework as much as possible. I only va-*

> *ried one assumption – the assumption concerning perfect information – and in ways which seemed highly plausible"* (Stiglitz 2002b: 519-20).

A truly heterodox understanding of economics is unlikely to be built on this foundation, and Stiglitz's early calls for a more interdisciplinary cooperation in economics (2002b: 520) – interpretable as a receptiveness to alternate methodologies[59] – have not reappeared in his work since the outbreak of the global financial crisis, despite its implications for the legitimacy of the mainstream. It should thus come as no surprise that for all of Stiglitz's emphasis on paradigm shift, we find no mention of heterodox literature in his work, much less of heterodox research programs.

3.2 Paul Krugman

Paul Krugman was born in 1953 in Albany, New York. After receiving his bachelor's degree in economics from Yale, he earned his Ph.D. at MIT in 1977 with a disseration on trade theory supervised by Rüdiger Dornbusch. Since then, Krugman has held positions at various elite universities, including MIT and Princeton, and was a member of the Council of Economic Advisors (CEA) under Reagan from 1982 to 1983. In 1991 he received the John Bates Clark medal from the American Economic Association, and in 2008 he was awarded the Noble Prize in Economics for his work in developing New Trade theory (NTT). The parallels between the careers of Stiglitz and Krugman are strikingly apparent – even if Krugman achieved much more at an early age, has held fewer positions (a possible indicator of influence in the economics community), has never been the editor of a major U.S. economics journal, and has only served as president of the marginally influential Eastern Economic Association (2010). While bibliographic rankings invariably name him as one of the world's top 50 economists, Kromphardt's (2013: 180) assertion that Krugman is 'the most in-

---

[59] Interestingly, much of this has been left out in the revised version of his Nobel Prize speech published in the American Economic Review (see Stiglitz 2002c: 486 - 87).

fluential Keynesian' is somewhat tenuous, given that Krugman is specialized in the somewhat peripheral subfield of international economics, and not in the core areas of macroeconomic theory.

Beyond his academic activities Krugman is also an author of books and columns geared to layman readers (see Krugman 1995, 1998, 1999, 2012). In his popular blog, Conscience of a Liberal, Krugman regularly engages in withering critiques of the economics profession. In a 2009 article in 'The New York Times' titled 'How Did Economists Get It So Wrong' Krugman offers up particularly pointed criticism. He not only chastises mainstream economists for failing to predict the global financial crisis; he also claims that their excessive faith in the efficiency of markets was a contributing factor in the crisis:

> *"As I see it, the economics profession went astray because economists, as a group, mistook beauty, clad in impressive-looking mathematics, for truth. Until the Great Depression, most economists clung to a vision of capitalism as a perfect or nearly perfect system. That vision wasn't sustainable in the face of mass unemployment, but memories of the Great Depression faded, economists fell back in love with the old, idealized vision of an economy in which rational individuals interact in perfect markets, this time gussied up with fancy equations. ... Unfortunately, this romanticized and sanitized vision of the economy led most economists to ignore all the things that can go wrong. They turned a blind eye to the limitations of human rationality that often lead to bubbles and busts; to the problems of institutions that run amok; to the imperfections of markets – especially financial markets – that can cause the economy's operating system to undergo sudden, unpredictable crashes; and to the dangers created when regulators don't believe in regulation"* (Krugman 2009).

Although Krugman does not directly address the need for paradigm shift, his statements exhibit the characteristics requisite for the rise of a heterodox paradigm (see Table 1): the abandonment of unrealistic core assumptions; skepticism toward reality-skewing formal deductivism; and the rejection of market efficiency and stability (the 'negative heuristic'). Yet in the same breath as Krugman stresses the difficulty of developing an alternate paradigm, he refers generally to 'behavioral finance' as "the kind of economics I have in mind" (Krugman 2009), without bothering to cite existing heterodox theories that could pave the way to a new paradigm. One doesn't have to agree with John Cochrane's (2011) fundamental critique of Krugman[60] to recognize that the 'dissenting' approaches advanced by Krugman have long since become part of the DSGE mainstream (see Table 1). Furthermore, the only paper by Krugman that points in the direction of establishing an alternate theoretical and methodological approach to economic questions is ultimately disappointing. In Eggertsson & Krugman (2012) he describes Keynesian 'phenomena' such as the short-term underutilization of resources as a result of underconsumption, and explains how it is impossible to return to optimal equilibrium through price flexibility. And while the paper also endorses several 'Keynesian recommendations' such as price rigidities as well as monetary and financial policy interventions, none of this is done on the basis of an alternate paradigm. Instead, the paper merely posits an exogenous shock, employs a number of selective assumptions, and distinguishes between short-term outcomes influenced by disequilibrium and long-term outcomes that are not. In short, despite Krugman's sharp anti-dogmatic rhetoric and frequent words of homage to Keynes[61] – which have lead some commentators to erroneously designate him as a post-Keynesian (see Rezende 2009) – there is a conspicuous absence of new theoretical content in his writings, as well as a total

---

[60] Cochrane writes, "Krugman isn't trying to be an economist: he is trying to be a partisan, political opinion writer … if you do not regard economics as a science; a discipline that ought to result in quantitative matches to data; a discipline that requires crystal-clear logical connections between the 'if' and the 'then,' … then his writing makes sense" (2011: 39).

[61] Krugman's high opinion of Keynes is particularly evident in his forward to the new American edition of *The General Theory*.

failure to engage with important heterodox literature (see also Vernengo 2010: 392-93).[62,63]

4. A Revolution in Economics in the Offing? Concluding Remarks

The global financial crisis has clearly been a matter of great consternation for the business-as-usual faction within the field of economics. In the years of the Great Moderation (see Summers 2005, Bernanke 2012), proponents of the mainstream heralded a veritable end of history in economics, with Robert E. Lucas (2003: 1) announcing that the "central problem of depression-prevention [has] been solved, for all practical purposes." The breakdown in economic systems witnessed from 2007 onward was practically unthinkable, and left many economists confused and uncertain. While this jolt to the complacency of mainstream thought led to some reflective works from establishment figures such as Olivier Blanchard (et al. 2010) and Michael Woodford (2010), the awarding of the Noble Prize in Economics to two proponents of the core doctrines of the DSGE mainstream in 2011 marked the end of this ruminative period[64]. Despite the signal sent by bestowing the Noble Prize on two committed ideologues, it is fairly certain that the pendulum will soon swing back toward neo-Keynesianism, as this school is better suited to addressing today's problems. Quite simply,

[62] The only heterodox source that Eggertsson & Krugman cite is Minsky (1986), and here we find only passing mention. As Palley (2013) correctly observes, this approach is all too common among defenders of the mainstream who endorse a heterodox viewpoint but then co-opt the critique by incorporating it into the dominant paradigm. Such economists attempt to establish their heterodox credentials by citing standard sources such as Minsky, yet they fail to acknowledge studies that elaborate on these standard sources, and demolish the mainstream approach. While Krugman's work points toward the need for a revolution in economic theory, closer inspection reveals that this revolution ought to be avoided. Krugman's calls for change might be characterized as 'rearranging the deck chairs on the Titanic'.

[63] Tellingly, Krugman's response to a friendly article about the heterodox economist Wynne Godley in the New York Times (see Schlefer 2013) shows little knowledge of his work and takes a rather hostile position (see Krugman 2013).

[64] Christopher Sims and Thomas Sargent, who received the Noble Prize for their work on cause and effect in macroeconomics, purport to demonstrate that political intervention is ineffective.

the current awareness of market imperfections implies the need for economic policy intervention, and neo-Keynesianism furnishes better insights into how stimlative measures influence macroeconomic growth (see Bean 2010). We can also expect the trend of studies assessing the financial system and its destabilizing potential to continue, and are likely to see further growth in the subfields of behavioral economics and behavioral finance (see Allington et al. 2011: 17).

Yet at the present time we have yet to see anything like a true paradigm shift, let alone a greater receptiveness to a plurality of views (see Galbraith 2013: 312) – an attitude Lakatos (and Feyerabend) believed was necessary for the advancement of knowledge. And the assessments of Stiglitz and Krugman, perhaps the two most prominent critical voices inside the American economics establishment, leaves little room for optimism:

1. Both Stiglitz and Krugman have strong reputations (see Table 2), yet neither of them appear influential enough to initiate a revolution in thought on their own[65].
2. A true change in the field of economics would require a shift in negative heuristics, which is to say, a shift in the axiomatic, methodological and epistemological openness of the discipline. While both Krugman and Stiglitz advocate a negative heuristic different from that of the mainstream, they do not support less rigorous formalism or more axiomatic openness.[66]
3. Ultimately, mainstream economists' ignorance of heterodox approaches (Colander 2010) needs to be countered with discussion of works by prominent researchers advocating novel approaches to economics. The near total absence of heterodox sources in papers authored by Krugman und Stiglitz underscores their reliance on mainstream views.

[65] Lebaron (20006) shows with reference to Gunnar Myrdal that not even the Nobel Prize safeguards against marginalization in an academic discipline.

[66] In this, both are different from other potential 'insider' critics of mainstream economics who are careful about their heuristic affiliation with mainstream economics and whose critique has been labelled as 'organized hypocrisy' (Vernengo 2010: 390).

Table 2: Stiglitz and Krugman

	Stance and Contributions	Academic Influence
Joseph Stiglitz	* Vehement critic of the mainstream * Author of important works on key theoretical issues (macroeconomics) * Proponent of a new information economy paradigm	* Nobel laureate (2001) * Editor of important professional journals: - *Journal of Economic Perspectives* (1986–93) * Co-initiator of the well-endowed Institute for New Economic Thinking * President of professional associations: - The Eastern Economic Association (2008–09) - The International Economic Association (2011–13) * Member of the Council of Economic Advisers (1993–97) * Author of influential textbooks: - *Economics* (with C.E. Walsh) - *Principles of Macroeconomics* (with C.E. Walsh) - *Economics of the Public Sector* (these textbooks discuss only the traditional canon of ideas)
Paul Krugman	* Vehement critic of the mainstream * Author of important works in trade theory, a non-core subject area in economics * Does not advocate for a specific alternate paradigm	* Nobel laureate (2008) * President of professional associations: - The Eastern Economic Association (2010) * Member of the Council of Economic Advisors (1982–83) * Author of influential textbooks: - *International Economics* (with Maurice Obstfeld) - *Macroeconomics* (with Robin Wells) - *Microeconomics* (with Robin Wells) (these textbooks discuss only the traditional canon of ideas)

In this paper, we sought to assess the likelihood of a revolution in thought emerging from the economics establishment in the U.S. – that is, from the dominant center of knowledge production in the discipline. For those who believe that productive change within a branch of knowledge hinges crucially on its receptiveness to a plurality of ideas, our findings are not encouraging. Yet the conclusion that innovation is unlikely from within the discipline merely implies that momentum for change is required from without. While this momentum could potentially emerge from a broad-based social movement (such as that seen in the 1960s; see e.g. Reich (1993: 45),

Lee (2004: 184ff), Mata (2009)), the adoption of new guidelines in academia (such as mandatory charters for intellectual diversity[67]), or massive financial incentives (such as special subsidies for heterodox research)[68], these topics lie beyond the scope of this paper. Nevertheless, one thing is clear: without meaningful change within the discipline, King's prediction that Post Keynesian economics may well be dead by 2020 is a likely scenario for the entire heterodox spectrum[69] (2002: 256).

---

[67] There is some evidence that university regulations advocating diversity were, at least, helpfull in hiring the so called ‚radical package' at the University of Massachusetts/Amherst in the early 1970s; see Katzner (2011: 118).

[68] The Institute for New Economic Thinking (INET) funded by George Soros appears to be based on these considerations. However, the very limited resources of INET can certainly not balance the economic capital position of heterodox economics with the mainstream assuming that INET really focusses on what has been classified as 'heterodox' here.

[69] It appears in this vein that Colander (2010) and Colander/Holt/Rosser (2010) argue in favour of a 'under-cover' inside-the-mainstream heterodoxy, which does not actively and in a hostile manner distinguish itself from the orthodoxy, yet remains critical to it. Although I am not convinced that such a 'Troian horse' strategy will work for it rests on the assumption that the differences (if not contradictions!) in methodology and heuristics can be successfully disguised, this may possible secure the odd academic position for some individuals but it certainly cannot contribute to what is at stake here: a paradigm shift or pluralisation in economics.

References

Abel, A.B., Bernanke, B.S. (2005); Macroeconomics, Boston

Allington, N.F.B., McCombie, J.S.L., Pike, M. (2011); The failure of the new macroeconomic consensus: from non-ergodicity to the efficient markets hypothesis and back; in: International Journal of Public Policy, Vol. 7, No. 1/2/3, pp. 4 - 21

Aslanbeigui, N., Oakes, G. (2007); The Editor as Scientific Revolutionary: Keynes, the Economic Journal, and the Pigou Affair, 1936- 1938; in: Journal of the History of Economic Thought, Vol. 29, No.l, pp. 15-48

Bean, C. (2010), Joseph Schumpeter Lecture The Great Moderation, The Great Panic, and the Great Contraction; in: Journal of the European Economic Association, Vol.8, pp. 289–325

Bernanke, B. S. (2010); On the Implications of the Financial Crisis for Economics; remarks delivered at a conference at Princeton University, available: http://www.federalreserve.gov/newsevents/speech/bernanke20100924a.pdf.

Bernanke, B.S. (2012); The Great Moderation; in: Koenig, E.F., Leeson, R., Kahn, G.A. (eds.); The Taylor Rule and the transformation of monetary policy, Stanford, pp. 145 - 162

Besley, T., Hennesey, P. (2009); Letter to HM Queen Elisabeth, The British Academy (available: http://memex.naughtons.org/wp-content/uploads/2010/09/economists_letter_to_hmq.pdf

Blanchflower, D. (2009); The future of monetary policy, open lecture at Cardiff University, March 24th 2009, available: http://194.61.178.65/publications/Documents/speeches/2009/speech382.pdf

Blanchard, O. (2006); Macroeconomics, New York

Blanchard, O. (2008); The State of Macro, NBER Working Paper 14259

Blanchard, O., Dell'Ariccia, G., Mauro, P. (2010): Rethinking Macroeconomic Policy, IMF Staff Position Note 10/03, Washington

Bourdieu, P. (1990); Homo Academicus, Cambridge

Bourdieu, P. (1991); Zur Soziologie symbolischer Formen, Frankfurt

Caballero, R.J. (2010); Macroeconomics after the Crisis: Time to Deal with the Pretense-of-Knowledge Syndrome; in: Journal of Economic Perspectives, Vol. 24, no.4, pp. 85 – 102

Cartwright, E. (2011); Behavioral Economics, Abingdon

Clower, R.; The Keynesian Counter-Revolution: A Theoretical Appraisal; in: Hahn, F.H., Brechling, F.P.R. (eds.); The Theory of Interest Rates, London 1965, pp. 103 - 125

Coase, R.H. (1994); Essays on Economics and Economists, Chicago

Cochrane, J.H. (2011); How Did Paul Krugman Get It So Wrong?; in: Economic Affairs, Vol. 31, No.2, pp. 36 – 40

Colander, D.C. (2010); Moving beyond the rhetoric of pluralism: suggestions for an 'inside-the mainstream' heterodoxy; in: Garnett, R., Olsen, E.K., Starr, M. (eds.); Economic Pluralism, London, pp. 36 - 47

Colander, D.C., Holt, R.C.F., Rosser, J.B. Jr. (2009); Introduction; in: Colander, D.C., Holt, R.C.F., Rosser, J.B. Jr. (eds.): Changing Face of Economics: Conversations with Cutting Edge Economists, Ann Arbor, pp. 1- 25

Colander, D.C., Holt, R.C.F., Rosser, J.B. Jr. (2010); How to win friends and (possibly) influence mainstream economists; in: Journal of Post Keynesian Economics, Vol. 32, No.3, pp. 397 - 408

Cronin, B. (2010); The Diffusion of Heterodox Economics; in: American Journal of Economics and Sociology, Vol. 69, No.5, pp. 1475 - 1494

Cross, R. (1982); The Duhem-Quine-Thesis, Lakatos and the Appraisal of Theories in Macroeconomics; in: Economic Journal, Vol. 92, pp. 320- 340

Davidson, P. (1984); Reviving Keynes' Revolution; in: Journal of Post Keynesian Economics, Vol. 6, No.4, pp. 561-575

Davidson, P. (2005); Responses to Lavoie, King, and Dow on What Post Keynesianism Is and Who Is a Post Keynesian; in: Journal of Post Keynesian Economics, Vol. 27, No. (3), pp. 393–408

Davis, J.B. (2006); The turn in economics: neoclassical dominance to mainstream pluralism?; in: Journal of Institutional Economics, Vol. 2, No.1, pp. 1 - 20

Deutsch, K.W., Platt, J., Senghaas, D. (1971); ConditionsFavoring Major Advances in Social Science; in: Science, Vol. 171, No. 3970, pp. 450 - 459

Eggertsson, G.B., Krugman, P. (2012); Debt, Deleveraging, and the Liquidity Trap: A Fisher-Minsky-Koo approach; in: Quarterly Journal of Economics, Vol. 127, No.3, pp. 1469 – 1513

Feyerabend, P. (1970); Consolations for the Specialist; in: Lakatos, I., Musgrave, A. (eds.); Criticism and the Growth of Knowledge, Cambridge, pp. 197 - 230

Feyerabend, P. (1975); Against Method. Outline of an Anarchistic Theory of Knowledge, London

Galbraith, J.K. (2013); The Thrid Crisis in Economics; Journal of Economic Issues, Vol. 47, No.2, pp. 311 - 322

Graham, H.D., Diamond, N. (1997); The Rise of American Research Universities. Elites and Challengers in the Postwar Era, Baltimore

Goodfriend, M. (2004); Monetary Policy in the new neoclassical synthesis: a primer; in: Economic Quarterly Federal Reserve Bank of Richmond, Summer, pp. 21 - 45

Hickel, R. (1986) (ed.); Radikale Neoklassik. Ein neues Paradigma zur Erklärung der Massenarbeitslosigkeit – die Vogt-Kontroverse, Opladen

Hutton, W. (1986); The Revolution that Never Was. An Assessment of Keynesian Economics, London

Katzner, D.W. (2011); At the Edge of Camelot. Debating Economics in Turbulent Times, Oxford/New York

Kazmierski, U. (1993); Grundlagenkrise in der Volkswirtschaftslehre; in: Ethik und Sozialwissenschaften Vol. 4, No. 2, pp. 283 - 295

Keynes, J.M. (1919); The Economic Consequences of the Peace, London

Keynes, J.M. (1925); The Economic Consequences of Mr. Churchill, in: The Nation and Athenaeum, May

Keynes, J.M. (1935); Letter to George Bernard Shaw of January, 1st 1935; in: Moggridge, D. (ed.); Collected Writings of John Maynard Keynes, Vol. XIII, London

Keynes, J. M. (1936); The General Theory of Employment, Interest and Money, London

King, J. (2002); A History of Post Keynesian Economics since 1936, Cheltenham

Kirman, A. (2010); The Economic Crisis is a Crisis for Economic Theory; in: CESIfo Economic Studies, Vol. 56, No. 4, pp. 498 - 535

Klein, L. (1947); The Keynesian Revolution, New York

Koppl, R., Luther, W.J. (2012); Hayek, Keynes, and modern macroeconomics; in: The Review of Austrian Economics, Vol. 25, No.3, pp. 223 -241

Kromphardt, J. (2013); Die größten Ökonomen: John Maynard Keynes, Konstant/München

Krugman, P. (1995); Peddling Prosperity: Sense and Nonsens in an Age of Diminished Expexpectations, New York

Krugman, P. (1998); The Accidental Theorist and other Dispatches from the Dismal Science, New York

Krugman, P. (1999); The Return of Depression Economics, New York

Krugman, P. (2009); How Did Economists Get It So Wrong?, in: The New York Times of September, 6th 2009

Krugman, P. (2012); End this Depression Now!, New York

Krugman, P. (2013); Wynne Godley and the Hydraulics; in: The New York Times of September, the 13th

Kuhn, T. S. (1962); The Structure of Scientific Revolutions, Chicago

Lakatos, I. (1970); Falsification and the Methodology of Scientific Research Programmes, in: Lakatos, I. & Musgrave, A. (eds.); Criticism and the Growth of Knowledge, Cambridge, pp. 91-195

Lawson, T.(2006); The Nature of Heterodox Economics; in: Cambridge Journal of Economics, Vol. 30, No.4, pp. 483 – 507

Lebaron, F. (2006); 'Nobel' Economists as Public Intellectuals. The Circulation of Symbolic Capital; in: International Journal of Contemporary Sociology, Vol. 43, No.1, pp. 87 - 101

Lee, F.S. (2000); The organizational history of Post Keynesian economics in America, 1971 – 1995, in: Journal of Post Keynesian Economics, Vol. 23, No.1, pp. 141 – 162

Lee, F.S. (2004); History and Identity: The Case of Radical Economics and Radical Economists, 1945 – 70; in: Review of Radical Political Economics, Vol. 36, No.2, pp. 177 - 195

Lee, F.S. (2009); A History of Heterodox Economics: Challenging the Mainstream in the Twentieth Century, Abingdon

Lucas, R. E jr. (2003); Macroeconomic priorities; in: American Economic Review, Vol. 93, No.1, pp. 1 - 14

Lucas, R. E. jr. (2009); In defence of the dismal science; in: The Economist of August 6th 2009

Mata, T. (2009); Migrations and Boundary Work: Harvard, Radical Economists and the Committee on Political Discrimination; in: Science in Context, Vol. 22, No.1, pp. 115 – 143

Mearman, A. (2012); Heterodox economics' and the problem of classification; in: Journal of Economic Methodology, Vol. 19, No. 4, pp. 407-424

Middleton, R. (1998): Charlatans or Saviours? Economists and the British Economy from Marshall to Meade, Northampton

Minford, P. (2010); The Banking Crisis as Dynamic Stochastic General Equilibrium; in: CESIfo Economic Studies, Vol. 56, No.4, pp. 554 – 574

Minsky, H.P. (1986); Stabilizing an Unstable Economy, New Haven

Mishan, E. J. (1963); Say's Law and Walras' Law once more; in: Quarterly Journal of Economics, Vol. 77, No.4, pp. 617-625

Moggridge, D. (1990); Keynes as Editor; in: Hey, J.D., Winch, D. (Hrsg.); A Century of Economics: 100 Years of the Royal Economic Society and The Economic Journal, Oxford, pp. 143- 157

Palley, T.I. (2013); Gattopardo economics: The crisis and the mainstream response to change, IMK Working Paper No. 112, Düsseldorf

Peabody, G.E. (1971); Scientific Paradigms and Economics; An Introduction; in: Review of Radical Political Economics, Vol. 3, pp. 1 - 16

Pessaran, M.H., Smith, R.P. (2011); Beyond the DSGE Straitjacket; in: The Manchester School, Vol. 79, pp. 5 - 16

Pigou, A.C. (1941); Employment and Equilibrium, London

Pressman, S. (1999); Fifty Major Economists, London

Reich, M. (1993); Radical Economics in Historical Perspective; in: Review of Radical Political Economics, Vol. 25, No.3, pp. 43 - 50

Rezende, F.C. (2009); Keynes's Relevance and Krugman's Economics, in: Blog in 'New Economic Perspectives', erhältlich unter http://new-economicperspectives.org/2009/08/keyness-relevance-and-krugmans.html

Robinson,]. (1976); Michal Kalecki: A Neglected Prophet, in: New York Review of Books, 4th of March

Rosser, J.B., Holt, R.P.F., Colander, D. (2010); European Economics at Crossroads; in: Rosser, J.B., Holt, R.P.F., Colander, D. (eds.); European Economics at Crossroads, Cheltenham, pp. 3- 28

Schlefer, J. (2013); Embracing Wynne Godley, an Economist Who Modelled the Crisis; in: The New York Times of September, the 10th

Schmidt, C. M. and N. aus dem Moore (2010), Die Methodendiskussion in den Wirtschafstwissenschaften vor dem Hintergrund der Finanzkrise; in: Jens, U., Romahn, H. (eds.), Methodenpluralismus in den Wirtschaftswissenschaften. Marburg, pp. 143-182

Schneider, J. (1988); Kritische Neoklassik: Ergebnisse und Perspektiven; in: Vogt, W. (ed.); Politische Ökonomie heute, Regensburg 1988, pp. 183 - 220

Schultze, Ch. L. (1996): The CEA: An Inside Voice of Mainstream Economics, in: Journal of Economic Perspectives, Vol. 10, pp. 23-39

Smith, V. L. (2003); Constructivist and Ecological Rationality in Economics; in: Frängsmayr, F. (ed.); The Nobel Prizes 2002, Stockholm, pp. 502- 561

Stiglitz, J.E. (2002a); Globalization and its Discontents, New York

Stiglitz, J.E. (2002b); Information and the Change in the Paradigm in Economics; in: Frängsmayr, F. (ed.); The Nobel Prizes 2001, Stockholm, pp.472 – 540

Stiglitz, J.E. (2002c); Information and the Change in the Paradigm in Economics; in: American Economic Review, Vol. 92, No.3, pp. 460 - 501

Stiglitz, J.E. (2003); The Roaring Nineties, New York

Stiglitz, J.E. (2006); Making Globalization Work, New York

Stiglitz, J.E. (2008a); The End of Neoliberalism, Project Syndicate, July

Stiglitz, J.E. (2008b); It doesn't Take Nostradamus; in: Economist's Voice, November

Stiglitz, J.E. (2008c); Markets Can't Rule Themselves; in: Newsweek v. 31. Dezember

Stiglitz, J.E. (2009a); Moving Beyond Market Fundamentalism to A More Balanced Economy; in: Annals of Public and Cooperative Economics, Vol. 80, No. 3, pp. 345-360

Stiglitz, J.E. (2009b): The Current Economic Crisis and Lessons for Economic Theory, in: Eastern Economic Journal, Vol. 35, No. 3, pp. 281 - 296

Summers, P.M. (2005); What caused the Great Moderation? Some Cross-Country Evidence; in: Federal Reserve Bank of Kansas City Economic Review, Vol. 90, No.3, pp. 5 – 32

Vernengo, M. (2010); Conversation or monologue? On advising heterodox economists; in: Journal of Post Keynesian Economics, Vol. 32, No. 3, pp. 389 - 396

Vogt, W. (1986); Theorie der kapitalistischen und einer laboristischen Ökonomie, Frankfurt

Williamson, O. (1997); Comments, in: Coats, A.W. (Hrsg.); The Post-1945 In-ternationalization of Economics, Durham

Woodford, M. (2010); Financial Intermediation and Macroeconomic Analysis; in: Journal of Economic Perspectives, Vol. 24, No.4, pp. 21 - 44

Worland, S.T. (1972); Radical Political Economy as a 'Scientific Revolution'; in: Southern Economic Journal, Vol. 39, No. 2, pp. 274 - 284

Yonay, Y. (1998); The Struggle Over the Soul of Economics: Institutionalist and Neoclassical Economists in America Between the Wars, Princeton

Three

The short rise and long fall of heterodox economics in Germany after the 1970s. Explorations in a scientific field of power and struggle*

1. Introduction

In 1992 a group of economists published a 'Plea for a Pluralistic and Rigorous Economics' in the *American Economic Review* which was also signed by several Nobel laureates (including Franco Mogdiliani, Paul Samuelson and Jan Tinbergen). Although the 'mainstream' criticized in this plea as an intellectual monopoly is not explicitly named, there is no doubt that the authors were alluding to the 'dynamic stochastic general equilibrium model' (DSGE), usually referred to as 'neoclassical economics' (cf. Düppe/Weintraub 2014: XII). This model not only provided the foundation for the vast majority of all research articles, but also constituted the canon in the widely used textbooks of (mainly) American authors (e.g. Mankiw's *Introduction to Economics* and Samuelson/Nordhaus's *Economics*).

There are two interesting things about this 'plea.' Firstly, it asserts the dominance of a scientific paradigm in economics ('intellectual monopoly'), though this is occasionally challenged with regard to numerous 'axiomatic variations.'[70] Secondly, it deplores this dominance, an attitude which is also not universally shared. Olivier Blanchard (2008), for example, quite recently described the state of economics as 'good,' primarily because a consensus model had been successfully established within the DSGE paradigm. This seemed not only to settle the long-lasting quarrel between the 'Keynesians' and the 'neoclassical economists,' but also provided the basis for an economic policy allowing a historically unprecedented stability of growth ('Great Moderation'; cf. Summers 2005). In the terms of the much-quoted philosopher of science Thomas Samuel Kuhn, a

---

* Originally published: Journal of Economic Issues, Vol. 50, No. 4, 1105-1130
[70] Cf. especially Colander (2000) and Colander/Holt/Rosser (2004).

'normal science' had developed, and economics had thus attained the status of a 'mature' science. According to this understanding, pluralism is a sign of immaturity or of a revolutionary paradigm shift within a science, while monism is a mark of maturity and 'normality' in the business of science.

Since the last global financial crisis, everything has changed. The self-assurance of mainstream economics has gone: within the discipline, there are calls for changes,[71] while external critics ask why the crisis was not predicted, and why there are no ready-made recipes for dealing with crises on the scale of the latest global financial crisis and the resulting European debt crisis.[72] Critics are calling into question the universal validity of a paradigm that is ontologically defined by an optimistic faith in self-regulation, and is almost completely fixated on allocative questions, instead of calling into question the conditions and risks of stability (cf. Lucas 2003: 11).

The aim here is not to argue for the pluralization of economics on the basis of the theory and philosophy of science;[73] the plea for pluralization in 1992, just like numerous other memoranda and appeals published by academics and students since then,[74] is sufficient indication of the lack of plurality and the continued existence of a monistic consensus in the community of economists. Instead, the central question will be why the state of pluralization that was apparent in surveys of economists at the beginning of the 1980s (cf. Frey/Humbert/Schneider 2007), was not maintained or

---

[71] Cf. amongst others Blanchard/Del'Arricia/Mauro (2010), Caballero (2010), Galbraith (2013), Stiglitz (2009a; 2009b; 2011; 2014).

[72] Particular prominence was attained by the question the Queen of England put to her economists in the British Academy of Science: why, she asked, was there not sufficient warning of the global financial crisis? (cf. Besley/Hennessy 2009). But German Chancellor Angela Merkel expressed similar criticisms at the 5th Lindau conference of Nobel laureates in economics (cf. Merkel 2014).

[73] The list of studies dealing with this is long. To give a small selection: Davis (1994), Backhouse (2001), King (2002a), Kellert/Longino/Waters (2006).

[74] The list of relevant appeals is equally long: see e.g. Auroi et al. (2011), Chesney et al. (2011), Thielemann et al. (2012). There are also numerous appeals from students, such as the 'Petition Autisme Economique' in 2000, 'opening up economics' by the Cambridge 27 in 2001, and the latest appeal, 'An international student call for pluralism in economics' by the International Student Initiative for Pluralism in Economics (2014).

indeed expanded when many faculties of economics were effectively re-founded at the East German universities after German reunification in the 1990s.[75] To do this, we need to briefly describe, in section 2, the concept of scientific plurality used here, in order to be able to distinguish between 'axiomatic variation' and 'genuine plurality.' This will also allow us to categorize other terms often used in this context: 'mainstream,' 'orthodoxy,' 'dissenter' and 'heterodoxy.' In section 3 we trace the paradigmatic development of economics in Germany (in light of the object of this study, pluralism), and its position in the universities, in the institutional context of changing structures of university governance. The focus, then, is exclusively on the academic discipline of economics, as represented by professorial positions at public universities.[76] In section 4 we will seek explanations for this development in an unpretentious Bourdieuian analytical framework. Section 5, finally, gives a brief conclusion.

2. Plurality versus variation

From a philosophy of science perspective, the concept of 'plurality' or 'pluralism' is opaque. Sometimes there is talk of a plurality of methods, sometimes of theoretical or paradigmatic pluralism. Following the concept of pluralism found in critical rationalism, and the philosophy of science principles of the theorists of pluralism, Imre Lakatos (1978) and Paul Feyerabend (1975), plurality is to be understood here as a multitude of paradigms, in the sense of a 'battle of the paradigms' for a better interpre-

---

[75] A new survey at the beginning of the 2000s showed that 80% of the economists surveyed now based their views on neoclassical economics – and these were significantly more young economists than old ones close to retirement (cf. Frey/Humbert/Schneider 2007). A similar development can also be observed for the USA, however; cf. Colander/Klamer (1987) und Klamer (2007: 230).

[76] Private universities, the first of which were established in the mid-1980s, cannot be taken into consideration here. This is because of the limited access to reliable data, but also because of the completely marginal influence they have had so far in Germany. Universities of applied sciences (*Fachhochschulen*) are not examined because they are not authorized to award doctorates and therefore cannot contribute to the reproduction of scientific paradigms.

tation or approximation of reality. Using Lakatos's scientific research program (srp)[77] as a frame of reference, the following dimensions of classification can be described: (cf. Tab. 1, Chap. 3): 1) a particular methodology, which is regarded as acceptable (and therefore scientific); 2) in epistemological terms, it is possible to identify certain core assumptions (axioms) underlying the formation of models; 3) a 'negative heuristic,' according to which the postulates of the research program, which have been derived from the core assumptions, are not (allowed to be) called into question.

The DSGE mainstream – which is made up of new classical macroeconomics and neo-Keynesianism[78] – is unanimously based on the core assumptions that characterize the paradigm of social exchange theory. These are rationality, ergodicity and substitutionality (cf. Davidson 1984), the exclusive acceptance of a formal mathematical-deductive, positivist reductionism (cf. Lawson 2006). After the 'empirical turn' of the last two or three decades, these have been combined with sophisticated micro- and macro-econometrics, or with experimental arrangements (cf. Schmidt/ aus dem Moore 2010), such as are familiar from the leading natural sciences (physics and chemistry). The postulate of stability and optimality (acceptance of Walras's law), which is implemented a priori in the core assumptions, serves as a 'model solution,' and thus functions as a marker of a *negative heuristic* (cf. Sargent 1979: 67 – 70). The apparently very different model prognoses of new classical macroeconomics (hyper-balanced and hyper-stable) on the one hand, and of standard and neo-Keynesianism (unbalanced, open to intervention) on the other hand are based on changes to assumptions in the 'protective belt' (e.g. about the speed of adjustment, the rigidity of prices and quantities, the formation of expectations etc.), but do not actually point to a different paradigmatic origin of the two schools

---

[77] For the problems involved in translating Lakatos's concept to economics, see Cross (1982). For an overview of the discussion on the application of philosophy of science concepts to economics, see Drakopoulos/Karayiannis (2005).

[78] Combining (neo-)Keynesian and neoclassical models in a single paradigm may sound strange to some readers, but will hopefully become plausible when discussed in more detail below. As Davidson (1992; 2005) has shown, placing these in the same paradigm highlights the unsuitability of the use of the term 'Keynesian' for neo-Keynesian models (which can thus be seen as fraudulent labeling).

of theory.[79] It is important to understand that the heuristic device of market stability as 'model solution' does neither preclude the existence of disequilibria as theoretical outcome based on particular assumptions (i.e. due to factors located in the *epistemological dimension* of paradigms) nor the use of non-equilibrium approaches in the *methodological dimension* as long as such disequilibria are covered by Walras's law (cf. Arthur 2010: 164; Greenfield 1986).

Criticism of the core assumptions of the mainstream is occasionally answered with the argument that these are still valid for the DSGE model used in education and training, but not for the model used in research. The latter, it is argued, has long since incorporated approaches from behavioral economics, neuroeconomics or the economics of complexity, and assumptions of, for example, limited rationality. Since the proponents of these approaches – sometimes referred to as 'dissenters,' sometimes as the 'periphery' – accept the (often methodological) limitations of the mainstream, and (observing the 'negative heuristic') do not venture to voice any fundamental criticism of the mainstream as a 'model solution,'[80] they are recognized

---

[79] Consequently, both approaches can be found in modern textbooks, with a distinction being made between short term (neo-Keynesian model) and long term (neoclassical model); cf. e.g. Abel/Bernanke (2005); Blanchard/Johnson (2013). Especially noteworthy is information economics, which also shares the core assumptions and methodology of the mainstream, but nonetheless rejects the ideal of stability and optimality as a negative heuristic. This apparently inconsistent finding is not based on the proof of deductive weaknesses in the theoretical derivation of the postulates of stability and optimality, but in the special emphasis placed on the distribution of information to economic subjects (who are no longer permitted to be seen as representative agents). This is raised to the rank of a – divergent – core assumption.

[80] 'Loyalty' to the mainstream is attested either by refusing to generalize the proof one has just given of the untenability of certain assumptions (mostly the assumption of rationality) (cf. Smith (2002, p. 505) for behavioral economics), or by explicitly stating that this is not an alternative to the dominant mainstream, but simply an addition (cf. e.g. Hermann-Pillath (2002, p. 21) for evolutionary economics and Arrow (1988: 275ff.), Blume/Durlauf (2001) and Arthur (2010) for complexity economics). This may be why Colander/Holt/Rosser (2004) view these approaches as the 'changing face of mainstream economics' rather than a paradigm shift. However, there are other voices which are more inclined to rate some of these 'dissenters' (particularly the evolutionary and complexity economists) as heterodox: cf e.g. Barkley Rosser (2004) and Fontana (2008). This difference in judgement may be due to different conceptions of complexity (cf. Bronk 2011):

by the mainstream,[81] and occasionally even held up as the dynamic front line of mainstream research (cf. Colander/Holt/Rosser 2009).[82] The same does not apply to those dissenters within the mainstream who share its core axioms and the optimistic belief in stability and optimality, but not the methodological requirements of a rigorous formal deductivism. The economics of order (*Ordnungsökonomik*), but also the 'Austrian school,' based on the work of Hayek, are largely marginalized as worthy, but methodologically weak and no longer up-to-date (cf. Schmidt/aus dem Moore 2010, pp. 170ff.).

Heterodoxy is characterized by the rejection of some (or all) of the mainstream axioms, methodological openness to less formal, narrative deductions and inductive techniques, and, consequently, the repudiation of the stability and optimality of the market coordination solution (repudiation of Walras's law[83]). Theoretical schools that can undoubtedly be regarded as

---

those, who refer to 'epistemological complexity' highlight the fact that no economic agent has the ability to collect and process all the information necessary to act fully rational – the world is simply too complicated. Those, however, who refer to 'ontological complexity' highlight the fact that not all information – particularly those about future events – are available because they are part of human action – i.e. the world is complex (to the dimension n) in the sense that it is an open system (with n possible paths of evolution). The former conception appears to be reconcilable with mainstream economics, while the latter appears to be irreconcilable. Therefore, we have rated evolutionary and complexity economics partly as (dissenters from) mainstream, partly as heterodox.

[81] This means, primarily, that representatives of these approaches are able to publish their work in the major mainstream journals (which are, in turn, part of the economic and symbolic capital of a paradigm).

[82] Both Kuhn's 'paradigm' and Lakatos's 'scientific research programs' are terminologically ambiguous. Here we wish to understand the concepts as efforts to explain the economy as a whole, in which all aspects of economics are embedded – theories of the labor market, distribution and growth, as well as theories of foreign trade, money or finance. From this perspective, however, it seems questionable whether, for example, behavioral economics or the economics of complexity actually constitute independent paradigms, or whether they are just partial theories, which may in some cases have connections to various paradigms (see footnote 80).

[83] The insight that a real paradigmatic alternative implies the rejection of Walras's law goes back to Robert Clower (1965). But even before that, 'heterodox' economists such as Karl Marx or Thomas Robert Malthus had begun to question the classical predecessor of

heterodox include post-Keynesianism, neo-Marxist regulation theory and theories of social economy[84]. Neo-Ricardianism, which goes back to Piero Sraffa, also conceives itself as heterodox, since its proponents reject the mainstream postulate of stability and optimality, while nonetheless accepting the research methodology and core axioms of the mainstream. This apparently inconsistent result can be explained by the fact that the neo-Ricardians, in the so-called Cambridge Capital Controversy (CCC), provided the proof that the stable equilibrium solutions based on the core assumptions of the DSGE mainstream, which are also shared (or at least not called into question) by the neo-Ricardians, are only valid in very limited circumstances.[85] In short, this rocked the entire deductive foundation of the mainstream – but without offering any plausible alternative.

The dual classification into orthodoxy/mainstream and heterodoxy/non-mainstream has the advantage of allowing clear distinctions between model-theory-based variations within a paradigm (i.e. intraparadigmatic plurality, which can also encompass the so-called 'dissenters') and interparadigmatic plurality. Heuristics turn out to be a key point of differentiation: only those models and theories that do not question the heuristic of the DSGE – i.e. the postulate of stability manifested in Walras's law as a 'model solution' – are orthodox/mainstream or are accepted by the mainstream, and only those models and theories that explicitly reject this heuristic can be regarded as heterodox/non-mainstream[86]. In this sense, real

---

Walras's law, Say's law; for the relationship between Walras's law and Say's law, see Mishan (1963).

[84] We have already pointed out the ambigious position of evolutionary and complexity economics. Sometimes, feminist and ecological economics are also ranked among the heterodox approaches (cf. Dobusch/Kapeller 2012) – however, these research programmes are obviously different as they are not necessarily ordered around shared epistemological, methodological and heuristic dimensions but rather a shared subject of inquiry. As much as 'international economics' or 'labor economics' is neither *per se* heterodox nor mainstream, 'feminist economics' or 'ecological economics' would only be counted as heterodox once heterodox approaches are applied (which, however, is often the case).

[85] One would have to either live in a one-commodity world (such as Ricardo's corn economy), or make specific assumptions about the capital intensity of the subsistence commodity industry and all of its input producers – neither of which is especially realistic.

[86] Drawing the demarcation line between heterodox and orthodox schools of thought in such a way allows to avoid the counter-intuative results of, for instance, having to rate

plurality, in contrast to 'axiomatic variation,' means the acceptance of all heuristics – orthodox and heterodox – that are based on rigorous modeling, which can be intersubjectively reconstructed and empirically falsified.

3. Development of economics in West Germany after 1945

With Hesse (2007; 2010), we can observe that economics and business studies were subject to multiple layers of development at German universities in the post-war years:

a) The number of students of *Wirtschaftswissenschaften* (economics + business studies) exploded from around 9000 in 1950 to 31,000 in 1965 (= + 244%), then to 52,000 in the 1974/75 winter semester (= + 68%).[87] To begin with, the number of professors did not keep pace, rising only from 54 in 1950 to 78 in 1960 (= + 44%). With the wave of new institutions being founded, however, this number also rose quite considerably by the mid-1970s, to 243 (= + 211%) giving young researchers an extremely powerful position in the market for academic economists (cf. Hesse 2007: 125). From the mid-1970s, this picture changed dramatically – access for young academics was now more or less blocked until around the end of the 1990s.[88]
b) The formalization and mathematization of the discipline was accompanied by a methodological and epistemological 'professionalization,' which was meant to allow economics to rise to the rank of a *Leitwissenschaft* or leading science (at least among the social sciences) (cf. e.g. Schipper 2013). Since this process was mainly driven by the US, the new scientific hegemon, it is often referred to as 'Americanization.' However, in view of the efforts of German

---

Neoricardianism as orthodox or Austrian economics as heterodox as would be the case if the methodological requirement of formalism would be the distinctive ingredient as advocated by Lawson (2006) or if heterodoxy would simply be taken as a „collection of different, non-neoclassical schools of thought" (Dobusch/Kapeller 2012: 1036).

[87] Due to a change in the classification system in 1972, the student numbers are not completely comparable over time.

[88] During the wave of foundation of new institutions, around 70 per cent of *Assistenten* (research assistants/ junior researchers) had a chance of gaining a professorship. Once these new institutions had been founded, from the mid-1970s, only 9 per cent of them had this chance; cf. Finkenstaedt (2010: 157).

economists to catch up with developments that had been missed during the Nazi period (especially the younger generation, most of whom had been trained in the US), it can also be understood at least in part as a process of 'self-Americanization' (cf. Hesse 2007: 128f.; Rosser/Holt/Colander 2010: 8).

c) Separation of economics from legal studies (previously combined in faculties of *Staatswissenschaften*, literally 'state sciences'), and internal specialization within economics faculties.

The aspect of professionalization, in conjunction with self-Americanization, requires further attention here[89]. On the one hand, this reflects the largely normal development of a science from the pre-paradigmatic stage to that of a more 'mature' science (cf. Kuhn 1970: 256ff.). On the other hand, however, professionalization also refers here to the transition from an evaluative normativism ('advocacy') to a (supposedly) objective positivism ('objectivity') – especially in light of the ongoing development of empirical testing methods, and the emergence of econometrics. The driving force of this development originally lay in the US, in the attempt to gain legitimation and acceptance for an academic discipline that was still in its infancy. Since – in contrast to Europe and in particular Germany – it was not the institution of the university that give the discipline or its representatives the necessary legitimation, generally accepted scientific criteria such as rigor and epistemological exactness had to be borrowed from other, successful disciplines ('leading sciences') – especially, of course, the natural sciences (cf. Busch 1959: 80ff.; Mirowski 1989). Thus formal-

[89] One referee was surprised to read so much about the development of economics in the US in a chapter on the development of economics in West Germany. However, the US hegemony in science in general and economics in particular has long been confirmed (cf. Graham/Diamond 1997, Rosser/Holt/Colander 2010) and it can certainly not be ignored for the evolution of economics in Germany after World War 2. The same referee critized ‚self-Americanization' as too individualistic a conception and referred to alternative explanations such as the cold war environment (cf. Garnett 2006). Although it certainly cannot be claimed that any evolutionary process is one-dimensional (cf. Backhouse 2005: 384), it must be stressed that it is the ontological process of forming a ‚normal science' in economics which is considered here not the ideological process of the rise of free market economics within that paradigm.

ization, axiomatization, and empirical monitoring were taken as the methodological and epistemological boundaries of what was legitimately allowed to call itself economics (cf. Fourcade-Gourinchas 2001: 426). Since, however, the process of knowledge acquisition is culturally bound, professionalization also implies a heuristic demarcation of boundaries: the special social position of the market as an instrument of coordination and a meritocratic justification for economic distribution outcomes in the US meant that an academic discipline hoping to gain social acceptance could not afford to fundamentally challenge the superiority of the market over other mechanisms of coordination and distribution (cf. Fourcade 2009: 35ff., 78ff.).[90] The equilibrium and welfare economics developing at the end of the 19th century, based on the work of Jevons, Menger, Walras and Pareto, increasingly replaced American institutionalism as the dominant paradigm in US economics. Although the German university as an institution, and the professor as a 'mandarin,' had lost much of their authority after the experiences of the Nazi period, and were subjected to further challenges, especially during the student movement, the phenomenon of 'self-Americanization' is probably to be ascribed more to German economists' feelings of inferiority in the international context[91] than to any urgent need to acquire legitimacy in the national social and political arena.[92] What happened, then, was an importing of norms which had no cultural basis in Germany – but which are defended, to this day, by those scholars who reject the idea of greater methodological openness.[93] Astonishingly, the argument given is that specific national approaches (*nationale*

[90] An American business journalist sums it up neatly: "To be an economist in the United States, you have to believe that the market works most of the time. The situation in which markets don't work, or cannot be made to work, is really quite exceptional, and not all that interesting to study" (Fourcade 2009: 61).
[91] Hesse (2010: 320ff.) refers to a large number of sources that show these feelings of inferiority, thus suggesting that Americanization was part of a semantics of progress.
[92] The German 'economics of order' (*Ordnungsökonomik*), which still resists the claims to axiomatization and formalization made by mainstream economics, was quite influential in the early phase of West Germany history (cf. among others Ptak 2004: 155ff.).
[93] Rosser/Holt/Colander (2010: 18) bemoan this US-centeredness as a source of second-class imitation rather than first-class innovation.

Sonderwege) would undermine the international competitiveness of German economists.

Although the theoretical foundations of equilibrium and welfare economics were laid in the second half of the 19th century, and came to occupy a dominant position in Great Britain,[94] it is nonetheless the period after the Second World War that has to be seen as the real phase of professionalization of economics, in the sense used above – and in both politics and academia, this phase was mainly dominated by one economist: John Maynard Keynes (cf. Solow 1986; Snowdon/Vane 1997). The construction of macroeconomic theories on the basis of Keynes's magnum opus – the *General Theory* (Keynes 1936) – left room not only for formalization and econometric expansion,[95] but also for appropriation by the (neo-)classical orthodoxy which Keynes had criticized.[96] Keynesian principles of economic management also allowed a promising combination of scientific objectivity and added value for society. The sentence ascribed to Paul Samuelson, "We are all Keynesians now," was roughly applicable to West Germany in the 1960s, where just over two thirds of the available professorships had been filled, even straight after the war, by academics who had completed their *Habilitation* either after 1945 (one third) or between 1933 and 1945 (another third) (cf. Hesse 2010: 191). The 1960s, however, saw the beginning of a process that would intensify in the 1970s, the struggle for paradigmatic supremacy – the second phase in the maturation process of economics, in the sense of the contested emergence of a 'normal science.' On the one hand, the voices questioning the neoclassical synthesis

---

[94] This is due, in particular, to the position of Alfred Marshall and Arthur Cecil Pigou at one of the world's foremost elite universities at the time. Thus there was already talk of 'orthodoxy' (cf. Keynes 1936: V) or of a 'citadelle' (cf. Keynes 1934: 488) in the first quarter of the 20th century.

[95] In the US, Lawrence Klein was arguably one of the most important exponents of the combination of econometrics and Keynesian macroeconomics.

[96] John Hicks's well-known IS-LM model can be seen as formalizing Keynesianism and reconciling it with neoclassical orthodoxy. Paul A. Samuelson eventually became the most prominent and influential representative of this "neoclassical synthesis," the harmonization of Keynes and neoclassical theory, in the US. In Germany, this version of Keynesianism was mainly propagated by Erich Schneider, Erich Preiser, Fritz Neumark and Karl Schiller.

as the standard interpretation of Keynesianism were growing louder; these critics saw it instead as a 'bastard Keynesianism' (Joan Robinson), which could not claim to give an accurate rendering of Keynesian macroeconomics. On the other hand, the Italian economist Piero Sraffa, a member of the circle surrounding Keynes, had published a slim volume in 1960 (Sraffa 1960), which dealt a severe blow to neoclassical equilibrium economics. He did this by pointing out deductive inconsistencies in the central argumentative field of neoclassical economics (and of the neoclassical synthesis): the price-based mechanism of equilibrium undoubtedly only works under unrealistic conditions. For the acceptance of a paradigm in a science that lays claim to exactness and rigor as its basis for legitimation, deductive weaknesses had to be fatal.[97] In addition to this, Sraffa set out to remedy the central weakness of classical political economy – the objective theory of value – with the *formally* exact description of an invariant measure of value. This led to a renaissance of classical political economy of Ricardian, but also Marxist provenance, whose proponents criticized not only the theoretical weaknesses of neoclassical equilibrium economics, but also its tenuous link with reality (cf. Vogt 1973: 12).

The German physicist and Nobel laureate Max Planck (1928: 22) argued that new scientific insights do not become widely accepted because the proponents of the old paradigm change their minds, but because they grow old and disappear, and because the next generation of scholars are familiar with the new paradigm. In keeping with this, the sudden increase in chairs and professorships during the wave of new universities, and the not-yet completed generational changeover in the existing ('old') universities, can be seen as an institutional starting point for a potential pluralization of economics in Germany. At first glance, the reform of the German higher edu-

[97] The 'fightback' against the alleged theoretical falsification, in defense of the embattled neoclassical position, was initially led by Paul A. Samuelson and Robert Solow, later by Christopher Bliss and Frank Hahn. Although they had to acknowledge the validity of the criticism put forward by Sraffa, they were so successful in downplaying the significance of this controversy for the rigor of neoclassical equilibrium theory that Sraffa is now not even mentioned in studies on the development of modern macroeconomics, let alone in standard textbooks; cf. Cohen/Hartcourt (2003).

cation landscape taking place at the same time as the 'battle of the paradigms' had more to do with organizational structures and educational objectives. On the level of economics faculties or departments, however, ideas of reform relating to socio-political orientation can certainly be linked with a type of economics that saw itself as an alternative to neoclassical equilibrium economics, even in its standard Keynesian version, or which at least called for pluralistic openness in the 'battle of the paradigms.'

In the founding phase of new universities in the 1960s and 1970s, a paradigmatic opening-up of economics coincided with the organizational opening-up of universities, especially certain 'reform' universities (*Reformuniversitäten*), which created space to consolidate the process of pluralization by appointing professors. Due to high demand for professorial candidates, which the existing supply of *habilitierte Privatdozenten* could not even come close to meeting[98], the elite system 'university' temporarily opened up. Recruitment practices based on habit and social structures were replaced by practices based on science and research policy,[99] particularly in those universities that had been founded as part of a movement to reform society, but also in universities – even traditional ones – where representatives of the students or research assistants had substantial involvement in decision-making, thanks to the short-lived principle of *Drittelparität* (one-third parity) in the governing bodies of the university. The university system at the beginning of the 1970s can be roughly divided into the following categories:[100] 1) traditional old universities with little likelihood of pluralization, 2) old universities where reform-oriented status groups have a strong influence; low to medium likelihood of pluralization, 3) newly

[98] In the mid-1970s, around one fifth of all university professors had not completed a *Habilitation* (the ordinary formal qualification required to become university professor); cf. Hesse (2007: 124).

[99] Cf. von der Vring (1975: 113 and 262), Gräfing (2012: 72ff.). What occasionally happened, however (at the University of Bielefeld, for example), was that other humanities faculties intervened in the recruitment process for individual chairs in economics, under the slogan of 'interdisciplinarity.' This probably led to a different orientation than would have been the case if only economists had been involved.

[100] For more on this and on the coding of the university types and their likelihood of pluralization, see Heise et al. (2015: 74ff.).

founded universities, designed to relieve pressure on existing universities, no aspirations to reform; low likelihood of pluralization, 4) newly founded universities based on Humboldt's ideal[101], low likelihood of pluralization, 5) newly founded universities with aspirations to reform in relation to social openness and practical relevance; medium likelihood of pluralization, and 6) newly founded universities with aspirations to socio-political reform; high likelihood of pluralization (cf. Tab. 3).

Table 3: University status and likelihood of pluralization to be expected

	Classification	**Likelihood of pluralization**
1	Traditional 'old university'	Low
2	Old universities strongly influenced by reform-oriented status groups	low-medium
3	Newly founded universities, designed to relieve pressure on existing universities, no reform aspirations	Low
4	Newly founded universities based on Humboldt's ideal	Low
5	Newly founded universities with aspirations to reform in relation to social openness and practical relevance	Medium
6	Newly founded universities with aspirations to socio-political reform	High

The upshot of this is that we cannot expect any nationwide pluralization of economics as an academic discipline in Germany, but a heterogenization of both the access routes and the paradigmatic orientation of the professorships, with considerable regional variation. This, but also the bypassing of the *Habilitation* as the normal path to a professorship,[102] temporarily made it impossible to close the elite system of the university 'from below,' i.e. with a qualification requirement monitored by the system itself. This led

[101] The University of Bielefeld and Konstanz University were founded with the explicit objective to create small-sized, research-oriented 'elite' universities adopting the ideals of 19th century German university reformer Wilhelm von Humboldt.

[102] On the one hand, this is a unique feature of the German-language university system, which is not internationally relevant. On the other hand, alternative recruitment paths via junior professorships and so-called 'tenure-track' systems have not yet been able to make any great headway against the path dependencies of tradition; cf. Bloch/Burkhardt (2011).

to pressure for standardization, linking recruitment to self-determined standards. Whether this form of closing the system 'from above' reproduces the heterogeneity which is to be expected, perhaps even extending it spatially, or whether it instead leads back to a broad paradigmatic homogeneity, depends very much on the developments on the 'battlefield of the paradigms.' It also depends, of course, on the range of possible dispositions in the field of power of 'economics.' The battlefield of the paradigms saw a wave of further developments of orthodoxy: from monetarism and new classical macroeconomics to neo-Keynesian modeling and, finally, the new neoclassical synthesis. Alongside this, however, a few 'dissenters' also emerged, variations on the neo-classical mainstream, who differed from the mainstream in their epistemology or methodologies but not their heuristics: neo-Austrian, neo-Schumpeterian, neo-institutionalist theories and, more recently, behavioral and complexity economic approaches. Heterodoxy developed various post-Keynesian and left-Keynesian positions,[103] neo-Marxist theories such as the (French) regulation school or the (American) 'social structure of accumulation' approach. In Germany, however, the latter received little attention, and no professorial backing within economics departments.[104] In his history of post-Keynesian economics, John King (2002: 140) claims that there was no significant group of post-Keynesian economists in Germany, but that "...neoclassical orthodoxy rules...". Fred Lee (2009), in his history of heterodox economics, also comes to the conclusion that – in terms of the number of heterodox economists – Germany plays a fairly unimportant role both internationally and in Europe. The following sections will investigate the reasons for this.

4. The marginalization of heterodoxy after 1970

At the end of the 1960s, many economists (especially younger ones) felt that their discipline was in a crisis, and therefore believed that they were on the verge of a scientific revolution. Their point of reference here was the frequently quoted text by the philosopher of science Thomas S. Kuhn

---

[103] For a more exact description of the heterodox research programs in Germany, see Heise (2010: 36f.).

[104] If at all, these paradigms were represented in social science faculties or departments (e.g. at the University of Frankfurt).

(cf. Kuhn 1962). Such an 'attack' on the 'dominant economics' was only possible because of the efforts made over the previous two decades to 'mature' economics into a paradigmatic science. Its microeconomic core in general equilibrium theory had been decisively summarized by Kenneth Arrow, Gerard Debreu and Frank Hahn, and its macroeconomic superstructure described theories of economic cycles and growth with a standard Keynesian focus. The massive expansion of the university system in Germany from the mid-1960s seemed to offer the chance to achieve a paradigm shift without waiting for the generational changeover which Max Planck had seen as the precondition for such cases. Instead it seemed possible to bring about a faster transition to the new paradigm by recruiting the younger generation, "which is familiar with the truth from the start" (Planck 1928: 22; own translation). The reliance on Kuhn, however, seems unfortunate. On the one hand, this is because the 'empirical anomaly' – the major economic crisis of the 1930s, as the basis of a state of crisis – was already so long ago that collective memory in the middle of the 'golden age of capitalism' had long since suppressed it. On the other hand, the 'logical anomaly' – the evidence of theoretical inconsistency provided in the framework of the Cambridge Capital Controversy – could not fulfill the conditions of a constructive alternative which Kuhn had seen as necessary to trigger a paradigm shift. Hence Imre Lakatos's concept of competing 'scientific research programs' seems better suited to examining the development of economics in general and heterodox economics in particular. This is especially true if one insists, like Paul Feyerabend, that this 'battlefield' – at least in the social sciences – cannot be objectively divided into 'progressive' and 'degenerate' research programs, and that paradigmatic plurality ('anything goes') should be allowed. From such a perspective, the 'field of power' in which the battle of the paradigms is fought becomes particularly important: to borrow from Pierre Bourdieu's field theory (cf. Bourdieu 1990, Bourdieu 1986), a paradigmatic development would then not be tied to objective (Kuhn) or objectifiable criteria (Lakatos), but would mainly depend on the actors' endowment with or access to different forms of capital such as economic, social, symbolic or cultural capital[105].

The next step will be to show that the hope of a broad opening up of theoretical approaches, or a paradigmatic change in what was from then on to be understood as 'dominant economics' (mainstream, normal science), was not able to be fulfilled even after the quantitative expansion and the substantive reform of the German university system from the mid-1960s.[106] Instead, the old universities largely closed themselves to this pluralization despite the generational changeover and the quantitative expansion – except in those cases where there were effective promoters such as active student bodies and representatives of the *Mittelbau* (non-tenured academic staff), who, with the institutional support of the short-lived system of *Drittelparität* (one-third parity), influenced the way professors were recruited. The example of the University of Bonn shows that recruiters were willing to put up with longer vacancies or a certain fluctuation, in order to restrict intake to those (junior) researchers who conformed to the disciplinary culture that was developing there at the time (mathematization). The result was an extremely unequal pluralization of economics at German universities (cf. the following Tab. 4 and Figure 1). At traditional old universities and at those new universities that had been founded solely to expand capacity, and were largely without aspirations to reform, heterodox econ-

---

[105] A truly in-depth Bourdieuian analysis taking all different forms of capital endowment and the personal biographies (‚habitus') of heterodox and orthodox economists into account cannot be offered here – Bourdieu himself was quite aware about the limitations in application of his field theory; cf. Bourdieu (1995: 184).

[106] The following statements are based on a comprehensive survey of all economics professors at economics departments or faculties in German universities from 1954 onwards as published in the various editions of the *Vademecum deutscher Lehr- und Forschungsstätten* and a postal survey of all (living) economists that had been identified as heterodox (to be counted as heterodox one needed to have published at least one book/article based on theories classified as heterodox in Tab. 1.). The response rate (47,8%) and the distribution of respondents across the different types of universities (see Tab. 2) allow us to take the results as fairly representative. Additionally, an in-depth comparison between a selected heterodox economics department (University of Bremen as heterodox stronghold) and an orthodox one (University of Bonn as orthodox stronghold) has been made; cf. Heise at al. (2015).

omists could only be appointed *by chance*, or these scholars only developed a heterodox orientation after their appointment. The chances of pluralism were somewhat higher when the relevant promoters encountered a 'culture of openness,' internal organizational democracy, and external political support, as for example at the University of Frankfurt, where a chair in 'Marxist economic theory' was even established, or at the FU Berlin, where several heterodox professors were appointed.

Table 4: Relative frequency of heterodox economists

Classification	**Locations (number)**	**Heterodox economists (number)**	**Heterodox economists per location**
Not classified (traditional old university)	43	13	0.3
Newly founded university based on Humboldt's ideal	2	4	2
New university founded to relieve pressure on existing institutions, no aspirations to reform	12	1	0.1
Old university strongly influenced by groups with socio-political orientation	6	8	1.3
Newly founded university with aspirations to reform in relation to social openness and practical relevance	8	12	1.5
Newly founded university with aspirations to reform in relation to socio-political orientation	2	15	7.5
Σ	**73**	**53**	
Average			**0.8**

Figure 1: Distribution of heterodox economists in the university field; 1954 – 2013

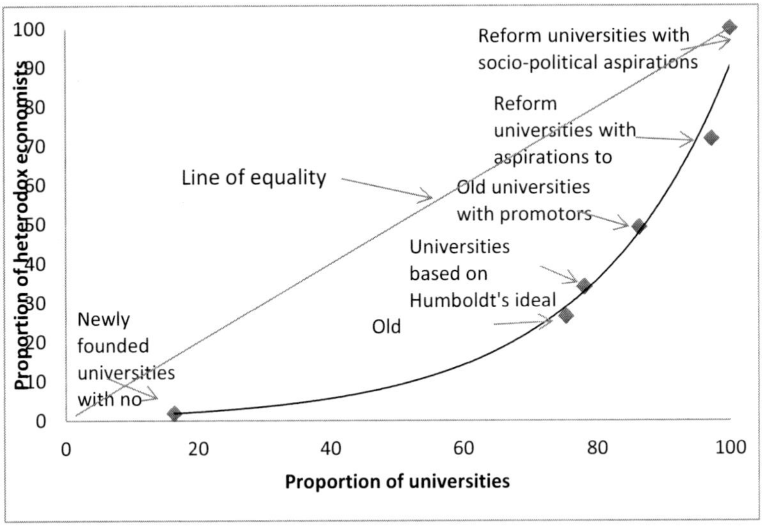

Source: Own calculations

At the 'comprehensive universities' (*Gesamthochschulen*[107]) in North Rhine-Westphalia and Hesse, which saw themselves as 'reform' universities with a focus on practical relevance, professorial recruitment policies could allow heterodox economists to be taken into consideration – depending on specific local circumstances such as the position of the founding dean and the personnel policies at the predecessor institutions. The crucial factor here was the expectation that those economists who stood for (social) reforms and practical relevance – i.e. critical or heterodox economists – could be better for a reform university than those economists who stood

[107] The German sytem of higher education falls under authority of the German *Bundesländer*. Some *Bundesländer* – namely those ruled by social-democratic governments at the time – experimented with a new form of higher education institution: the 'comprehensive university' which combinded academic units of universty status with academic units of 'Fachhochschul' status ('universities of applied science' which are the German pendant to British polytechnics and US liberal arts colleges).

for the preservation of the traditional university model with its claims to value-neutral science – i.e. the mainstream economists. At the two reform universities with socio-political aspirations – the University of Bremen and the Hochschule für Wirtschaft und Politik (HWP) in Hamburg – these aspects came together in a way that was particularly favorable for pluralism, and thus permitted the emergence of two bastions of heterodoxy.

Figure 2: Professorial appointments of heterodox economists 1954 to 2013

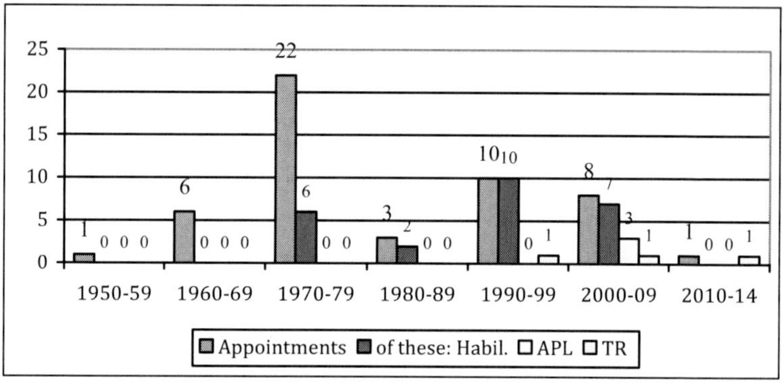

Notes: Habil. = Habilitation; Apl. = außerplanmäßige (extra-ordinary, non-tenured) professorships; TR = Transformation professorships, resulting from the fusion of universities of applied science and universities

Source: Own representation

At three quarters of all German universities with economics faculties or departments, then, heterodox economists were virtually unrepresented; of the remaining quarter, nearly 30% are to be found in the two 'bastions' of heterodoxy (Bremen and HWP). The pluralization is not only extremely unequal but quantitatively limited: at no point in time could more than 10% of economics professors at German universities be classified as belonging to the heterodox camp. And the development over time only tells a story of further marginalization (cf. Fig. 2): The number of appointments of heterodox economists after the 1970s declined rapidly,[108] and as the 'first generation' grow old and retire, their numbers are shrinking more and more. At the same time, heterodox economists were completely overlooked when the economics faculties of East German universities were effectively re-founded after the German reunification in the early 1990ies: out of 80 newly appointed professorships only 4 (!) could be ranked as 'heterodox'.[109] And finally, of the two bastions of heterodox economics (Bremen and HWP), one was practically shut down as a unit for teaching undergraduate economics, and the other was adapted to the mainstream after the generational changeover by being converted into another organizational unit.

Economic capital endowment

This story of marginalization must, however, be read with reference to the dispositions in the field of power. The community of economists exerted an enormous pressure to conform on their heterodox colleagues: for many years, the universities at which most of them were employed were denied membership of the *Deutsche Forschungsgemeinschaft (DFG).* The DFG is the major publically funded, self-governing organization for science and research in Germany. Members are German universities and research institutions. Membership is acquired through application and acceptance by the DFG governing bodies. Membership is required to be able to be represented in the decision-making bodies of the DFG. While the 2 newly

---

[108] The 1990s should not be interpreted as an 'interim high'; instead they hint at the quantitative extent of 'accidental' appointments. The low number of heterodox appointments in the 1980s is due to the high degree of saturation of the university market after the wave of new universities had been founded.

[109] Furthermore, three of the four heterodox professors at East German universities did not go through the normal appointment procedures, but are *außerplanmäßige* (extraordinary) *Professoren* (professorial title which universities may bestow on academics who have suitable qualifications for a professorship but are not actually employed as such) or arrived at their function when a university of applied science (*Fachhochschule*) fused with a university (or was transformed into a university). Finally, the 3 heterodox professors had been appointed by those 3 faculties or departments where the founding dean was no economist but had a different academic background (business informatics or sociology). In the other faculties or departments where the founding dean was a West German (mainstream) economist, heterodox economists had virtually no chance to be appointed.

founded university based on Humboldt's idea were immediately granted DFG membership, the newly founded universities with aspiration to reform in relation to social openness and practical relevance had to wait 17 years on average before being allowed into the DFG and those with aspirations to reform in relation to socio-political orientation had to wait 15 years (University of Bremen) or were never accepted as members (HWP). Therefore, heterodox economists never held influential positions within the decision-making bodies of the DFG. This substantially reduced their economic, social and symbolic capital.

Table 5: Research funding of heterodox economists

Institution	**Applied for funds (in %)**		**Approved (in %)**			
	Yes	No	0	< 50%	>50%	All
DFG	60	40	50	25	8	17
Alternative external sources	75	25	7	7	29	57

Source: Own calculations based on Heise et al. (2015)

The latter is also reflected in the fact that heterodox economists – predictably – have poor chances of obtaining funding from the DFG, and are thus dependent on alternative, yet financially much scarcer, external sources. Many heterodox economists have submitted research proposals to the DFG, but their chance of success is low, or in any case lower than for applications to alternative research funding institutions (cf. Tab. 5): According to our survey, only 17% of DFG applications by heterodox economists were fully approved, as opposed to 57% of applications to alternative institutions. 50% of all applications to the DFG were completely rejected, but only 7% of applications to alternative external sources. This means that critical research – in the sense of 'heterodox' – can only really be achieved by means of such alternative external sources of funding. However, DFG funding as distinct from alternative sources of funding has acquired particular prestige, and therefore, is also becoming symbolic capital on its own.

Of particular importance for the reproducibility of a scientific paradigm is the 'production' of disciples, i.e. the number of doctorates and *Habilitationen* which are successfully completed during the tenure of a professorship, creating the potential to recruit the next cohort of professors. Although it is also fundamentally possible to complete one's doctorate or *Habilitation* as an external scholar, the financial and human resources of an academic unit (faculty, department, institute or chair) are still the most significant parameter of reproducibility. This category of 'economic capital' was a further area in which the heterodox economists were not on an equal footing with the representatives of the mainstream – and this is vividly illustrated by a comparison between the two strongholds of orthodoxy and heterodoxy, the universities of Bonn and Bremen.[110] On the one hand, those reform universities where heterodox economists were most likely to be found had far fewer resources than the traditional 'professorial' universities (*Ordinarienuniversitäten*).[111] On the other hand, in places where heterodox economists had access to comparable resources (e.g. in the case of

[110] Despite limited information, it can be stated that fewer than 10 junior researchers received their *Habilitation* in economics at the economics department of the University of Bremen in the period from 1971 to 2014. In the substantially shorter period from 1984 to 2014, more than three times as many economists (over 30 of them) completed a *Habilitation* at the University of Bonn, and most of these went on to obtain a professorship at a German university. This goes for fewer than half of those who did their *Habilitation* in Bremen (of which merely one could be identified as 'heterodox').

[111] At the University of Bremen, for example, one of the elements of reform was to reduce the dependency of junior researchers on the chairs or professors. Sometimes professors were not given any postgraduate or postdoctoral research staff (*wissenschaftliche Mitarbeiter* or *Assistenten*) at all. It was not until the mid-1980s that a turnaround in staffing policy occurred and the (mainly heterodox) professors were granted a small number of positions for research staff. According to the Statistisches Bundesamt, professors of economics in Germany had an average of 3.71 postgraduate and postdoctoral research staff in 2011 (cf. Stabu 2012: 96). Our survey of heterodox professors in Germany found an average of 2.32 research staff. The discrepancy evident here in the resourcing of orthodox and heterodox professors – especially with postdoctoral staff – is likely to have been even greater in the past: while the average level of resourcing is decreasing overall (for the economists at the University of Bonn, the rate was 4-5 research positions per professor in the 1980s and 1990s; in the more recent past this has been considerably reduced to 2-3,

the University of Bielefeld), 'production' of disciples was made difficult, at least at the level of the *Habilitation.* And even at those locations where reproduction was successful as far as the *Habilitation* – at old and comparatively well-resourced universities such as the University of Frankfurt or the FU Berlin –, those who had gained their *Habilitation* seldom achieved the breakthrough to a regular professorship. Such scholars have often chosen alternative strategies: emigrating, moving into professorships at universities of applied science, or even shifting to other departments (sociology, political science).

Social and symbolic capital endowment

Lastly, heterodox economists quickly began networking at the beginning of the 1970s: among others, the *Arbeitsgruppe Alternative Wirtschaftspolitik* (Working Group for Alternative Economic Policy, also referred to as the 'Memogruppe') and the *Arbeitskreis Politische Ökonomie* (AK PolÖK, Working Group for Political Economy) were founded, as were numerous local *'Rote Zellen Ökonomie'* (Red Cells for Economics). Moreover, numerous economics and social science journals with pluralistic or 'critical' aspirations were established, including *Mehrwert – Beiträge zur Kritik der Politische Ökonomie, Prokla – Probleme des Klassenkampfes, Hefte für Politische Ökonomie, Das Argument, Leviathan – Zeitschrift für Sozialwissenschaft* and *Jahrbuch für Ökonomie und Gesellschaft*. However, the heterodox economic community never succeeded in using these networks as a base for penetrating the reviewer networks of the DFG or to establish their journals as reputed outlets of academic research.[112]

---

by the large-scale introduction of 'junior,' fixed-term and minimally-resourced professorships; cf. Heise et al. 2015), the heterodox professors tend to report a slight improvement. Of course this development has to be viewed in the light of the above-mentioned zero endowment of many heterodox professorships in the founding phase of the reform universities, and a subsequent 'normalization.'

[112] Some of the named journals have terminated publication since, none of the journals made it into the *Handelsblatt* ranking list which is becoming an ever more crucial instrument in the measurement of research output, the allocation of funds and the recruitment process at German universities.

True, a number of heterodox economists are involved in the *Verein für Socialpolitik* (VfS, Social Policy Association[113]), especially in the committees for evolutionary economics and the history of economic thought. In the more prestigious committees for economic theory and economic policy, however, which play a crucial role in determining the influential members of the decision-making bodies of the DFG (*Fachausschüsse* or 'review boards') their involvement within the VfS (based on electoral selection) is minimal. And symbolic capital, the assumption of important and therefore symbolic positions in scientific, economic or political organizations (e.g. the *Wissenschaftsrat* (German Council of Science and Humanities), or the scientific advisory councils of the German federal government or the *Deutsche Bundesbank*), have remained largely closed to the heterodox economists. Thanks to the nominating rights of the German Trade Unions, two heterodox economists had been delegated to the *Sachverständigenrat zur Begutachtung der gesamtwirtschaftlichen Entwicklung* (SVR, German Council of Economic Experts) since it was founded, but here too, their role was that of the outsider (cf. Kampe 1983)[114].

In summary, heterodox economics had to compete with mainstream economics in a very 'uneven field of power.' This development is also embedded in the increasingly influential model of a competitively organized university landscape, in which universities compete with each other, as 'enterprises,' for scarce financial resources. This is why research, today, is not defined by a striving for knowledge, but by 'usability' (*Verwertbarkeit*), in the sense of the ability to attract external funding. This and

---

[113] The *Verein für Socialpolitik* is historically the (inofficial) professional organisation of academic economists of the German speaking world.

[114] Out of ten members of the SVR which the Trade Unions had a right to nominate since its establishment in 1967, only two came from the ranks of ‚heterodox economists' while the other eight nominees can almost entirely be categorized as 'mainstream' of 'neo-Keynesian' orientation. The fact that even Trade Unions referred to mainstream rather than heterodox economists may on the one hand be taken as evidence for the degree of non-acceptance within the academic community: although Trade Unions had a nomination right, the other (mainstream) members of the SVR had a right to reject nominees – heterodox nominees were always endangered to be rejected. On the other hand, from an economic policy perspective, neo-Keynesians were seen as cricital enough to oppose the free market orientation of the majority of the SVR.

(partly as a result of this) the lack of reproduction and consolidation of heterodox structures has exacerbated the 'unevenness' of the above-mentioned field of power of economics.

5. Conclusion

The development of a scientific discipline is dependent on many determinants. As in every creative process, idiosyncratic factors within the personality of the individual scholar are especially important when it comes to explaining specific innovations or insights. A vital role is also played, of course, by the circumstances at the time, the economic or social developments that affect the research process – this may take the form of an especially urgent problem that requires scholarly examination. But empirical anomalies, as we have known since Thomas S. Kuhn, have also frequently changed the direction and paradigmatic orientation of a science. Furthermore, distinctive features of a discipline must also be taken into account, e.g. the stage of development already reached, or the object of study itself. An immature, pre-paradigmatic science seems more open to new epistemic processes or methodological approaches than a more mature science in a paradigmatic state.

Furthermore, the manner in which a society tends and protects its underlying institutions (e.g. the market) has an effect on the acceptance of theoretical and paradigmatic approaches – quite irrespective of their actual explanatory power (cf. Fourcade 2009: 35ff.). The sum of these factors describes what Imre Lakatos described as the 'scientific battlefield.' Depending on the specific circumstances of the time, idiosyncratic influencing factors, and the specifics of the discipline, this battlefield may be characterized by particularly intense interpretive struggles between different research programs (Lakatos), or may find itself in the calm waters surrounding a dominant hegemon, described by Kuhn as a 'normal science.' And, lastly, there is one further determinant of the development of a scientific discipline: the dispositions in the field of the science in question, which must be understood in Bourdieuian terms as a 'field of power,' in which the various types of capital possessed determine the conditions in which the contest on the 'battlefield' is fought.

This explanatory background helps to understand the development of economics at the beginning of the 20th century: The microeconomics-based equilibrium and welfare theory which was taking shape at the time co-existed with classically Marxist approaches and with the still-dominant 'Historical School.' The rise of Keynesianism to (worldwide) prominence in the early post-war period to around the mid-20th century cannot be explained without the global economic crisis of the 1930s, and the special position of John Maynard Keynes as an economist at one of the world's most prestigious universities, a statesman, and the editor of what was at the time the most influential economics journal in the still relatively small community of economists. But equally, the specific interpretation of Keynesian macroeconomics as an outlier of neoclassical equilibrium theory, which had a major influence on the professionalization and paradigmatic development of economics, especially in Germany, cannot be explained without the increasing hegemony of American scholarship after the Second World War, and the position of Paul Samuelson at an elite US university, as well as the massive worldwide success of his textbook, *Economics* (cf. Skousen 1997; Davidson 2015). Economics had thus developed from a pre-paradigmatic, plural and evaluative science ('advocacy') to a mono-paradigmatic and positivist one ('objectivity'). The co-opting of Keynes by general equilibrium theory satisfied the cultural requirements of a science whose hegemon could not have legitimated any really fundamental criticism of the underlying institutions of its society. It was, however, this very domestication of the Keynesian paradigm, and the increasing theoretical criticism of its equilibrium-centered heuristics, that determined the development of economics in the middle of the 20th century. The 'battle of the paradigms' was influenced by the simultaneous expansion and reform of the universities, a broad social liberation movement, which also affected the universities, and dispositions in the field of power in the economic discipline.

The result was, at the beginning of the 1970s, a paradigmatic opening up of economics in Germany, which took an extremely uneven course. While the traditional old universities only appointed heterodox economists by chance, two bastions of heterodox economics emerged at the University of

Bremen and the Hochschule für Wirtschaft und Politik (HWP) in Hamburg. In addition to these, a few newly founded universities – especially the 'comprehensive universities' in North Rhine-Westphalia and Hesse – and a few existing universities, in which reform-oriented status groups were particularly active, allowed at least some steps to be taken towards a pluralization of economics. However, at no point were more than 10 percent of economics professorships filled by heterodox economists. Although heterodox economics quickly developed its own institutions and networks, by founding organizations and journals, the following 40 years saw an overall marginalization of heterodoxy in Germany. This was also reflected in the overlooking of heterodox economists during the restaffing of East German economics departments after the unification of Germany. The following factors must be taken into account here:

1. The number of heterodox research programs represented in German universities, especially in the 1980s, does not suggest that heterodoxy became quantitatively insignificant because its approaches were beaten on the 'battlefield of the paradigms.' Moreover, empirical anomalies – such as the increasingly permanent presence of unemployment despite increasing flexibilization of the labor markets (cf. Heise/Kromphardt/Priewe 1998) – remained significant enough to encourage the continuing search for alternative explanations (within, but also outside the mainstream).

2. German economics surrendered completely to the hegemony of American economics after the Second World War. On the one hand, this was intended to offset actual deficits caused by the exodus of important scholars and the country's isolation during the Nazi period. On the other hand, German economics could not escape the hegemonic claims to standardization asserted by certain elite US universities and their journals. Even today, this '(self-) Americanization' lingers on under the catchphrase 'international competitiveness,' which is thought to preclude specific national paths (*Sonderwege*) – or national scientific cultures. Under these conditions, the marginalization of heterodox economics in the US had to be seen as, at least, a limiting parameter for developments in Germany.

3. Heterodoxy and the mainstream coexisted, without any acknowledgement of heterodoxy by the mainstream or any extensive penetration of the

mainstream by heterodoxy. This non-acknowledgement is manifested in the long-standing refusal to admit pluralistic reform universities to the DFG, the ongoing denial of decision-making positions in DFG committees to heterodox economists, the general impossibility of accessing financial resources from the DFG, and the severely restricted access to publishing opportunities in journals which promise a high level of recognition, and which are supposedly not affiliated to any school. This denial of recognition became a standardized, institutionalized part of the allocation of university resources during the transition of university governance from committee-led to competitive universities, thus making this marginalization virtually automatic, and above all, legitimizing it. The failure of heterodoxy to penetrate the mainstream is shown in the refusal of many heterodox economists to accept organizations such as the Verein für Socialpolitik (VfS) as representatives of the economics community with no paradigmatic affiliations. It should be mentioned, though, that the distribution of the heterodox VfS members over the committees of the VfS (the vast majority are members of the committee on the history of dogma) suggests that the specific rite of admission to the VfS imposed clear restrictions on access to the core areas of the VfS and was therefore also an instrument for denying recognition.

4. The reproduction of heterodox economists remained well below the average. The reason for this was the below-average number of positions available for junior researchers (*Qualifikationsstellen*), and the severe restrictions on access to DFG resources. But the orientation of many heterodox economists, who preferred to have an influence on society (through research transfer) than on the academic community (through research), is also likely to have played a part. The recruitment process in the economics faculties of East German universities after the German unification makes it clear, however, that it is not only the below-average reproduction of heterodoxy – i.e. a problem of supply –, but also the very much below-average level of recruitment – i.e. a problem of demand – that have to be taken into account as important factors.

5. Due to the special significance of the University of Bremen and the HWP for the development of heterodoxy, their specific circumstances have to be examined. These show the same thing that has happened, so far,

to all attempts to influence traditional economics with a new orientation: in the end, the denial of recognition by the academic community led to a loss of political-social support and, ultimately, to the dissolution or at least total marginalization of the heterodox academic unit.

The representatives of heterodox economics did not succeed in establishing pluralization as part of the 'cultural capital' of the German community of economists, and were thus unable to claim recognition for the heuristic divergence of their own paradigmatic approach in relation to the mainstream focus on self-regulation. Their chances of winning the 'battle of the paradigms' were hopeless, given their vast inferiority in terms of every kind of capital: *economic* (professorships and the associated positions for junior researchers, access to financial resources from the DFG etc.), *social* (networks based on VfS membership, editorial boards of journals, influential scholarly organizations such as scientific advisory committees of federal ministries, boards of reviewers of the DFG etc.) and *symbolic* (presidents of important economic research institutes, members of scientific advisory boards in federal ministries, members of the SVR (German Council of Economic Experts), etc.). Nor were they able to prevent the establishment of scientific standards which *systematically* belittled the value of heterodox economics, thus perpetuating the marginalization of heterodoxy and ensuring the monistic idealization of the mainstream. In short, the setting of paradigmatic standards has been used to close the academic system, after previous attempts to close it by means of socio-structural attributions had failed due to the sudden expansion of the universities in the early 1970s.

References

Abel, A.B., Bernanke, B.S. (2005); *Macroeconomics*, Boston

Abramovitz, M. et al. (1992); Plea for a Pluralist and Rigorous Economics; in: *American Economic Review*, Vol. 82, No.2, p. XXXV

Arrow, K.J. (1988); Workshop on the Economy as an Evolving Complex System: Summary; in: Anderson, P.W., Arrow, K.J., Pines, D. (eds.); *The Economy As An Evolving Complex System*, Redwood

Arthur, W.B. (2010); *Complexity, the Santa Fe approach, and non-equilibrium economics*; in: History of Economic Ideas, Vol. 18, No.2, pp. 149 - 166

Auroi, C. et al. (2011); 'Aufruf: Forschung **un**d Lehre in Wirtschaftswissenschaften, Finance und Management sollen erneuert werden mit dem Ziel, dem Allgemeinwohl besser zu dienen,' Geneva, Fribourg, Zurich (http://www.responsiblefinance.ch/aufruf/)

Backhouse, R. E. (2001); On the credentials of methodological pluralism; in: Biddle, J.E./Davis, J.B./Medema, S.G. (eds.); *Economics Broadly Considered: Essays in Honor of Warren J. Samuels*, London, pp. 161 – 181

Backhouse, R.E. (2005); The Rise of Free Market Economics: Economists and the Role of the State since 1970; in: *History of Political Economy*, Vol. 37, pp. 355 - 392

Barkley Rosser, J. Jr. (2004); Introduction; in: ibid (ed.); *Complexity in Economics. Methodology, Interacting Agents, and Microeconomic Models*, Cheltenham, pp.

Besley, T., Hennessey, P. (2009); Letter in response to a question of Queen Elizabeth, British Academy of Science, London

Blanchard, O. (2008); The State of Macro, NBER Working Paper 14259

Blanchard, O., Dell'Ariccia, G., Mauro, P. (2010): Rethinking Macroeconomic Policy, IMF Staff Position Note 10/03, Washington

Blanchard, O., Johnson, D.R. (2013); *Macroeconomics*, New York (6th edn.)

Bloch, R., Burkhardt, A. (2011); Arbeitsplatz Hochschule und Forschung für wissenschaftliches Personal und Nachwuchskräfte; in: Hans-Böckler-Stiftung (ed.); *Expertise für die Hochschule der Zukunft*, Bad Heilbrunn, pp. 401 – 478

Blume, L., Durlauf, S. (2001); The Interaction-Based Approach to Socioeconomic Behavior; in: Durlauf, S., Young, P. (eds.); *Social Dynamics*, Cambridge (Mass.)

Bourdieu, P. (1986); The Forms of Capital; in: Richardson, J. (ed.); *Handbook of Theory and Research for the Sociology of Education*, New York, pp. 241 - 258

Bourdieu, P. (1990); *Homo Academicus*, Cambridge

Bourdieu, P. (1995); *The Rules of Art. Genesis and Structure of the Literary Field*, Stanford

Bronk, R. (2011); *Epistemological difficulties with neoclassical economics*, paper presented at the Southern Economic Conference, 20th November 2011 (available at: http://eprints.lse.ac.uk/39423/)

Busch, A. (1959); *Die Geschichte des Privatdozenten. Eine soziologische Studie zur großbetrieblichen Entwicklung der deutschen Universitäten*, Stuttgart

Caballero, R.J. (2010); Macroeconomics after the Crisis: Time to Deal with the Pretense-of-Knowledge Syndrome; in: *Journal of Economic Perspectives*, Vol. 24, no.4, pp. 85 – 102

Chesney, M. et al. (2011); Baseler Manifest für ökonomische Aufklärung, Zentrum für Religion, Wirtschaft und Politik, Basel

Clower, R.; The Keynesian Counter-Revolution: A Theoretical Appraisal; in: Hahn, F.H., Brechling, F.P.R. (eds.); *The Theory of Interest Rates*, London 1965, pp. 103 – 125

Cohen, A.J., Harcourt, G.C. (2003); Whatever Happened to Cambridge Capital Theory Controversies? In: *Journal of Economic Perspectives*, Vol. 18, No.1, pp. 199 - 214

Colander, D.C., Holt, R.C.F., Rosser, J.B. Jr. (2009); Introduction; in: Colander, D.C., Holt, R.C.F., Rosser, J.B. Jr. (eds.): *Changing Face of Economics: Conversations with Cutting Edge Economists*, Ann Arbor, pp. 1- 25

Colander, D., Klamer, A. (1987); The Making of an Economist, in: *Journal of Economic Perspectives*, Vol.1, No.2, pp. 95 – 111

Cross, R. (1982); The Duhem-Quine-Thesis, Lakatos and the Appraisal of Theories in Macroeconomics; in: *Economic Journal*, Vol. 92, pp. 320- 340

Davidson, P. (1984); Reviving Keynes' Revolution; in: *Journal of Post Keynesian Economics*, Vol. 6, No.4, pp. 561-575

Davidson, P. (1992); Would Keynes be a New Keynesian?; in: *Eastern Economic Review*, Vol. 18, No.4, pp. 449 - 463

Davidson, P. (2005); Responses to Lavoie, King, and Dow on What Post Keynesianism Is and Who Is a Post Keynesian; in: *Journal of Post Keynesian Economics*, Vol. 27, No. (3), pp. 393–408

Davidson, P. (2015); What was the primary factor encouraging mainstream economists to marginalize post Keynesian theory?; in: Journal of Post Keynesian Economics, Vol. 37, No.3, pp. 369 - 383

Davis, J.B. (1994); Pluralism in social economics, in: *History of Economic Ideas*, Vol. 2, Nr. 3, pp. 119 - 128

Dobusch, L., Kapeller, J. (2012); Heterodox United vs. Mainstream City? Sketching a Framework for Interested Pluralism in Economics; in: *Journal of Economic Issues*, Vol. XLV, No.4, pp. 1035 - 1057

Drakopoulos, S.A., Karayiannis, A.D. (2005); A Review of Kuhnian and Lakatosian 'Explanations' in Economics; in: *History of Economic Ideas*, Vol. 12, No.2, pp. 51 - 73

Düppe, T., Weintraub, E. R. (2014); *Finding Equilibrium. Arrow, Debreu, McKenzie and the Problem of Scientific Credit*, Princeton

Feyerabend, P. (1975); *Against method*, London

Finkenstaedt, T. (2010); Die Universitätslehrer; in: Rüegg, W. (ed.); *Geschichte der Universität in Europa*, Vol. IV: Vom Zweiten Weltkrieg bis zum Ende des 20. Jahrhunderts, Munich, pp. 153 – 188

Fontana, M. (2008); *The Complexity Approach to Economics: A Paradigm Shift*, Working paper No.8, Department of Economics, University of Torino

Fourcade, M. (2009); *Economists and Societies. Discipline and Profession in the United States, Britain and France, 1890s to 1990s*, Princeton

Fourcade-Gourinchas, M. (2001); Politics, institutional structures, and the rise of economics: A comparative study; in: *Theory and Society*, Vol. 30, pp. 397 – 447

Frey, B.S., Humbert, S., Schneider, F. (2007); Was denken deutsche Ökonomen? Eine empirische Auswertung einer Internetbefragung unter den Mitgliedern des Vereins für Socialpolitik im Sommer 2006, in: *Perspektiven der Wirtschaftspolitik*,Vol. 8, Nr.4, pp. 359–377

Galbraith, J.K. (2013); The Third Crisis in Economics; *Journal of Economic Issues*, Vol. 47, No.2, pp. 311 – 322

Garnett, R.F.Jr. (2006); *Paradigms and pluralism in heterodox economics*; in: Review of Political Economy, Vol. 18, No.4, pp. 521 - 546

Gräfing, B. (2012); *Tradition Reform. Die Universität Bremen 1971 – 2001*, Bremen

Graham, H.D., Diamond, N. (1997); *The Rise of American Research Universities. Elites and Challengers in the Postwar Era*, Baltimore

Greenfield, R.L. (1986); *Walras's law and Macroeconomic Disequilibrium*; in: Austrialian Economic papers, Vol. 25, Issue 47, pp. 257 - 260

Heise, A. (2010); Krise der Wirtschaftswissenschaft – Raum für Alternativen? Plädoyer für einen Pluralismus in der Ökonomik; in: Jens, U., Romahn, H. (eds.); *Methodenpluralismus in den Wirtschaftswissenschaften*, Marburg, pp. 33 - 50

Heise, A., Hirte, K., Ötsch, W., Pühringer, S., Reich, A., Sander, H., Thieme, S. (2015); Ökonomen und Ökonomie. Eine wissenschaftssoziologische Entwicklungsanalyse zum Verhältnis von Ökonomen und Ökonomie im deutschsprachigen Raum ab 1945. Abschlussbericht eines HBS-Projektes, Hamburg/Linz (unpublished manuscript)

Heise, A., Kromphardt, J., Priewe, J. (1998); Alternative Konzeptionen makroökonomischer Politik im Spannungsfeld von Arbeitslosigkeit, Globalisierung und hoher Staatsverschuldung; in: Eicker-Wolf, K. et al. (eds.); *Die arbeitslose Gesellschaft und ihr Sozialstaat*, Marburg

Hermann-Pillath, C. (2002); *Grundzüge der Evolutionsökonomik*, München

Hesse, J.-O. (2010); *Wirtschaft als Wissenschaft. Die Volkswirtschaftslehre in der frühen Bundesrepublik*, Frankfurt

Hesse, J.-O. (2007); Hochschulreformgeschichte als Disziplingeschichte – Das Beispiel der Wirtschaftswissenschaften; in: A. Franzmann, B. Wolbring (eds.); *Zwischen Idee und Zweckorientierung. Vorbilder und Motive von Hochschulreformen seit 1945*, Berlin, pp. 121 – 135

Kampe, D. (1983); ‚Fünf Weise' in der Wirtschaft – Sachverstand live erlebt; in: Hickel, R., Mattfeldt, H. (eds.); *Millionen Arbeitslose! Streitschrift gegen den Rat der Fünf Weisen. Eine Bilanz nach zwanzig Jahren*, Reinbeck b. Hamburg

Kellert, S., Longino, H., Waters, K. (eds.)(2006); *Scientific Pluralism*, Minneapolis

Keynes, J.M. (1934); Poverty in Plenty, in: *The Listener* v. 21. November 1934 (this quote from Moggridge, D. (ed.); *Collected Writings of John Maynard Keynes*, Vol. XIII, London 1973, pp. 485 – 492)

Keynes, J.M. (1936); *The General theory of Employment, Interest and Money*, London

Keynes, J.M. (1973); *General Theory of Employment, Interest and Money*, London (1st edn. 1936)

King, J.E. (2002a); Three arguments for pluralism; in: *Journal of Australian Political Economy*, Vol. 50, pp. 82 – 88

King, J.E. (2002b); *A History of Post Keynesian Economics Since 1936*, Cheltenham

Klamer, A. (2007); Does this Have to Be our Future?; in: Colander, D.; *The Making of an Economist, Redux*, Princeton, pp. 227 – 233

Kuhn, T.S. (1962); *The Structure of Scientific Revolutions*, Chicago

Kuhn, T.S. (1970); Reflections on my Critics, in: Lakatos, I., Musgrave, A.; Criticism and the growth of knowledge. Proceedings of the International Colloquium in the Philosophy of Science, Cambridge, pp. 231-278.

Lakatos, I. (1978); Falsification and the methodology of scientific research programmes; in: Worrall, J., Currie, G. (eds.); *Imre Lakatos. The Methodology of Scientifc Research Programmes. Philosophical Papers Vol. I*, Cambridge, pp. 8 - 71

Lawson, T. (2006); The Nature of Heterodox Economics; in: *Cambridge Journal of Economics*, Vol. 30, No.4, pp. 483 – 507

Lee, F. (2009); *A History of Heterodox Economics: Challenging the Mainstream in the 20th Century*, New York

Lucas, R.E. jr. (2003); Macroeconomic Priorities; in: *American Economic Review*, Vol. 93, No.1, 1 – 14

Merkel, A. (2014); Rede von Frau Bundeskanzlerin Merkel zum 5. Treffen der Nobelpreisträger; available at: http://www.bundesregierung.de/ Content/DE/Rede/2014/08/2014-08-20-lindau.html

Mirowski, P. (1989); *More heat than light. Economics as social physics: Physics as nature's economics*, Cambridge

Mishan, E. J. (1963); Say's Law and Walras' Law once more; in: *Quarterly Journal of Economics*, Vol. 77, No.4, pp. 617-625

Möller, C. (2013); Wie offen ist die Universitätsprofessur für soziale Aufsteigerinnen und Aufsteiger?; in: *Soziale Welt*, Vol. 64, pp. 341 - 360

Planck, M. (1928); *Wissenschaftliche Autobiographie*, Leipzig

Ptak, R. (2004); *Vom Ordoliberalismus zur Sozialen Marktwirtschaft. Stationen des Neoliberalismus in Deutschland*, Opladen

Rosser, J. Barkley Jr., Holt, R.P.F., Colander, D. (2010); *European Economics at a Crossroads*, Cheltenham

Sargent, T.J. (1979); *Macroeconomic Theory*, New York

Schipper, L. (2013); Marx im Regen; in: *Frankfurter Allgemeine Zeitung* (8 October 2013), online: http://www.faz.net/-gyq-7i47e [12 June 2014]

Schmidt, C. M. and N. aus dem Moore (2010), Die Methodendiskussion in den Wirtschaftswissenschaften vor dem Hintergrund der Finanzkrise; in: Jens, U., Romahn, H. (eds.), *Methodenpluralismus in den Wirtschaftswissenschaften*. Marburg, pp. 143-182

Skousen, M. (1997); The Perseverance of Paul Samuelson's Economics; in: *Journal of Economic Perspectives*, Vol. 11, No.2, pp. 137 – 152

Smith, V. L. (2003); Constructivist and Ecological Rationality in Economics; in: Frängsmayr, F. (ed.); *The Nobel Prizes 2002*, Stockholm, pp. 502- 561

Snowdon, B., Vane, H.R. (1997); The development of modern macroeconomics, in: Snowdon & Vane (eds.); *A Macroeconomic Reader*, London, pp. 1 - 25

Solow, R. (1986); What is a Nice Girl Like You Doing in a Place Like This? Macroeconomics after fifty years; in: *Eastern Economic Journal*, Vol. 12, No. 3, pp. 191 – 198

Sraffa, P. (1960); Production of Commodities by Means of Commodities, London

Stabu (2012); Fachserie 11, Reihe 4.4, Wiesbaden

Stiglitz, J.E. (2009a); Moving Beyond Market Fundamentalism to A More Balanced Economy; in: *Annals of Public and Cooperative Economics*, Vol. 80, No. 3, pp. 345-360

Stiglitz, J.E. (2009b): The Current Economic Crisis and Lessons for Economic Theory, in: *Eastern Economic Journal*, Vol. 35, No. 3, pp. 281 - 296

Stiglitz, J.E. (2011); Rethinking Macroeconomics: What Failed and How to Repair It; in: *Journal of the European Economic Association*, Vol. 9, No. 4, pp. 591-645

Stiglitz, J.E. (2014); The Lessons of the North Atlantic Crisis for Economic Theory and Policy; in: Akerlof, G.,Blanchard, O., Romer, D. Stiglitz, J.E. (eds.); *What Have We Learned? Macroeconomic Policy after the Crisis*, Cambridge (Mass.) and London, pp. 335-347

Summers, P.M. (2005); What caused the Great Moderation? Some Cross-Country Evidence; in: *Federal Reserve Bank of Kansas City Economic Review*, Vol. 90, No.3, pp. 5 – 32

Thielemann, U. et al. (2012); Für eine Erneuerung der Ökonomie. Memorandum besorgter Wissenschaftlerinnen und Wissenschaftler, Berlin (http://www.mem-wirtschaftsethik.de/memorandum-2012/)

Vogt, W. (1973); Einleitung; in: Vogt (ed.); *Seminar: Politische Ökonomie. Zur Kritik der herrschenden Nationalökonomie*, Frankfurt

von der Vring, T. (1975); Hochschulreform in Bremen, Bericht des Rektors über Gründung und Aufbau der Universität Bremen während seiner Amtszeit von 1970 – 1974, Frankfurt/Cologne

Woodford, M. (2010); Financial Intermediation and Macroeconomic Analysis; in: *Journal of Economic Perspectives*, Vol. 24, No.4, pp. 21 – 44

Four

'Why has economics turned out this way?' A socio-economic note on the explanation of monism in economics*

1. Introduction

As several studies have shown, pluralism in economics is a bygone assumption (see e.g. Heise/Thieme 2016, Lee 2009). This statement assumes that economics had been characterized by pluralism in earlier times. Indeed, the period until World War II is often described as a pluralistic period (see e.g. Morgan/Rutherford 1998), and the 1960s and 1970s also experienced a rise in pluralism after what has been dubbed the 'The Second Crisis in Economic Theory' (see Robinson 1972). For some, most notably the heterodox faction of the economic scientific community and many students, this is a lamentable development and claims for a re-pluralization have been made[115]. For others, it is the necessary and therefore applauded result of a science reaching maturity.

Much ink has been spilled on the discussion about the need for pluralism and the effects (cost or benefit respectively) of its loss (see e.g. Salanti/Screpanti 1997, Garnett/Olson/Starr 2010), much less has been written to provide a clear conceptualization of pluralism (see e.g.Garnett 2006)[116], and even less investigated is the reason for or background forces of the development from 'inter-war pluralism to post-war neoclassicism' (Morgan/Rutherford 1998). For those who believe economics ought to be

* Originally published: The Journal of Philosophical Economics; vol. X, No. 1, 2016

[115] Most recently, this has been done in a volume titled 'Reclaiming Pluralism in Economics' edited by Courvisanos/Doughney/Millmow (2016)

[116] One of the major problems in the discussion on pluralism versus monism is the obscurity of the terms used. Pluralism (and the same holds for monism) may be applied to theories, methods, methodologies, epistemologies, ontologies and paradigms – all conveying a different meaning. If not stated otherwise, the term pluralism (or monism) used here always refers to paradigmatic pluralism. This implies the existence and tolerance of adversarial scientific research programs with respect to their heuristic dimensions beyond mere epistemological or methodical variations within a paradigm; for a more detailed discussion see Heise (2017) and Fullbrook (2013).

monist, in the sense that it eventually spawns a 'normal science' of the Kuhnian type, there simply is no question to reflect upon (see e.g. Goodfriend 2007). For those, however, who advocate pluralism (see e.g. Salanti/Screpanti 1997, Kellert/Longina/Waters 2006, Fullbrook 2008, Garnett/Olsen/Starr 2010), its absence must be disturbing, and an explanation is badly needed in order to propose remedies that might reverse the process of de-pluralization in the future.

John King, a staunch defender of pluralism, is among the few who has provided an answer to "why economics has turned out this way"; nevertheless, he concedes: "and I am still not sure to have the full answer" (King 2016: 7). He highlights two reasons:

- the pretention that economics is a 'rigorous science' demands a single, generally accepted representation of the 'truth' based on formal reasoning and sophisticated empirical testing (i.e. the methodology of positivistic fallibilism)
- the economic discipline touches too much on vested interests to allow for a free investigative project pursuing every possible trail of thought.

While both explanations may appear intuitive to critical minds, they are not entirely convincing on closer inspection from a perspective not so inclined, or, rather, they need further argumentative support to become more appealing. That is what this short research note seeks to provide: In the next two sections, I will scrutinize the arguments and point out deficiencies. In a fourth and fifth section, I will unfold a socio-economic theory of the 'market for economic ideas' and provide some evidence for restraints on competition (or, sociologically speaking, an uneven battlefield) which will support King's explanations. This will serve as a foundation for some proposals for re-claiming pluralism.

2. Methodological ineptitude and the quest for monism

Although economics is arguably the strictest social science in its methodological rigour (see e.g. Freeman 1999; Colander 2005), economists are usually not very well trained in terms of methodology (see Caldwell 1988). By that I mean that in relying on positivistic fallibilism, economics emulates the natural sciences in its search for 'the one and only truth'. The insistence on positivistic ('scientific') 'objectivity' as opposed to normative 'advocacy' marked the beginning departure of economics from economic sociology as a result of the *'Methodenstreit'* which took place in Germany and elsewhere at the end of the 19th century (see Moore 2003). Economics turned into a science – emphasizing methodological unity with the natural sciences (see e.g. Mirowski 1989)[117] – claiming to be "a body of systematized knowledge concerning what is" (Keynes 1891: 34) or, as Milton Friedman stated in his famous article 'The Methodology of Positive Economics':

> *"Positive economics is in principle independent of any particular ethical position or normative judgement. ... Its task is to provide a system of generalizations that can be used to make correct predictions about the consequences of any change in circumstances. ...Its performance is to be judged by the precision, scope, and conformity with experience of the predictions it yields. In short, positive economics is, or can be, an 'objective' science, in precisely the same sense as any of the physical sciences"* (Friedman 1953: 4).

Based on such a fallacy, economics is pursued by most economists[118] as a science that ultimately will provide a single, generally accepted, historically unspecific answer to all economic problems (see e.g. Middleton 1998: 344, Schultze 1996: 26, Williamson 1997: 365); i.e. something that can be taken as 'truth':

> *"...a thumbnail sketch of what a genuine science of economics would amount to: it would ideally be a discipline that sought a complete, objective account of the 'laws of motion' which would causally explain the 'characteristics' and 'function(ing)' of the investigator-independent economic 'system' in its parts and as whole. Although this conception of an economic science does not deny ontological complexity and diversity and does not deny human fallibility, it does lend itself to*

[117] It has been claimed, though, that many natural sciences such as Physics have undergone a ‚pluralistic turn‘ in the past which the economic discipline is still lacking; see Fullbrook (2014).

[118] It must be condeded that this perspective cannot solely be attributed to mainstream or orthodox economists but is also assumed by many heterodox economists; see e.g. Van Bouwel (2004), Freeman/Kliman (2006), Holcombe (2008).

> *an ultimately monistic paradigmatic vision of the future of the economics discipline"* (Mariyani-Squire/Mossa 2015: 200).

This strong scientific claim matches neither the necessary ontological and epistemological preconditions that the object of inquiry – the economic order – must fulfil if 'truth' is to be established nor a similarly rigorous methodological exigency that is critically disclosed (see Heise 2017). The foundation of scientific monism, the 'one world-one truth' principle, can be upheld only under very restrictive and unrealistic conditions: a) the existence of a single (economic) reality and the objectivity of its emergence, which is questioned by post-modern constructivism (see Berger/Luckmann 1966); b) the assumption that the economic order (or system) is a 'closed system' which would exclusively allow for (stochastic) predictions based on detectable links between system elements (constituting 'analytic judgement a priori' in a Kantian sense). Although this assumption is highly dubious and definitely cannot be taken as an (unquestionable) axiom, this is exactly what mainstream economics[119] does:

> *"It is indeed the proclaimed virtue of general equilibrium reasoning that it takes into account all the possible interactions between all the elements that are included in the model; therefore, if uncertainty about future possibilities appears to prevent the completion of the set of connections between present decisions and their full set of consequences, then we must agree that the imaginative response of Arrow and Debreu in extending the set of elements to include all future dates and all possible states of the world – which are fully connected to every other element in the model – was methodologically appropriate"* (Loasby 2003: 291).

However, what is methodologically appropriate for concise model-building is not necessarily appropriate for the representation of reality.

If the ontological and epistemological requirements for a monist approach are too demanding to be fulfilled, one could still hope for a clear-cut discrimination between theoretical approaches by empirical testing – which

[119] As is common, I take the 'dynamic stochastic general equilibrium model' as the core of mainstream economics; see e.g. Carlin/Soskice (2006: 574ff.) who dub it the 'neoclassical benchmark model' covering neo-Keynesian as well as new classical macroeconomics based on microeconomic foundations.

by itself can only establish provisional or conjectural knowledge but no 'truth'. Yet, due to the 'problem of induction' and the so called 'Duhem-Quine' thesis, an objective demarcation between 'truth' and 'non-truth' or a similar objective discrimination between competing theories or theoretical systems (paradigms) is simply impossible (see Blaug 1980: 26). This does not ultimately imply the complete rejection of the existence of objective knowledge (as constructivists would claim), but undoubtedly it implies the end of certainty concerning the establishment and proof of objective knowledge – which is thus replaced by the admittance of ontological and epistemological pluralism as a scientific imperative of economics.

Monism, therefore, is not the logical result of the pretence that economics is like the natural sciences and the indicator of its maturity; rather it follows from a methodological error regarding the ontological and epistemological constraints of the discipline, thus making paradigmatic pluralism indispensable.

3. Vested interests and economics

There is no doubt that economics covers topics that are deeply affected by vested interests. Moreover the 'knowledge' provided by economics surely helps special interest groups to gain the upper hand in disputes about policy-making and the provision of public goods which simply cannot serve in a 'neutral (or merely functional) way' the general welfare of society for the reason that such a thing – the welfare of society – cannot coherently be conceptualized. Since Kenneth Arrow's seminal book (Arrow 1951), we know that what contributes to the welfare of a society is, at best, determined by the majority or, more realistically, by the minority who are able to frame their particular interests as the common interest of the wider society (see e.g. Bartels 2008; Hacker/Pierson 2010; Häring/Douglas 2012). This framing process requires considerable resources which can better be provided if one is successfully participating in the market – which, in turn, results in a pro-market bias. Taking into consideration that universities, the major organisations of knowledge-creation, are in many countries private enterprises, it appears difficult to deny that economic research and education at these private universities may well also display a pro-market bias and disparage more critical approaches – not necessarily as a downright conspiracy but rather as the result of a cultural constraint imposed by the patrons of the private universities[120]. But even if this description were right, how would that translate into a general discrimination against critical approaches if it is conceded that the vast majority of universities around the world are public organizations which are free to follow other – less pro-market oriented theories and paradigms – currents? Why should that part of the economic scientific community not under its patrons' tutelage still reject scientific pluralism given that monism is clearly untenable?

4. The market for economic ideas

The practice of basic economic research and education is concentrated in universities. The market for economic ideas is, therefore, determined by the way scientific personnel (as 'factors of production') – mainly professors – are recruited and the way university researchers conduct their research in a methodological and paradigmatic manner (as 'production programme' or 'technology'). The output provided by the market for economic ideas – basic economic research – is a pure public good (see Eggertsson 1995: 206) with the particular characteristic of a credence good unveiling its value to the consumer only after consumption, if at all. Although these characteristics imply that it has no price, it means neither that basic research will not be privately supplied nor that there are no means to govern the market for economic ideas.[121] What it means is that the demand side of the market is not controlled by those who pay for its provision – which, at least in most public universities, is the general tax payer or, if tuition is charged, the student – but by the scientific community itself (see Menand 1996: 7) which enjoys academic freedom.

The private provision of the public good 'basic economic research' is motivated either by being a joint-product of academic education or because it serves an ideological purpose (see above) benefitting the financier of the private universities. And because the price does not regulate the market, rewards such as attention and reputation must take its place. And again, it

---

[120] For a classical account of the governance of universities acting as business corporations see Veblen (1918). For a historical account of some cases of individual harassment leading ultimately to the foundation of the American Association of University Professors in 1915 particularly promoting academic freedom see Haskell (1996).

[121] Some authors (e.g. Albert 2006, Mirowski 2004: 60, Wible 1998) question the applicability of economics to the investigation of the procurement of knowledge as insinuated by the metaphor of a 'market of ideas'. This position is not assumed here as economics provide helpful tools to conceptualize public goods such as 'economic ideas'.

is the scientific community, not the tax payer or the student, that bestows such attention and reputation on the producer since the basic economic research is a credence good. This, of course, constitutes the need for standards determining what is good scientific practice and output and measuring its quality as the basis for reputation-assignment. Moreover, the 'market for economic ideas' is distinguished further by characteristics that call for the introduction of standards in order to govern it: at most times, it shows the combination of high supply (of academics qualified to take a professorship) and low demand (for tenured professors) resulting in a quasi-permanent excess-supply ('shrink market')[122] and rendering it very risky. This is particularly the case because the attainment of a (tenured) professorship requires the acquisition of high and very specific human capital that can hardly be utilized in any other profession (see Eggertsson 1995: 203) and is, thus, associated with high sunk cost.

From this accrues a demand for standard-setting which mitigates the risks involved by providing guidelines for ontological, epistemological and methodological constraints that mark the boundaries between 'good' and 'bad/no' economics. On the other hand, due to network externalities, learning effects, and high sunk cost, the market for economic ideas is prone to develop ontological, epistemological, and methodological path-dependencies (see Morgan 2015), creating a situation of 'lock-in' which can be interpreted as a process of implicit standardization (see Arthur 1989). While in former times, when the scientific community was a very small, close-knit elite group of people knowing each other, gate-keeping into the academic system of economics had been provided by networking based on sociodemographic similarities ('habitus') and direct personal control[123], this no longer functions after academic education has become mass education and the scientific community has been inflated enormously. Now, gate-keeping is provided by ontological, epistemological, and methodological standardization, which is a rational regime from the perspective of the individual researcher (minimizing his risk) but may be dangerous from the perspective of the discipline if it strangulates the competition of ideas

[122] This characteristic of the market for economic ideas at the level of professorial appointments is not coincidental but necessary to the academic recruitment principle of 'selection of the best'.

[123] Eggertsson (1995: 204) reports – with reference to Keynes – on the influence which Alfred Marshall had on the professorial appointments at British and overseas universities in the English-speaking world.

on paradigmatic grounds. And the process of 'product differentiation' which usually evolves in order to transform a 'shrink market' into a 'niche market' (characterized by a situation of 'excess-demand'), may provide theoretical variation within the 'standard' paradigm but not the required paradigmatic pluralism.[124]

Yet, even if the market for economic ideas were prone to market failures which are disclosed in restricting paradigmatic competition, would not the victor – i.e. the one who manages to set the standards – be coincidental? Or, put differently, why should a market-apologetic paradigm prevail as King predicted (with reference to Karl Marx)[125]?

5. Power, hierarchy and the economic battle field

If one wants to predict the outcome of a process of standardization, one needs to know the direct benefits of different candidates (i.e. competing paradigms) to its (potential) users and the benefit that results from network externalities (i.e. the use that stems from the fact that the paradigm is used by others) which are related to the number of users (see e.g. Elsner 2012: 166ff.). In this very setting, the process of standardization may become random, once the initial conditions satisfy a high degree of equality throughout the distribution of users across different paradigms. But even if that were the case – which, of course, is not very realistic - other factors may contribute: the endowment of different paradigms (or, rather, their academic representatives) with economic (e.g. professorial positions and third party funding), social (e.g. networks within and without the scientific community), cultural (e.g. editorial board memberships on important journals) and symbolic capital (e.g. awards or highly visible positions beyond the university) will impact on the choice of and adherence to a paradigm as much as the weight that must be assigned to network externalities, assuming that some users are more powerful than others in the economic field.

---

[124] For the distinction between 'variation' and 'pluralism' see Heise (2014: 74ff.), Heise (2017).

[125] See King (2016: 8) who cites Marx (1867: 10): "In the domain of Political Economy, free scientific inquiry meets not merely the same enemies as in all other domains. The peculiar nature of the material it deals with, summons as foes into the field of battle the most violent, mean and malignant passions of the human breast, the Furies of private interest".

Recent work on the socio-economics of economics has been very illuminating in this respect: Taking 'economic ideas' as being an international public good (see Eggertsson 1995: 207) and the economic system as being strictly hierarchically structured (see Fourcade/Ollion/Algan 2015: 96ff.), a handful of private, elite US universities became the key-players in the standardization game. They control the journals which frame topics and bestow excellence on research(ers), they set the curriculum of Ph.D. programmes world-wide where the ontological, epistemological, and methodological tool-kit is passed on to the next generation of researchers (see Hodgson/Rothman 1999). These universities are not only extremely well equipped with economic capital (each elite US university commands a hundred times more financial resources compared to public universities world-wide), they rose to excellence under the cultural pretence that universities need to be beneficial to the society in order to gain legitimacy and acceptance. In a society – the USA – in which the market as the core constituent plays a crucial role in determining not only output and prices, but in legitimizing income aspirations and wealth distribution in a purely meritocratic way[126], it is hard to see how the economic discipline could not have developed a pro-market bias (see Fourcade 2009: 33ff.). And even after their strong grip on the system had been loosened slightly (and, only temporarily, as it turned out) during the 1960s, when the combination of political movements and the vast extension of the higher education system opened a 'window of opportunity' for economic pluralism, the situation could not be sustained as long as the endowment with the different kinds of capital remained as unequal as before.[127] Moreover, standardization as a gate-keeping measure became ever more important after personal control ceased to work in a world in which half of each age cohort takes up university study. In some countries (such as the UK), this standardization has become rather formal (see e.g. Lee 2007, Lee/Pham/Gu 2013). In others (such as Germany), it remained mainly informal, yet no less effective (see e.g. Heise/Sander/Thieme 2016). Although this research note is only concerned with the market for economic ideas, one might argue that the gist of the argument put forward here would presumably apply equally to other

[126] This is part of the 'American dream' and a founding principle of the United States of America, based on settlers escaping from feudal Europe with its social stratification based on descent (see e.g. Hochschild 1995 and Hacker 2008).

[127] For the development of heterodox economics see Lee (2009), King (2002) and Heise/Thieme (2016), Heise/Sander/Thieme (2016) with particular reference to Germany.

disciplines of the social sciences such as sociology or political science which, nevertheless, have remained pluralistic. I believe closer inspection would prove the crucial differences between the market for economic ideas and the markets for ideas of other social sciences: The other social sciences are in general more 'applied' (real world) sciences than economics[128], requiring the accumulation of less specific but more general human capital with lower sunk cost. Moreover, the scientific pretentions of economics as compared to the other social sciences are different: None of the other social sciences would claim to provide 'the one and only truth' ('erklären'; requiring a monist vision of the world) but rather a historically and institutionally backed understanding ('verstehen') of the social order, including the advocacy of normative positions (requiring a pluralism of approaches). Additionally, none of the other social sciences have developed axiomatic epistemologies that could claim to become a 'normal science' of Kuhnian type and, finally, none of the other social sciences is as hierarchically structured as economics (see e.g. Fourcade/Ollion/Algan 2015: 96ff.). Therefore, even if there was a demand for standardization within the other social sciences, this demand could not be met by a paradigmatic standardization along the lines of epistemological, ontological, and methodological monism.

6. Re-claiming pluralism in economics

John King is brave enough to concede that he is not sure of the answer to the question of why economics turned into a monist discipline based on a pro-market paradigm. And he is even less sure of what can be done to change this situation, yet proposes the following strategies: "...closer co-operation with each other (among the heterodox economists, A.H.), more interdisciplinary collaboration with the other social sciences, and pressure for political economy to be taught as a discipline in its own right, separate from departments of (mainstream) economics" (King 2016: 9). Although the quest to strengthen the ties among those members of the economic scientific community who are being discriminated against and to extend the ties beyond the disciplinary borders towards the more open-minded political and social sciences appears a sensible and comprehensible strategy, in combination with the proposal to claim heterodox economics as a distinct

[128] Economics, for instance, has much more often than other social sciences been criticized for relying overtly on formal rigorousness than on relevance or realism.

scientific discipline ('Political Economy'), it can only be rated as surrender and retreat, i.e. a Dunkirk strategy.[129]

Now that a socio-economic approach to economics has been presented, it must be accepted that a market such as the market for economic ideas, which is prone to market failure and is showing an extremely uneven battlefield in terms of the distribution of economic, social, cultural and symbolic capital, self-regulation in the sense of 'good economic theories will eventually assert themselves', cannot be expected.[130] However, rather than deserting the market entirely, it might be better to try first to regulate the market in order to overcome its failures. As it would be naive to hope for a re-distribution of economic, social, cultural and symbolic capital in the economic field in the nearer future, regulation must create and secure a place for all economic theories and paradigms, including heterodox economics which bows to the methodological requirements of positivistic fallibilism[131] in economics departments. This could, for instance, be achieved by introducing a 'pluralism codex' requiring the appointment of scientific staff from different paradigmatic backgrounds. This, again, could be controlled by 'equal opportunity commissions' and reinforced by providing financial incentives through public research funding bodies.

Of course, to hope for such regulation may be judged equally naïve, considering the way the economics profession is. Still, there appears to be one gateway for the introduction of formal regulations: at the root of 'self-regulation' of the scientific community lies 'academic freedom'. However, academic freedom not only passively safeguards the actors in the market for economic ideas against inappropriate interventions from the state; the concept of academic freedom also involves the obligation of the members of the scientific community (and the state) to create conditions under

---

[129] It should be conceded that a Dunkirk strategy – as in the name-giving event – can be a successful retreat to a more defensible position. However, it would still involve surrendering the economic discipline to the mainstream.

[130] Goldman/Cox (1996: 30f.) distinguish between 'competition of ideas in an unregulated (free) market' and an 'adversarial system of discourse', which are often confused. The former does not provide – due to the market failures put forward in part 2 – an optimal acquisition of knowledge, while the latter needs a regulatory framework in order to do so. It is this 'adversarial system of discourse' which only scientific pluralism can guarantee.

[131] This concession is necessary to prevent a methodological 'anything goes' (which, at least, would clash with the scientific pretences of the economic discipline) and to avoid the ordinary accusation that pluralism means obscurantism (see Tirole 2014).

which the procurement of knowledge can be provided free from discrimination or harassment (see Mason/McCallum/Haiven 2015: 9ff.)[132]. Based on the meta-theoretical foundations laid out in part 2, an appropriate organisation of the economics discipline must guarantee ontological, epistemological, and methodological pluralism in research and education, not only as an ethical principle but as a scientific imperative – non-compliance must be judged as a violation of academic freedom.

Until now, the violation of academic freedom with respect to a lack of pluralism has been perceived only, if at all, at the level of a specific department (as, for instance, in the case of the University of Manitoba; see Mason/McCallum/Haiven 2015). It ought to become a general device including the principle of 'negative discrimination' until a certain degree of pluralism has become established in every economics department and scientific pluralism has become a part of the 'cultural capital' of the discipline.

[132] Coase (1974b) draws our attention to the fact that regulating commodity markets is viewed far less critically than regulating markets for ideas. The reason is that regulating markets for ideas is often feared to undermine the freedom to express such ideas. As we have argued, in case of the economics discipline, it is the special features of the market for economic ideas which are exactly undermining academic freedom if the market is left to self-regulation. We would still need to find an appropriate form of regulation, though, in order to avoid substituting one form of market failure with another.

References

Albert, M. (2006); Product quality in scientific competition, Discussion Papers on Strategic Interaction 2006-6, Max-Planck-Institut für Ökonomik, Jena

Arrow, K.J. (1951); Social Choice and Individual Values, New Haven (:Yale University Press)

Arthur, B. (1989); Competing Technologies, Increasing Returns, and Lock-In by Historical Events; in: The Economic Journal, Vol. 99, pp. 116 - 131

Bartels, L.M. (2008); Unequal Democracy. The Political Economy of the New Gilded Age, Princeton (:University Press)

Berger, P.L., Luckmann, T. (1966); The Social Construction of Reality. A Treatise in the Sociology of Knowledge, Garden City (NY)

Caldwell, B.J. (1988); The case for pluralism; in: N. de Marchi (Hg.); The Popperian Legacy in Economics, Cambridge (:University Press), S. 231 – 244

Carlin, W., Soskice, D. (2006); Macroeconomics. Imperfections, Institutions and Policies, Oxford (:University Press)

Coase, R. H. (1974a); The Lighthouse in Economics; in: Journal of Law and Economics, Vol. 17, No. 2, pp. 357 – 376

Coase, R.H. (1974b); The Market for Goods and the Market for Ideas; in: American Economic Review, Papers & Proceedings, Vol. 64, No.2, pp. 384 - 391

Colander, D. (2005); The Making of an Economist Redux; in: Journal of Economic Perspectives, Vol. 19, No. 1, pp. 175 – 198

Courvisanos, J., Doughney, J., Millmow, A. (eds.) (2016); Reclaiming Pluralism in Economics, Abingdon(: Routledge)

Eggertsson, T. (1995); On the economics of economics; in: Kyklos, Vol. 48, No.2, pp. 201 – 210

Elsner, W. (2012); Microeconomics of Interactive Economies, Cheltenham (: Edward Elgar)

Fourcade, M. (2009); Economists and Societies. Discipline and Profession in the United States, Britain and France, 1890s to 1990s, Princeton (:University Press)

Fourcade, M., Ollion, E., Algan, Y. (2015); The Superiority of Economists; in: Journal of Economic Perspectives, Vol. 29, No.1, S. 89 – 114

Freeman, A., Kirman, A. (2006); Beyond talking the talk: Towards a critical pluralist stance; in: Post-Autistic Economics Review, No. 40, article 4

Freeman, R.B. (1999); It's better being an Economist (But Don't Tell Anyone); in: Journal of Economic Perspective, Vol. 3, No.3, pp. 139 – 145

Friedman, M. (1953); The Methodology of Positive Economics; in: ders.; Essays in Positive Economics, Chicago (: University Press), S. 3 – 42

Fullbrook, E. (2008); Pluralist Economics, London (: Zed Books)

Fullbrook, E. (2013); New paradigm economics, in: real-world economics review, issue no. 65, pp. 129 - 131

Fullbrook, E. (2014); New Paradigm Economics versus Old Paradigm Economics; Interview with Edward Fullbrook, Conducted by Paul Rosenberg, in: real- world economics review, issue no. 66, pp. 131 - 143

Garnett, R. F. jr. (2006); Paradigms and pluralism in heterodox economics; in: Review of Political Economy, Vol. 18, No.4, S. 521 - 546

Garnett, R., Olsen, E.K., Starr, M. (eds.) (2010); Economic Pluralism, Abingdon(: Routledge)

Goldman, A.I., Cox, J.C. (1996); Speech, Truth, and the Free Market for Ideas; in: Legal Theory, Vol. 2, pp. 1 - 32

Goodfriend, M. (2007); How the World Achieved Consensus on Monetary Policy; in: The Journal of Economic Perspectives, Vol. 21, No.4, pp. 47 - 68

Hacker, J.S. (2008); The Great Risk Shift. The New Economic Insecurities and the Decline of the American Dream, Oxford (: University Press)

Hacker, J.S., Pierson, P. (2010); Winner-Take-All Politics. How Washington Made the Rich Richer – And Turned Its Back on the Middle Class, New York (: Schuster & Simon)

Häring, N., Douglas, N. (2012); Economists of the Powerful – Convenient Theories, Distorted Facts, Ample Rewards, London (: Anthem Press)

Haskell, T.L. (1996); Justifying the Rights of Academic Freedom in the Era of 'Power/Knowledge'; in: Menand, L. (ed.); The Future of Academic Freedom, Chicago (: University Press), pp. 43 - 90

Heise, A. (2014); The Future of Economics in a Lakatos-Bourdieu framework; in: International Journal of Political Economy, Vol. 43, No. 3, pp. 70 – 93

Heise, A. (2017); Defining Economic Pluralism: Ethical Norm or Scientific Imperative?; in: International Journal of Pluralism and Economics Education, Vol. 8, No. 1 (forthcoming)

Heise, A., Sander, H., Thieme, S. (2016); Ende der Heterodoxie?, Wiesbaden (:VS Verlag)

Heise, A., Thieme, S. (2016); The short rise and long fall of heterodox economics. Explorations in a scientific field of power and struggle; in: Journal of Economic Issues (forthcoming)

Hochschild, J.L; Facing Up to the American Dream. Race, Class, and the Soul of the Nation, Princeton (: University Press)

Hodgson, G. M., Rothman, H. 1999. The editors and authors of economics journals: a case of institutional oligopoly? Economic Journal, vol. 109, no. 2, pp.165–86

Holcombe, R. (2008); Pluralism versus heterodoxy in economics and the social sciences; in: Journal of Philosophical Economics, Vol. 1, No.2, pp. 51 - 72

Kellert, S.H., Longino, H.E., Waters, K.C. (Eds.) (2006); Scientific Pluralism, Minneapolis (: University of Minnesota Press)

Keynes, J.N. (1891); The Scope and Method of Political Economy, London

King, J. E. (2002); A History of Post Keynesian Economics since 1936, Cheltenham (: Edward Elgar)

King, J.E. (2016); Pluralist Economics in my Lifetime; in: Courvisanos/Doughney/Millmow (2016), p. 3 – 14

Lee, F.S. (2007); The Research Assessment Exercise, the state and the dominance of mainstream economics in British universities; in: Cambridge Journal of Economics, Vol. 31, pp. 309 - 331

Lee, F.S. (2009); A History of Heterodox Economics: Challenging the Mainstream in the Twentieth Century, London and New York (: Routledge)

Lee, F.S., Pham, X., Gu, G. (2013): The UK Research Assessment Exercise and the narrowing of UK economics. In: Cambridge Journal of Economics, Vol. 37, No.4, 693-717

Loasby, B. (2003); Closed Models and Open Systems; in: Journal of Economic Methodology, Vol. 10, No.3, S. 285 – 306

Manson, A., McCallum, P., Haiven, L. (2015); Report of the Ad Hoc Investigatory Committee into the Department of Economics at the University of Manitoba, Canadian Association of University Teachers (CAUT), Ottawa

Mariyani-Squire, E., Moussa, M. (2015); Fallibilism, Liberalism and Stilwell's Advocacy for Pluralism in Economics; in: Journal of Australian Political Economy, Vol. 75, S. 194 – 210

Marx, K. (1867); Preface to the first German edition of 'Capital', Vol. 1, Moscow (: Foreign Languages Publishing House, 1961)

Menand, L. (1996); The Limits of Academic Freedom; in: Menand, L. (ed.); The Future of Academic Freedom, Chicago (: University Press), pp. 3 - 20

Middleton, R. (1998); Charlatans or Saviours? Economists and the British Economy from Marshall to Meade, Northampton (:Edward Elgar)

Mirowski, P. (1989): More heat than light. Economics as social physics: Physics as nature's economics. Cambridge (: University Press).

Mirowski, P. (2004); The effortless economy of science, Durham (: Duke University Press)

Moore, G. (2003); John Neville Keynes's Solution to the English Methodenstreit; in: Journal of the History of Economic Thought, Vol. 25, No.1, S. 5 – 38

Morgan, J. (2015); Is Economics Responding to Critique? What do the UK 2015 QAA Subject Benchmarks Indicate?, in: Review of Political Economy, Vol. 27, No. 4, S. 518-538

Morgan, M.S., Rutherford, M. (eds.) (1998); From Interwar Pluralism to Postwar Neoclassicism, Durham (: Duke University Press)

Robinson, J. (1972); The Second Crisis in Economic Theory; in: American Economic Review, Vol. 62, No.1/2, pp. 1 - 10

Salanti, A., Screpanti, E. (Hrsg.) (1997); Pluralism in Economics. New Perspectives in History and Methodology, Cheltenham (: Edward Elgar)

Schultze, Ch.L. (1996); The CEA: An Inside Voice of Mainstream Economics; in: Journal of Economic Perspectives, Vol. 10, pp. 23 – 39

Tirole, J. (2015); Letter to the French Minister of Education Fioraso. (http://assoeconomiepolitique.org/wp-content/uploads/Lettre-de-jean-Tirole.pdf , retreaved 22.02.2016)

Van Bouwel, J. (2004); Explanatory pluralism in economics: Against the mainstream?; in: Philosophical Explorations, Vol. 7, No. 3, pp. 299 - 315

Veblen, T. (1918); The Higher Learning in America. A Memorandum on the Conduct of Universities by Business Men, New York (:B.W. Huebsch)

Wible, J.R. (1998); The economics of science – methodology and epistemology as if economics really mattered, London (: Routledge)

Williamson, O. (1997); Comments, in: Coats, A.W. (Hrsg.); The Post-1945 In-ternationalization of Economics, Durham (:Duke University Press)

Five

Re-Claiming the University: transforming economics as a discipline*

Economics as a discipline is in disarray. In the aftermath of the global economic crisis, academic experts, students, commentators, practitioners, and politicians all questioned the status of academic economics and many called for a 'new economic thinking' (see e.g. Dow 2012).

There are a range of scientific research programmes (SRPs) that might be considered potential candidates to replace the neoclassical DSGE model as a mainstream paradigm and the basis of a new orthodoxy. These include post-Keynesianism, complexity economics, and evolutionary economics. Some commentators have nonetheless claimed that what is needed now is not just another mainstream model, but rather a more thoroughgoing transformation of economics into a pluralist social science in which no dominant mainstream can marginalise other paradigms simply because they employ a different ontology (see e.g. Fullbrook 2003: 8-9).

Nearly a decade after the onset of the financial crisis, however, there is little evidence of any transformation in economic research and teaching (see e.g. Yalcintas 2016, Stillwell 2016). Furthermore, economic policy based on mainstream economics is still prevalent (see e.g. Crouch 2011; Mirowski 2013). What is needed, then, is not simply another plea for pluralism in economics and a demonstration of its advantages (if not necessity; see e.g. Heise 2017a), but rather a consideration of the conditions of a transformation of the economic discipline and an explanation of the resilience of the current mainstream (see e.g. Stützle 2016)[133].

---

* Originally published: The Journal of Philosophical Economics: Reflections on Economic and Social Issues , Vol. XI, No. 2, 2018, 37-66

[133] It has been argued that economics is currently in a transitional state characterised by a battle for hegemony (see Decker 2018). Assuming that this is not an overly optimistic

To this end, it is first of all crucial to clarify what it would mean to *transform* economics as a discipline, since this is an ill-defined term that has been interpreted in very different ways. From a practical perspective, ambiguity and misunderstanding as to what is meant by such a transformation may provoke unnecessary opposition to it. From an academic perspective, it may also give rise to very different methodological approaches and subsequently to highly divergent conceptions of the road ahead.

The first section of the paper will clarify the concept of transformation. The second will discuss the desirability of transformation, and on this basis will discriminate between different transformation paths and single out one preferred path. In section three, the conditions of a successful transformation will be elaborated with reference to both intra-disciplinary and extra-disciplinary factors. Finally, section four will draw a number of conclusions concerning the potential steps that may be taken toward transforming the discipline, as well as considering further interdisciplinary research efforts that may promote pluralism within and beyond the epistemic community of academic researchers.

1. Transforming Economics

In order to shed some light on the potential ways in which economics as a discipline might be transformed,[134] we first need to begin with its ambitions as a science. If science is a means of generating knowledge that can not only claim to objectively establish 'truth' but also to do so in an inter-

---

view of the state of the discipline, the present article considers a number of possible paths towards its transformation. It should be emphasised at this point that the article only addresses those paths that are related to pluralism in economics. Other transitional paths, such as a transformation in favour of ethical economics (see e.g. DeMartino 2011; DeMartino/McCloskey 2016), are not considered here.

[134] The transformation paths outlined in the following sections (see tab. 6) have all been discussed in the literature on economic pluralism. If we assume with Jackson (2018) that economics is presently marked by an 'orthodox/heterodox divide' (where heterodox economics is dominated, yet tolerated by mainstream economics), we can also imagine another transformation resulting in an 'orthodox hegemony' (i.e. the exclusion of heterodox economics). This transformation is not considered here, firstly because I believe this is already a more accurate description of the status quo, and secondly because such a transformation would clearly not fulfil the requirements outlined in the introduction.

subjectively verifiable way, then economics is in trouble. From a constructivist perspective, no such objective truth exists; what is considered truth is in fact socially constructed and the 'one world one truth' hypothesis is simply rejected. From a positivist perspective, by contrast, objective knowledge does exist, yet on account of the nature of the object of enquiry (the economic system as an 'open system') and the methodological restrictions of the discipline (as a non-experimental science, it is subject to the Duhem-Quine-thesis), there is no ultimate method of discriminating between different paradigmatic approaches (Heise 2017a: 22ff.). The best we can hope for is therefore conjectural knowledge, which can be regarded as the 'truth' as long as it has not been clearly falsified by empirical evidence or deductive shortcomings. A plurality of alternative, competing, and potentially incommensurable paradigms is thus not only possible, but also desirable in a discipline that sees competition as facilitating new insights (Hayek 1968). It also follows that the relativism of the constructivists – which calls the discipline's scientific status into question simply through its rejection of objective truth – is not a necessary position, though not an entirely refutable one either. On the other hand, the monist 'one world one-truth paradigm' is only tenable under the restrictive and rather implausible assumption that the economic system is a 'closed' and exhaustively analysable system.

Radical Pluralism

One potential approach would seek to transform economics from a discipline dominated by a monist, 'one world one truth' paradigm into an endeavour predicated on a relativist and radical pluralist 'no objective truth' paradigm (see e.g. Samuels 1997). Since this approach not only denies the 'one world one truth' hypothesis but also rejects fallibilist positivism in favour of an 'anything *necessarily* goes' methodology (Samuels 1997: 68; emphasis in the original), it leaves itself open to being labelled 'obscurantist'. Moreover, it should be emphasised that such a transformation would not be supported by those who defend the discipline's scientific status.

Paradigm Pluralism

Another form of transformation would involve rejecting the monist approach as too restrictive and untenable, and instead advocating paradigm pluralism as a scientific imperative (see e.g. Heise 2017a). This form of transformation would not question the methodological necessity of fallibilist positivism nor the 'one world one truth' hypothesis. It would nonetheless contend that the aim of enquiry is not to establish 'objective truth,' but rather to provide 'conjectural knowledge' that may well be plural. In order to distinguish this form of transformation from that outlined under the heading of 'radical pluralism', it would be necessary to agree on a set of standards determining which paradigms should be allowed to compete within this pluralist framework and which would have to be rejected as 'obscure,' so as not to jeopardise the discipline's scientific status.

Scientific Revolution

A third kind of transformation could be described as a 'scientific revolution'. It would involve replacing the now-dominant neoclassical DSGE paradigm with any other paradigm, while continuing to regard positivist fallibilism as an adequate methodology and leaving the monist 'one world one truth' claim intact (see e.g. Davidson 2004). This transformation would regard the recent global financial crisis as the empirical anomaly that generated a crisis in neoclassical economics, and would aim to establish another paradigm, such as post-Keynesianism, Marxism or complexity economics as the new orthodoxy. Such a transformation would be in line with Kuhn's contentions concerning scientific progress, yet rather than helping to establish a pluralistic discipline, it would only serve to replace one dominant paradigm with another. As Max Planck (1928: 22) noted, such transformations are not supported by the successful proponents of the old mainstream, but rather by a younger generation of scientists aware of the shortcomings of the old paradigm and the potential of the new.

Methodological Pluralism

The fourth potential form of transformation would have a far more limited scope. In the course of the professionalisation of economics during the first half of the 20th century, not only did fallibilist positivism come to be accepted as the methodology appropriate to the discipline's claim to be a 'quasi-natural science'; formal deductivism also came to be established as the only acceptable method of theorising (see e.g. Debreu 1991; Mirowski

1991). Mathematics thus came to be regarded as the only acceptable language of economic theory, to such an extent that formal deductivism has been described as the most comprehensive characteristic of mainstream neoclassical economics (see Lawson 2013) – to the detriment of all approaches that reject such mathematical formalism. The fourth form of transformation would therefore aim to establish a methodological pluralism, so that non-formal and potentially narrative-based approaches (such as the economics of order ('*Ordnungsökonomik*') or Hayekian and Austrian economics, which reject formal inquiry as a 'pretence of knowledge' would also receive acceptance (see e.g. Rosen 1997: 147ff.; Erlei 2015).

Critical Political Economy

Finally, a fifth form of transformation might aim to subvert the discipline's scientific pretension to establish objective knowledge in the name of a desire to normatively intervene in the process of societal development and reform (see e.g. Stilwell 2016; Jakobson 2017), thus replacing 'objectivity' with 'advocacy'. Such a transformation would to a certain extent take us back in time to the economic debates of the end of the 19th century. At this time, proponents of the German historical school and of ('old') American institutionalism made the case within their respective scientific societies (the American Social Science Association and the Verein für Socialpolitik) for the necessity of a methodological foundation oriented toward 'political economy,' which would replace 'objective knowledge' based on deductive theorising with 'historical understanding' derived from historico-empirical investigations (see e.g. Furner 2011; Fourcade 2009: 78ff.). These historical *'Methodenstreits'* led to a separation between economics, which stressed its scientific 'objectivity', and economic sociology, which lowered its scientific ambitions and focussed on acquiring an understanding of historically and institutionally specific situations and phenomena, as well as on social reform (see e.g. Stilwell 2016: 45). The fifth form of transformation would therefore aim to secure the (interdisciplinary) reintegration of economic sociology into economics, or at least the blurring of the methodological division between the disciplines.

Table 6: Different Forms of Transformation

	Key emphasis	Sphere Concerned	Scope	Institutional incentives/ obstructions	Actors involved
1. Transformation from neoclassical to post-Keynesian, Marxist, or other paradigm dominance	Scientific revolution	Internal (to the academic economic community)	Accepting positivistic fallibilism, rejecting constructivism/ relativism	Path dependencies	(young) economists
2. Transformation from formal deduction to narrative-based abduction	Methodological pluralism	Internal	Accepting positivistic fallibilism, rejecting constructivism/ relativism	Standardisation/ professionalisation	epistemic community of economists
3. Transformation from monism to pluralism	Paradigm pluralism	Internal and external (society as a whole; pluralist interest groups)	Accepting positivistic fallibilism, rejecting constructivism/ relativism	Standardisation, ontological ignorance and resistance	economists, students, institutions (e.g. trade unions,), political actors (seeking to aid academic freedom)
4. Transformation from objective enquiry to advocacy	Critical political economy	Internal and external (science always embedded in broader social structures)	Rejecting positivistic fallabilism, accepting constructivism/ relativism	Methodological resistance (charges of 'relativism/ obscurantism')	Social scientists
5. Transformation from monism to radical pluralism	Radical pluralism	Internal and external	Rejecting positivistic fallabilism, accepting constructivism/ relativism	Methodological resistance	Social scientists

Internal and External Agents of Change

The different forms of transformation (see tab. 6) clearly differ greatly in terms of their scope. Two of these transformation types – scientific revolution and methodological pluralism – can be described as 'internal', since the relevant agents of change and their motivations are firmly rooted within economics as a discipline. In the case of a scientific revolution in the Kuhnian sense, the agents of change would be the younger generation of scientists who would decide to pursue a new paradigm. The older generation, by contrast, would continue to defend the old hegemonic paradigm simply because a paradigm shift would devalue their human capital and scientific merits. Such a transformation would not be based on a collective, organised movement but on the activities of individuals. Methodological pluralism, on the other hand, would be supported by those who value methodological freedom more than the constraints imposed by the demand for professionalisation and standardisation. It would be opposed by those who see it as endangering the scientific legitimacy of the discipline. The chances of these transformations succeeding would depend on the power exerted by the older, mainstream generation in their function as gate-keepers (of journals, universities, and so on) and on the availability of formal or informal incentives such as journal publishing opportunities and third-party funding allocations. In an academic discipline as hierarchically structured as economics (see e.g. Fourcade/Ollion/Algan 2015), internal resistance can be expected to be strong, and a collective (internal) struggle would potentially be required to effect transformation.

The other three forms of transformation – paradigm pluralism, critical political economy and radical pluralism – involve both internal and external motives. Internally, paradigm pluralism can be seen as imperative[135] to the advancement of the discipline. Critical political economy and radical pluralism, on the other hand, lack a sound – i.e. scientific – basis for their implementation. The particular ontological premises of radical pluralism

[135] It is important to emphasise that paradigm pluralism is not a position based on an ethics of fairness and tolerance and advocated by those marginalised by the dominant mainstream, but rather a scientific imperative that is crucial for the flourishing of the discipline. This needs to be recognised and acknowledged by academic economists from all theoretical and paradigmatic backgrounds, not only those from the heterodox camp.

and the interdisciplinary claims of critical political economy, which serve to blur methodological boundaries, need not and likely will not be shared by the academic economic community. Radical pluralism and critical political economy are fundamentally interdisciplinary in nature, and many of the relevant agents of change are situated within academic disciplines outside economics, such as sociology, political science, and philosophy. Likewise, a shift toward paradigm pluralism would have to contend with an ontologically standardised discipline and would also need to rely on external support. This might come from consumers of economic insights and education such as students, trade unions, and other social groups who are dissatisfied with mainstream equilibrium analysis and market apologetics and hungry for other approaches. In addition, the state in its regulative capacity has a responsibility to ensure that the discipline is appropriately organised and governed so that it can remain pluralistic and allow academic freedom to prevail.

2. Which Form of Transformation Should We Pursue?

In light of the range of possible forms of transformation, it is necessary to choose a preferred path that is not simply arbitrary, but rather consistent and comprehensible. Which option we should pursue of course depends on our priorities: The likelihood of success? The path of least resistance? The path with the broadest support? Since transformation is not in itself an objective but only a means of leaving behind an undesirable state of affairs for a more desirable one, the desirability of the outcome could be used as a criterion here. But isn't desirability a purely subjective criterion that cannot serve as a basis for a consistent and comprehensible decision? This would certainly be the case if our tastes and inclinations were to frame our desire. What we are concerned with here, however, is the desired state of an academic discipline with its own unique history, development, and nature. Desirability in this instance does not therefore depend on the subjective preferences of individuals or groups but rather refers to developments that are either inevitable from a functional perspective or collectively acceptable insofar as the decision maker's own academic position is unknown (i.e. hidden behind a 'veil of ignorance'[136]).

Do We Need a Paradigm Shift?

Against this backdrop, let us first turn to the purely internal forms of transformation, which we have labelled 'scientific revolution' and 'methodological pluralism'. According to Thomas S. Kuhn, a scientific revolution has two necessary preconditions: firstly, the dominance of the mainstream paradigm needs to be undermined either by empirical evidence that is difficult to reconcile with the existing body of mainstream theory or by a flaw in its deductive reasoning that calls into question the accuracy of its conclusions. Secondly, since science does not allow for a theoretical vacuum, there needs to be a competing paradigm that not only explains all the evidence adequately explained by the dominant paradigm to date, but also sheds light on the empirical or theoretical trigger of the crisis in this dominant paradigm[137]. These preconditions, however, are necessary but not by themselves sufficient. Whether a *momentum crucis* should spark a scientific revolution depends on the capacity of the dominant paradigm to resolve those problems with which it is faced and/or on its ability to call into question its potential competitors.

In a non-experimental science such as economics, paradigms cannot be falsified by empirical anomalies. Such anomalies may necessitate repair work within the 'protective belt' of the paradigm's auxiliary assumptions, but are not able to oblige its followers to abandon it without further ado. They may nonetheless cast doubt on the 'progressiveness' of the dominant paradigm and tempt younger researchers in particular to try out other more promising approaches[138]. Such an evolution, which may ultimately lead to

[136] This concept was of course first introduced by John Rawls to objectify the wholly subjective concept of 'justice' (see Rawls 1971).
[137] It might be argued that Sraffa's critique of neoclassical capital theory did not depose neoclassical economics as the dominant mainstream paradigm (contrary to the expectations of many Sraffians) because it was purely critical and did not provide a constructive alternative capable of taking over from the neoclassical paradigm.
[138] I am aware that I am mixing Kuhnian and Lakatosian elements here. I believe Kuhn is

a paradigm shift, may still be obstructed if the gate-keepers of the scientific system remain attached to the old paradigm and are in a position to deter most (younger) researchers from engaging with alternatives. The recent global financial crisis has of course been described as a *momentum crucis* by many economists (e.g. Stiglitz 2017) and a number of theoretical approaches – such as information economics, complexity economics, and post-Keynesian economics – have been singled out as potential contenders for a new economic mainstream.

There are nonetheless three important countervailing forces that such a shift would have to contend with. Firstly, proponents of the DSGE mainstream have been quick to re-integrate the global financial crisis into their explanatory cosmos – either by simply denying that DSGE modelling cannot explain it (see e.g. Cochrane 2011a; Cochrane 2011b; Minford 2010) or by arguing that some additional elements may suffice to reconcile DSGE modelling with major economic disruptions (see e.g. Benes/Kumhof/Laxton 2014; Del Negro/Giannoni/Schorfheide 2014; and many of the contributions to the Spring-Summer 2018 issue of the Oxford Review of Economic Policy). Secondly, many competing paradigms such as complexity economics or information economics cannot be regarded as genuine paradigmatic alternatives to the DSGE, but must rather be understood as epistemological variations on the mainstream paradigm, even if they were formerly regarded as 'dissenters'(see e.g. Heise 2016; Heise 2017a)[139]. Thirdly, key gate-keepers in the academic economic field, such as influential scientists with significant symbolic capital (e.g. Nobel Prize winners) and influential economic institutions with considerable economic and social capital (e.g. elite US universities and high-ranking economic journals) have shown little inclination to overhaul their approaches and

more adept at coining memorable terms such as paradigm or paradigm shift, while Lakatos provides a more profound dimensional description of paradigms (i.e. 'scientific research programmes') and the temporary and changing status of paradigms as either 'progressive' or 'degenerative'. It therefore seems to me fruitful to make eclectic use of Kuhnian and Lakatosian concepts.

[139] Farmer (2017) even recently attempted to interpret post-Keynesianism as a DSGE variant.

their policies. Furthermore, outspoken critique of these influential individuals and institutions is often regarded simply as a means of gaining attention for dissenting approaches (see e.g. Heise 2014).

In sum, it would seem safe to say that a paradigm revolution in economics is neither likely[140] nor at present desirable. It is far more likely that the mainstream will become even more fragmented and varied than it already was on Colander/Holt/Rosser's 2004 description, as a result of the decisions of individual scientists.

More Methodological Pluralism?

Although economics has seen immense growth in methods on the back of the 'empirical and experimental turn' that has marked the last three decades (see Hamermesh 2013; Kim et al 2006), this has only strengthened the fallibilistic dimension of its positivistic methodology. Formal deductivism remains the backbone of economic research, such that non-formal theoretical papers are unlikely to be published in core mainstream journals and non-formal schools of thought such as the economics of order and constitutional economics (*'Ordnungsökonomik'*) and Hayekian or Austrian economics (which intentionally reject the mathemisation of economics as a 'pretence of knowledge') are unlikely to be accepted as part of 'modern economics'[141]. Insofar as economics has come to be regarded as an axiomatic, deductive science, it is no surprise that mathematics has become a key tool in economic enquiry: the rigor of its formal logic and its economy of exposition makes it attractive to researchers endeavouring to produce objective, interpersonally verifiable results that are 'right' in a formal sense[142].

---

[140] In a conversation between three Nobel Prize winners – Robert Solow, Michael Spence and Joseph Stiglitz – none of the participants mentioned any transformation of the discipline that could be regarded as a quest for a paradigm shift; see Andersen (2011).

[141] Schmidt/aus dem Moore (2010: 170ff.), for instance, emphasise the historical merits of a non-formal economics of order, but are sceptical of its future prospects within an internationalised (US-centered) modern economic discipline.

[142] Debreu (1986: 1261) acknowledges that "Deductive reasoning about social phenomena invited the use of mathematics from the first". And Paul Krugman (1996), who was awarded the Nobel Prize for his contributions to international trade theory, adds that "International trade in particular happens to be a subject in which a page or two of algebra

Nevertheless, in light of the long and inconclusive debate on the use and applicability of mathematics in economics (see e.g. Beed/Kane 1991), Dany Rodrik (2015: 31ff.) would seem a little naïve in claiming that:

> *"The reason economists use mathematics is typically misunderstood. It has little to do with sophistication, complexity, or claims to higher truth. Math essentially plays two roles in economics, neither of which is cause for glory: clarity and consistency. [...] So math plays a purely instrumental role in economic models. In principle, models do not require math, and it is not the math that makes the model useful or scientific".*

Rodrik may be right that mathematics plays a purely instrumental role in economics, yet its role is certainly not limited to making theory clearer and more consistent. In the context of the post-war professionalisation of the discipline, it surely also served to underscore the accuracy and objectivity of a science that has a host of significant political and social implications. Furthermore, the use of a language that is inaccessible to the layman or even to other social scientists served to make the discipline less accessible to non-experts (see Beed/Kane 1991: 603)[143].

Since mathematisation has been pursued particularly by proponents of (DS)GE modelling as a means of formalising allocation-oriented market solutions and optimisation problems, the quest for formalisation can also be interpreted as an attempt to maintain control over the epistemological and ontological core of economics as a discipline[144]. Whether this amounts to a hidden agenda or is simply an unintended consequence of mathemati-

---

and diagrams is worth 10 volumes of mere words".

[143] Krugman (1996) is again rather bold in this regard: "The opponents of mainstream economics dislike people like me not so much for our conclusions as for our style: They want economics to be what it once was, a field that was comfortable for the basic literary intellectual..."

[144] Tony Lawson in particular has repeatedly pointed out that a science's degree of formalisation depends on its ontology (see e.g. Lawson 2003). An insistence on a high level of formalisation is therefore at the same time an insistence on a particular ontology – in the present case, the ontology of social and economic exchange in a Walrasian context. Any call for formalisation as a means of ensuring 'quality' standards can then be seen as a simple screening device.

sation, this ought to be the starting point for a consideration of the desirability of (greater) methodological pluralism. It is worth bearing in mind that while it is impossible to make any scientifically tenable claim by wholly excluding non-formal, narrative methods of enquiry, there may be certain cases in which particular ontological premises make the application of formal reasoning questionable. Mathematics and the social sciences are not natural bedfellows (see Mirowski 1991: 53f.). Indeed, Habermas (1968: 143ff.) argues that only an ontological openness[145] that leaves space for abduction allows for rational scientific enquiry, while mathematical deduction is simply a form of applied logic that does not by itself provide any scientific knowledge. Ontological openness is therefore a necessary precondition for any economic discipline that claims to be a science rather than an art or a purely logical activity, and it is formal reasoning rather than narrative approaches that requires justification.

Any marginalisation of economic paradigms or schools of thought purely on the grounds that they use non-formal methods is entirely unjustifiable. On the other hand, the ontology of social and economic exchange presupposed by mainstream market economics lends itself to formalisation. As long as formalisation is not used to privilege a certain ontology, it should be tolerated and may indeed only serve an instrumental purpose. Both the historical proximity between Americanisation and mathematisation[146] and the fact that the ontological dimensions of economic paradigms have been almost completely neglected or lost in economic theorising since its post-war Americanisation seems to suggest a certain bias toward the use of formal methods in economics. By contrast, the number of Nobel prizes awarded to proponents of non-formal economics – including Elinor

[145] 'Ontological openness' means here that the essence of the object of inquiry is not determined in advance but is (potentially the most critical and creative) part of the knowledge creation process through which an academic discipline becomes a science. While mainstream economics rests on the ontological presupposition of (intertemporal) exchange relations, Marxian economics is based on power relations, and post-Keynesian economics on nominal obligations. Whether complexity economics' assumption that the economy is a 'complex adaptive system' can be seen as a distinct ontological presupposition (as Thornton (2017: 56) believes) remains an open question (see Heise 2017b).

[146] In Germany, for instance, the 'Americanisation' and 'mathematisation' of economics are used almost synonymously to connote its 'modernisation' (see e.g. Hesse 2012).

Ostrom, Robert Vogel, Douglass North, Amartya Sen, Daniel Kahneman, and James Buchanan – and the number of non-formal faculties even in the US (see e.g. Klamer 1995) seem to speak against the idea of a lack of methodological pluralism. A desire for a shift in emphasis towards non-formal, narrative methods in economics is then surely a reflection of personal inclinations rather than an objective necessity.

Anything Goes or Critical Political Economy?

If a transformation will not and need not come about purely by means of internal forces, perhaps it might be stimulated by other sources within philosophy and the social sciences. Constructivism argues that any reality, whether social or natural, is constructed and that the truth claims of science in general and the social sciences (including economics) in particular have to be rejected. From this perspective, no rigid methodological rule can be formulated or imposed on economics, and a radical form of pluralism is advocated instead. Furthermore, since scientific research cannot produce 'objective knowledge', economics is called upon to take a critical perspective on human circumstances and to attempt to intervene to improve living standards for all. Further justification for such a transformation of economics into a critical form of political economy and for an alliance with the other social sciences is often sought within a tradition stretching back to Adam Smith, David Ricardo and Karl Marx (see Stilwell 2016).

Unlike in the 1960s and 1970s, however, when the renaissance of classical political economy helped drive a temporary pluralisation of the discipline, the renewed interest in political economy today is not based on a desire to break a theoretical deadlock (as was the case with Sraffa's solution to the problem of finding a value-standard that would be independent of functional income distribution). The desire to transform economics into an interdisciplinary form of political economy rests entirely on individual preferences and cannot claim to be either functionally necessary or broadly acceptable on the assumption of a 'veil of ignorance'. Moreover, an anything-goes pluralism rests on fringe ontological assumptions that cannot possibly be accepted as necessary (Heise 2017a: 31).[147]

---

[147] This is not to say that such assumptions are to be rejected altogether. Yet just like the

Paradigm Pluralism and the Desirability of Transformation

If the extremes of paradigm monism[148] and radical pluralism are both rejected on the basis of their unrealistic assumptions, paradigm pluralism remains the only logical alternative. It would then be scientifically imperative for the flourishing of the discipline and the creation of an environment of academic freedom. Paradigm pluralism does not entail any eclectic paradigm usage nor the construction of a pluralist paradigm (whatever that may be), nor does it preclude the individual researcher's insistence on the superiority of the paradigm he or she has chosen to use[149]. It only requires us to accept that, due to the nature of economics' object of enquiry and its methodological restrictions, it may not be possible to determine that any one paradigm is superior to others and a plurality of paradigms must therefore not only be tolerated but also regarded as healthy for the discipline. In other words, paradigm pluralism must become part of the cultural capital of economics (as it is in the other social sciences).

In order to distinguish 'paradigm pluralism' from 'radical pluralism' and, moreover, to acknowledge the fact that science is conducted in epistemic communities with shared common beliefs about what makes the discipline scientific (see e.g. Kitcher 1993) – i.e. about the demarcation line between science and non-science and disciplinary boundaries – we need first to establish some commonalities (see e.g. Dow 2007). These help to prevent

---

closed system assumptions of mainstream exchange economics (which form the basis of the monist 'one world one truth' paradigm), the radical pluralists' assumption that there is no possible objective knowledge cannot form the ontological consensus of the epistemic community of economists.

[148] Which, incidentally, does not exclude a variety or even a plurality of methods, theories and epistemologies (see Heise 2017a: 24ff.). Contrary to what Vines/Wills (2018) appear to believe, however, this does not involve a pluralism in any genuine sense.

[149] It has been argued that pluralism might leave no room for rational choice between paradigms (see e.g. Langhe 2009), so that a form of paradigm indifference might come to paralyse the discipline. Nevertheless, paradigms differ in terms of their epistemological, methodological and ontological dimensions. It should therefore be regarded as rational to choose the paradigm whose axiomatic structure and pre-analytic vision suits the individual researcher best. In fact, given the nature of science in general and economics in particular, this is the only honest way to conduct research (as opposed to allowing it to be influenced by career or funding-related motives).

endless discussions within the epistemic community concerning the scientific content of research statements, though they also harbour the risk of suppressing valid criticisms and valuable new insights. In light of this trade-off, and the fact that the 'marketplace for economic ideas' is not a perfect market but rather an embattled field in which various actors endowed with vastly different quantities of economic, social and cultural capital compete very imperfectly (see e.g. Merton 1968; Knorr-Cetina 1982; Heise/Thieme 2016), these commonalities cannot be determined by (powerful) individual actors in this very field but must be arrived at using a heuristic device such as Rawls' 'veil of ignorance'. In order to be acceptable, such commonalities require the assent of all scientists, independently of their position in the field. Assuming that a researcher were in a weak position in the field, he or she would not accept any standard that would undermine his or her ability to gain the most significant reward within it: recognition and reputation. He or she would then oppose the imposition of restrictions on the ontological, epistemological, and methodological realms for fear of marginalisation. In truth, methodical and epistemological pluralisation is important in ensuring 'product differentiation' in the market for economic ideas, while ontological pluralisation lies at the very root of the knowledge creation process.[150] Nevertheless, the quest for methodological monism cannot be rejected if the scientific status of the economic discipline[151] and the demarcation line separating it from the other social sciences are to be left intact[152].

---

[150] As Schumpeter (1954: 41) states: "Analytic effort is of necessity preceded by a preanalytic cognitive act that supplies the raw material for the analytic efforts... This preanalytic cognitive act will be called Vision. It is interesting to note that vision of this kind not only must precede historically the emergence of analytic effort in any field but also must re-enter the history of every established science each time somebody teaches us to see things in a light of which the source is not to be found in the facts, methods, and results of the pre-existing state of the science".

[151] As Blaug (1980: 248) asks: "what events, if they materialized, would lead us to reject that program? A program that cannot meet that question has fallen short of the highest standards that scientific knowledge can attain".

[152] This clearly does not mean that other methodological approaches need to be refuted, but rather that research based on different methodological approaches is not economic in nature but rather sociological, historical, or philosophical (see e.g. Louzeck 2011: 459).

Following a series of *Methodenstreits* during the formative phase of the discipline around the turn of the 19th century,[153] the epistemic community of academic economists has ultimately clung to a methodological monism of the fallibilist positivist type as its common theoretical basis and disciplinary demarcation line (see Blaug 1980: 47ff). Accepting this paradigm was a necessary step in the consolidation and professionalisation of the discipline on the basis of a shared understanding of its scientific core. It nevertheless need not be allied with an ontological restriction to the principle (or pre-analytic vision) of social exchange as the basic constituent of economic interactions, as has been the case from the origins of economic theorising in ancient times[154].

3. What Are the Conditions of Transformation?

Now that we have established 'paradigm pluralism' as the most desirable state for economics as a social science, it is also important to note that there will only be seen to be a pressing need for such a transformation if there is a general consensus that the discipline is in a 'dire state'. Although studies have been conducted in various countries documenting the growing lack of paradigm pluralism, i.e. the marginalisation of heterodox approaches after the temporary, small-scale, and regionally very limited pluralisation of the 1960s and 1970s,[155] there have also been a number of statements

[153] For a historical account of the German *Methodenstreit* and the formation of economics as a discipline see e.g. Louzeck (2011); on the English *Methodenstreit* see e.g. Coats (1954); Moore (1999: 53), who writes: "The English Methodenstreit, or 'battle of methods', was a methodological debate between the historical economists, or historicists, and the orthodox economists (first the quasi-classical then the neoclassical) that took place over the period 1865 – 1914. The historicists called for a realist, inductive, relativist, dynamic, and sociological methodology, while the orthodox economists insisted upon an abstract, deductive, universalist, static, and isolationist methodology".

[154] Although the ontological basis of economic theory is very rarely addressed directly, money has been principally declared a 'medium of exchange' from the very beginning of 'academic' reflection upon it. Furthermore, theorising that is based on a Walrasian general equilibrium is clearly an analytic exercise in intertemporal exchange. Finally, the frequent use of the term 'market economy' to describe the essence of the object of economic enquiry provides a subtle indication of the predominance of an ontology of bartering or exchange.

[155] During the 1960s and 1970s, many countries witnessed the expansion of academic

and claims to the contrary. Colander/Holt/Rosser (2004; 2009), for example, have argued for some time that mainstream economics has been turning into what they call 'mainstream pluralism'. Others have claimed that there is no lack of pluralism (see e.g. Bachmann 2015) or that where there is such a lack, it is due to the failure of heterodox paradigms to establish themselves as genuine alternatives to mainstream economics (MacKenzie 2017)[156]. On closer inspection, however, all such claims that deny the discipline is in a 'dire state' are either based on a mistaken interpretation of pluralism (i.e. confuse theoretical, methodical, or epistemological plurality with paradigm pluralism) or fail to distinguish between variation and pluralism[157][158].

In light of the fact that economics was far closer to its ideal state in earlier phases of its development (before interwar pluralism transformed into post-war neoclassicism; see Morgan/Rutherford 1998), we need to examine the forces that drive the evolution of economic ideas at a paradigmatic rather than a theoretical level. As several studies have shown (see e.g. Goodwin 1998; Heise 2016; Kellecioglu 2017), these forces are as external as they are internal. Internally, we can only grasp the paradigmatic development of economics as a discipline once we appreciate the peculiarities of the 'market for economic ideas'. The output that is 'economic knowledge' is an international public good, which also has the character

education, which involved the founding of numerous new universities, the rise of the student movement and its campaign for student and civic rights, curricular reform, and a more critical stance among the (social) sciences, and the appointment of greater numbers of heterodox staff. Since then, however, the process of pluralisation has again been reversed; see e.g. Heise/Sander/Thieme 2017, Heise/Thieme 2016 for Germany, Corsi/D'Ippolito/Ludici (2010) for Italy, AFEP (2009) for France, and Klamer (2007) and Katzner (2011) for the USA.

[156] As MacKenzie (2017) maintains: "As for economists, we rejected Marx and Veblen about a century ago, not because of political views, which were varied, but rather because their theories were seen as fatally flawed". In fact, the theories of Marx and Veblen have not been refuted on theoretical or empirical grounds.

[157] While pluralism always involves some form of incompatibility, incommensurability, or general opposition, variation does not.

[158] There may of course be another reason why the lack of pluralism in today's academic economics is not seen as problematic, namely, because pluralism is mistakenly conflated with relativism and obscurantism; see for example the letter written by the 2014 Nobel Prize winner Jean Tirole to the French Minister of Science; Tirole (2014).

of a credence good. The market for such goods is not governed by price; its token is rather a form of 'recognition' or 'reputation' that is not awarded by the consumers of the good (i.e. by students or the public) but by fellow producers ('peers'). Furthermore, the academic job market tends to be a 'shrink market', i.e. a market in which there is a quasi-permanent excess of supply.[159] This renders it very risky - particularly when the specificity of the required human capital (and its high sunk costs) is taken into account.

Such a market calls for standardisation in order to more clearly distinguish between 'truth' and 'error' or 'objective knowledge' and 'unjustified claims'/'subjective values', and to reduce the risks of human capital investment. As we have previously argued, in order neither to eliminate the welfare enhancing effects of competition, nor to mitigate the process of 'product differentiation' (i.e. to transform a 'shrink market' into a 'niche market'), in a perfect 'market for economic ideas', standardisation would be limited to the methodological dimension. In the real world, however, network externalities and learning effects create path dependencies that serve as implicit standards (see e.g. Morgan 2015). In maximising individual utility but not overall welfare, these standards may impose ontological and even epistemological limitations. In other words, as long as the standardisation process is not regulated, the result will be determined by internal and external incentives that favour one paradigm over another.

This is where external factors become especially important, since they can significantly influence the potential benefits of using a given paradigm. These benefits either stem from its 'progressiveness' as a scientific tool (if 'truth seeking' is the driving force behind the research) or from the number of other researchers using the paradigm. The latter 'network effect' serves to maximise the potential recognition and reputation enjoyed by the paradigm's adherents. Although these motives need not exclude each other, they are not necessarily identical. On the one hand, this is because the 'progressiveness' of a paradigm is difficult to objectively determine and on the other, because financial incentives (in the form of academic positions or

[159] This is not an accidental feature but a necessary (and only rarely and temporarily unfulfilled) condition of the academic principle of 'selection of the best'.

funding) and non-financial incentives (such as publication space in journals or board membership at prestigious institutions) may influence the researcher's paradigm choice. Since the latter incentives can be classified as external to academic production, the standardisation process might easily come to reflect these external interests rather than internal requirements.

In sum, the dire present state of academic economics is due partly to internal and partly to external forces. The internal forces reflect the particularities of the 'market for economic ideas'; the external forces represent the intrusion of economic interests and normative values into a scientific discipline committed to objectivity and truth claims similar to those of the natural sciences. Goodwin (1998) has clearly described the transformation of US economics from a state of paradigm plurality at the beginning of the 20th century into one of neoclassical dominance from the 1950s on. As he puts it:

> *"It is difficult for the present-day academic economist, accustomed to teaching mainly the children of contented and politically conservative middle-class parents the wonders of the free market system, to appreciate that not long ago this discipline was widely feared as the seat of radicalism and the means to corruption of the young" (Goodwin 1998: 54).*

This process, which came about during the professionalisation of the discipline, is not the result of superior truth claims driving out inferior truth claims on the path toward a mature 'normal science' (in Kuhn's terms) or of a more 'progressive' scientific research programme superseding 'degenerative' programmes (in those of Lakatos). It rather reflects a cold war-era desire on the part of the (American) 'patrons of economics', namely higher education institutions, the government, the business community, and charitable foundations, to replace the 'bad guys' (i.e. heterodox economists of Marxian, Keynesian or institutionalist descent) with the 'good guy' of neoclassical economists, which "had all the virtues many of the 'plural' brethren lacked" (Goodwin 1998: 61). The aim in doing so was to ensure "...that traditional religious and economic values [...] – values that had made the nation great – had (no longer, A.H.) been banished from the training grounds of the elite" (Goodwin 1998: 59).

Furthermore, both the moderate flourishing of pluralism during the 1960s and 1970s and the ensuing marginalisation of heterodox paradigms demonstrate the importance of external forces. The civil rights and student movements, in conjunction with various theoretical developments[160] that undermined the theoretical rigour of mainstream neoclassical economics, served to pressure the 'patrons of economics' into letting some of the 'bad guys' back in to the US higher education system. Elsewhere, the massive expansion and reform of university systems and the temporary 'democratisation' of recruitment procedures at the professorial level facilitated the emergence of a number of pluralist strongholds, alongside a majority of traditional economic departments that held firm against the 'winds of change'. The subsequent marginalisation of heterodox economics took place largely through a vastly unequal endowment of economic, social and institutional capital (see Heise/Thieme 2016) and the triumph of ranking analyses and institutionalised forms of 'quality control' (which measure publication output by impact and citation scores). These clearly tend toward the 'mainstreamisation' of economics (see e.g. Lee 2007, Lee/Pham/Gyun 2013).

4. By Way of a Conclusion: Where Do We Go from Here?

Despite the discipline's miserable performance in predicting and coping with the recent global financial crisis, there would appear to be no need for a paradigm shift in economics. There is also no need to dispense with its strict methodological standards, or to seek to initiate an interdisciplinary, 'normative turn' towards an advocacy-oriented science. These forms of transformation may be desirable from various individual perspectives, but they are not otherwise necessary.

What the economic discipline does urgently require, however, is a transformation of its present state of paradigm monism. This is marked by an exceedingly dominant neoclassical DSGE mainstream that incorporates a number of dissenting epistemologies accepting a market-oriented ontology as a negative heuristic. This paradigm monism now needs to be transformed into a paradigm pluralism that remains open to other ontologies.

[160] Including Sraffa's 'Production of Commodities by Means of Commodities' and the resulting 'Cambridge capital controversy'.

What is called for, in short, is a 'pluralist turn'[161]. Pluralism in this sense is a scientific imperative in order to ensure academic freedom and to provide a stimulating environment for knowledge creation (or the competition of economic ideas). Furthermore, it is the only possible means of giving economics the status of a science, rather than merely an exercise in applied logic or – worse – pure empiricism.

There are nonetheless a range of strong internal and external forces that serve to undermine competition between economic ideas. This tends to result in some paradigms becoming dominant and others being marginalised. At the internal level, the peculiarities of the 'market for economic ideas' serve both to drive demand for and help supply some of the standards required to describe the required commonalities of an epistemic community. Nevertheless, if this standardisation process is not regulated, its outcome will be unlikely to reflect the collective assumptions of the community, and will instead favour the individual assumptions of those market actors who are endowed with a greater share of economic, social, and institutional capital, i.e. those that are more powerful. External factors, such as the provision of financial or other incentives by actors outside the epistemic community (whether charitable foundations, the business community, the government, or other collective actors influencing the researcher's paradigm choice) open the way to the intrusion of vested interests and ideologies into the discipline. At the same time, however, they may serve to counter-balance certain existing imbalances.

In order to successfully transform economics as a discipline, it is first and foremost necessary for the state, in its capacity as regulator, to step in to safeguard academic freedom. Academic freedom is not only a protective norm that prevents inappropriate external interventions, but also a constructive norm that obliges the state to make it possible for all members of the epistemic community to conduct their research, irrespective of the paradigm they choose to espouse. This entails a certain degree of paradigm pluralism, not necessarily within every academic unit (whether research

---

[161] As Fullbrook (2012) points out, it is only after such a pluralist turn that the economic discipline could really resemble its role model, physics.

centre, department, faculty, or university), but within the overall institutional scope of the legislator. This is not the place to go into the details of a possible regulatory framework. Ensuring an optimal regulatory design may require us to draw on the resources of constitutional economics and institutional economics, as well as mechanism design theory. It should be emphasised, however, that regulating commodity markets is usually regarded far less critically than regulating the market for (economic) ideas, since such intervention is often felt to undermine its own intention of promoting academic freedom (see e.g. Coase 1974). In this regard, Coase (1974: 386) offers an explanation of the frequent difference in views where commodity markets and ideas markets are concerned:

> *"The market for ideas is the market in which the intellectual conducts his trade. The explanation of the paradox is self-interest and self-esteem. Self-esteem leads the intellectuals to magnify the importance of their own market. That others should be regulated seems natural, particularly as many of the intellectuals see themselves as doing the regulating. But self-interest combines with self-esteem to ensure that, while others are regulated, regulation should not apply to them. And so it is possible to live with these contradictory views about the role of government in these two markets. It is the conclusion that matters. It may not be a nice explanation, but I can think of no other for this strange situation".* [162]

[162] When Bachmann (2017: 846) speaks of 'forced pluralisation' with respect to state-facilitated academic freedom, he appears to fall victim to exactly the kind of double standard that Coase refers to. Vanberg (2010: 46f.) likewise sees a need for the regulation of the market for ideas in order to guarantee its welfare enhancing functioning, yet he believes that such regulation will ultimately come about through epistemic self-regulation: "Temporary and local reward systems may well evolve or be established deliberately that distract from the unbiased pursuit of truth in science. Yet, however extended such periods and localities may be, it cannot prevent truth-seeking scientists at other times and in other locations to refute error and to push the frontiers of science closer to the truth. Likewise, temporary and local rules and incentive structures may evolve or be established deliberately in markets that favor other than consumer interests. Yet, this cannot and will not prevent advantage-seeking human beings from exploring more attractive alternative options ...the principles of selection that prevail in research institutes and universities, the constraints that national rules and regulations define for scientific work, and conventions

In order to draw the legislator's attention to the welfare enhancing effects of a regulated pluralism and to mitigate the sense of undue intervention, broad internal and external support should be mustered from the epistemic community, students, politicians, trade unions and (parts of) the business community to counterbalance the external forces favouring 'economics as usual'. In order to better assess the chances (and potential limitations) of making 'plural economics' the object of a civic movement and to design a promising strategy to lead the discourse on the 'future of economics' or 'new economic thinking', we might draw on the sociology of epistemic communities and movements, the Gramscian political theory of hegemonic discourses,[163] and political theories of system transformation. Ultimately, history has indicated the importance of these external forces (for better and worse) in shaping the economic profession.

that come to prevail in professions such as economics may be epistemically dysfunctional, but man's ineradicable interest in knowing how the world around him works will be an incessant force that tends to select in favor of more informative theories, and stubborn reality will be an inescapable ultimate selector between conjectures that are compatible with the facts and those that are not". In light of the above-mentioned characteristics of good 'economic knowledge' (as a credence good), Vanberg's optimism would seem not to be grounded in rigorous enquiry but in his arbitrary faith in self-regulation.

[163] Adopting a Gramscian perspective may, for instance, highlight the fact that the transformation of economics favoured here will only be truly successful if the transformation trajectory takes the form of a 'counter-hegemony' (see e.g. Carroll 2010). Another kind of trajectory, termed 'passive revolution' would seek to keep as much of the status quo (i.e. the dominance of the present mainstream), intact while superficially supporting pluralism as a 'new economic thinking'. This might be achieved by blurring the essential difference between paradigm pluralism and epistemological variation. Traces of such an approach can in fact be discerned in what has been called the 'changing face of mainstream economics' promulgated by initiatives such as the influential, Soros-sponsored 'Institute for New Economic Thinking' (INET); see e.g. (Haering 2014).

Literature

Andersen, C. (2011); Rethinking Economics in a Changed World; in: Finance & Development, June issue, pp. 50 – 52

Association Francaise d'Economie Politique (AFEP) (2009); Evolution of the economics professors' recruitment since 2000 in France. The End of Pluralism, available at: http://assoeconomiepolitique.org/wp-content/uploads/FAPE-State-of-Pluralism-in-France-Final-Version.pdf

Bachmann, R. (2015) *Erkennen, was Quatsch ist*; in: brand eins, 17.Jg., H.11, pp. 86 – 89

Bachmann, R. (2017); Zur aktuellen Pluralismusdebatte in der Ökonomik: Ansichten eines wohlwollenden Pluralismusskeptikers; in: Wirtschaftsdienst, Vol. 97, No. 12, pp. 843 - 847

Benes, J., Kumhof, M., Laxton, D. (2014); Financial Crisis in DSGE Models: Selected Applications of MAPMOD, IMF Working Paper 14/56

Blaug, M. (1980); The methodology of economics or how economists explain, Cambirdge

Carroll, W. K. (2010); Crisis, movements, counter-hegemony: in search of the new; in: Interface: a journal for and about social movements, vol. 2, No.2, pp. 168 – 198

Coase, R.H. (1974); The Market for Goods and the Market for Ideas; in: American Economic review, Vol. 64, No. 2 (Papers & Proceedings), pp. 384 - 391

Coats, A. W. (1954); The Historist Reaction in English Political Economy 1870 –

1890; in:Economica, Vol 21, pp.143 – 153

Cochrane, J. H. (2011a); How did Paul Krugman get it so wrong?; in: Economic Affairs, Vol. 31, No.2, pp. 36 – 40

Cochrane, J. h. (2011b); Understanding policy in the great recession: Some unpleasant fiscal arithmetic, in: European Economic Review, Vol. 55, No. 1, pp. 2-30

Colander, D., Holt, R.P., and Barkley Rosser Jr., J. (2004); The Changing Face of Mainstream Economics; in: Review of Political Economy, Vol. 16, No. 4, pp. 485 – 499

Corsi, M., D'Ippoliti, C., Lucisi, F. (2010); Pluralism at Risk? Heterodox Economic Approaches and the Evaluation of EconomicResearch in Italy; in: The American Journal of Economics and Sociology, Vol. 69, No. 5, pp. 1495-1529

Crouch, C. (2011); The Strange Non-death of Neo-Liberalism, Cambridge

Davidson, P. (2004); A Response to King's Arguments for Pluralism; in: Post-Autistic Economics Review, Issue 24, March, pp. 1 – 5

Debreu, G. (1986); Theoretical Models: Mathematical Form and Economic Content; in: Econometrica, Vol. 54, pp. 1259 – 1270

Debreu, G. (1991); The Mathematization of Economic Theory; in: American Economic Review Vol. 81, pp. 1 – 7

Decker, S. (2018); Towards a critical and transdisciplinary economic science?; in: Decker, S., Elsner, W., Flechtner, S. (Eds.): Advancing Pluralism in Economics. International Perspectiveson a Textbook science, London (forthcoming)

Del Negro, M., Giannoni, M.P., Schorfheide, F. (2014); Inflation in the Great Recession and New Keynesian Models, Federal Reserve Bank of New York Staff Reports No. 618

DeMartino, G.F. (2011); The Economists Oath. On the Need for and Content of Professional Economic Ethics, Oxford

DeMartino, G.F., McCloskey, D. (2016) (eds.); The Oxford handbook of professional economic ethics, Oxford

Dow, S.C. (2012); Foundations for New Economic Thinking, Basingstoke

Erlei, M. (2015) ‚Was ist richtig an der Kritik heterodoxer Ökonomen?‘ Wirtschaftliche Freiheit. Das ordnungspolitische Journal. 23rd September 2015 (available at: http://wirtschaftlichefreiheit.de/wordpress/?p=18020, accessed 23, January 2018)

Fourcade, M. (2009); Economists and Societies. Discipline and Profession in the United States, Britain and France, 1890s to 1990s, Princeton

Fourcade, M., Ollion, E., Algan, Y. (2015) 'The Superiority of Economists,' *Journal of Economic Perspectives*, Vol. 29, No.1, pp. 89 – 114

Fullbrook, E. (ed.) (2003): The Crisis in Economics. The Post-Autistic Economics Movement: The first 600 days, London

Fullbrook, E. (2012); To observe or not to observe: Complementing Pluralism in physics and economics; in: real-world economics review, issue no. 62, pp. 20 – 28

Furner, M.O. (2011); Advocacy and Objectivity: A crisis in the profesionalisation of American Social Science, 1865 – 1905, New Brunswick

Goodwin, C.D. (1998); The Patrons of Economics in a Time of Transformation; in: Morgan, M.S., Rutherford, M. (eds.); From Interwar Pluralism to Postwar Neoclassicism, Durham, pp. 53 - 81

Habermas, J. (1968); Erkenntnis und Interesse, Frankfurt

Haering, N. (2014); George Soros' INET: an institute to improve the world or a Trojan horse of the financial oligarchy?; in: real-world economics review, No. 67, pp. 90 – 96

Hamermesh, D. S. (2013); Six Decades of Top Economics Publishing: Who and How?; in: Journal of Economic Literature; Vol. 51, No.1, pp. 162- 172

Heise, A. (2014) 'The Future of Economics in a Lakatos-Bourdieu Framework,' *International Journal of Political Economy,* Vol. 43, No.3, pp. 70 – 93.

Heise, A. (2016) 'Why has economics turned out this way? A socio-economic note on the explanation of monism in economics', *Journal of Philosophical Economics*, Vol. 10, No.1, 81 - 101

Heise, A. (2017a); Defining economic pluralism: ethical norm or scientific imperative; in: International Journal for Pluralism and Economic Education, Vol. 8, No.1, S. 18 – 41

Heise, A. (2017b); Whither economic complexity? A new heterodox economic paradigm or just another variation within the mainstream; in: International Journal of Pluralism and Economic Education, Vol. 8, No.2, pp. 115 - 129

Heise, A. et al. (2015); ÖkonomInnen und Ökonomie. Eine wissenschaftssoziologische Entwicklungsanalyse zum Verhältnis von ÖkonomInnen und Ökonomie im deutschsprachigen Raum ab 1945, Hamburg and Linz (Manuscript)

Heise, A., Sander, H., Thieme, S. (2017); Das Ende der Heterodoxie? Die Entwicklung der Wirtschaftswissenschaften in Deutschland, Wiesbaden

Heise, A., Thieme, S. (2016); The short rise and long fall of heterodox economics. Explorations in a scientific field of power and struggle; in: Journal of Economic Issues, 50 (4), 1105 – 1130

Hesse, J.-O. (2012); The 'Americanisation' of West German economics after the Second World War: Success, failure, or something completely different?; in: The European Journal of the History of Economic Thought, Vol. 19., No.1, pp. 67 – 98

Jackson, W.A. (2018); Strategic Pluralism and Monism in Heterodox Economics; in: Review of Radical Political Economics, forthcoming (first published 01. November 2017, DOI 10.1177/0486613416670971)

Jakobson, O. (2017); Transformative Ecological Economics.Process Philosophy, Ideology and Utopia, Abingdon

Katzner, D.W. (2011); At the Edge of Camelot. Debating Economics in Turbulent Times, Oxford

Kellecioglu, D. (2017); How to transform economics? A philosophical appraisal; in: Journal of Philosophical Economics, Vol. 11, Issue 1, pp. 1 – 26

Kim, E.H. et al. (2006); What has Mattered to Economics since 1970; in: Jounrla of Economic Perspectives, Vol. 20, No. 4, pp. 189 – 202

Kitcher, P. (1993); The Advancement of Science: Science without Legend, Objectivity without Illusions, Oxford

Klamer, A. (1995); A Rhetorical Perspective on the Differences Between European and American Economists; in: Kyklos, Vol. 48, Fasc. 2, pp. 231 – 240

Klamer, A. (2007) 'Does this Have to Be our Future?' Colander, D. (Ed.); *The Making of an Economist, Redux*, Princeton University Press, Princeton, pp. 277 – 233

Knorr-Cetina, K. D. (1982); Scientific Communities or Transepistemic Arenas of Research? A Critique of Quasi-Economic Models of Science; in: Social Studies of Science, Vol. 12, pp. 101 – 130

Krugman, P. (1996); Economic Culture Wars; in: Slate, October (available at: http://www.slate.com/articles/business/the_dismal_science/1996/10/economic_culture_wars.html; retrieved: 21.11.2017)

Langhe, R. Why should I adopt pluralism; in: Garnett, R., Olsen, E.K., Starr, M. (eds.); Economic Pluralism, London, pp. 1 – 11

Lawson (2003); Reorienting Economics, London/New York

Lawson, T. (2013) 'What is this 'school' called neoclassical economics?,' *Cambridge Journal of Economics,* Vol. 37, No. 4, pp. 947 – 983

Louzek, M. (2011); The Battle of Methods in Economics: The Classical Methodenstreit—Menger vs. Schmoller; in: The American Journal of Economics and Sociology, Vol. 70, No. 2, pp. 439-463

MacKenzie, D.W. (2017); The case against pluralism; Foundation of Economic Education (available at: https://fee.org/articles/the-case-against-pluralism-in-economics; retrieved: 08.12.2017)

Merton, R. K. (1968); The Matthew Effect in Science. The reward and communication systems of science are considered; in: Science, Vol. 159, pp. 56 – 63

Minford, P. (2010); The Banking Crisis as Dynamic Stochastic General Equilibrium, *CESifo Economic Studies*, Vol. 56, Issue 4, pp. 554–574

Mirowski, P. (1991); The When, the How and the Why of Mathematical Expression in the History of Economic Analysis; in: Journal of Economic Perspectives, Vol. 5, pp. 145 – 157

Mirowski, P. (2013); Never let a serious crisis go to waste. How neoliberalism survived the financial meltdown, London

Moore, G.C. (1999); John Kells Ingram, the Comtean Movements and the English *Methodenstreit*; in: The History of Political Economy, Vol. 31, No.1, pp. 52 – 78

Morgan, J. (2015) 'Is Economics Responding to Critique? What do the UK 2015 QAA Subject Benchmarks Indicate?', *Review of Political Economy,* Vol. 27, No. 4, pp. 518-538

Planck, M. (1928); Wissenschaftliche Autobiographie, Leipzig

Rawls, J. (1971); A Theory of Justice, Cambridge/Mass.

Rodrik, D. (2015); Economics Rules. The Rights and Wrongs of the Dismal Science, New York/London

Rosen, S. (1997); Austrian and neoclassical economics: Any gains from trade?; in: Journal of Economic Perspectives, Vol. 11. No.4, pp. 139 – 152

Samuels, W. (1997); The case for methodological pluralism; in: Salanti, A., Screpanti, E. (eds.); Pluralism in Economics. New Perspective in History and Methodology, Cheltenham, pp. 67 – 79

Schmidt, C.M., aus dem Moore, N. (2010); Die Methodendiskussion in den Wirtschaftswissenschaften vor dem Hintergrund der Finanzkrise; in: Jens, U., Romahn, H. (eds.); *Methodenpluralismus in den Wirtschaftswissenschaften*, Metropolis, Marburg, pp. 143 – 182

Schumpeter, J.A. (1954); History of Economic Analysis, London

Stiglitz, J. E. (2017); Where Modern Macroeconomics Went Wrong, NBER Working Papers 23795, Washington D.C.

Stilwell, F. (2016); Heterodox Economics or Political Economy?; in: Real-World Economic Review, Issue 74, pp. 42 – 48

Stützle, I. (2016); Hätte, müsste, sollte – die Kritik der Neoklassik; in: Oxi – Wirtschaft anders denken of 21st of June 2016 (available at: https://oxiblog.de/kritik-der-neoklassik/; retrieved on 12.01.2018)

Thornton, T.B. (2017); From Economics to Political Economy. The problems, promises and solutions of pluralist economics, Abingdon

Tirole, J. (2014); Letter to Madam Fiorosa (available at: http://assoeconomiepolitique.org/wp-content/uploads/TIROLE_Letter.pdf; retrieved on 04.01.2018)

Vanberg, V. (2010); The 'science-as-market' analogy: a constitutional economics perspective; in: Constitutional Political Economy, Vol. 21, pp. 28 – 49

Vines, D., Wills, S. (2018); The rebuilding macroeconomic theory project: an analytical assessment; in: Oxford Review of Economic Policy, Vol. 34, Issue 1-2, , Pages 1–42

Yalcintas, A. (2016); Intellectual Path Dependence: Why Economists Do Not Reject Refuted Theories, London

Part Two

Critical Assessments

Six

Defining Economic Pluralism: Ethical Norm or Scientific Imperative?*

1. Introduction

The recent global financial crisis dealt a heavy blow to economics, criticized for its inability to foresee the crisis; its incapacity to offer a plausible retrospective explanation and to develop acceptable counter-measures against future crises (cf. Besley/Hennessey, 2009). In question here is the **practical serviceability of economics as the source of its legitimacy**. Those involved in economic affairs at the practical level have noted that certain theoretical notions (such as the theory of efficient financial markets and the system of rating financial assets based upon it) were partly responsible for the crisis, since they assumed a capacity for risk assessment and attributed to the financial markets a forecasting ability, that proved to be erroneous and fatal (cf. Cassidy, 2009).

In question here is the **responsibility** of economics. Furthermore, economics students have complained about the oppressive dominance of a single scientific paradigm and the lack of historical perspective (cf. ISIPE, 2014). Critical, heterodox academics, meanwhile, have voiced their dissatisfaction with the increasing marginalisation of non-mainstream approaches and the associated effects on their publication prospects, access to (public) funding and thus career prospects. Here it is a question of **academic independence and integrity** and a **right to academic freedom**.[164]

---

* Originally published: Int. J. Pluralism and Economics Education, Vol. 8, No. 1, 2017, 18 – 41(https://www.inderscience.com/jhome.php?jcode=ijpee)

[164] Academic freedom not only includes protection from restrictive state intervention in the practice of a discipline (a 'subjective right to defence'), but also the principle according to which the state is required to ensure free academic enquiry in its public and also private universities. This responsibility can in principle be entrusted to the academic community itself, but only when the latter does not erect its own barriers to access.

These criticisms of the current state of economics can be summarised in terms of a common demand: critics have lamented the lack of pluralism in the economic sciences and have therefore called for the pluralisation of the discipline (Sent, 2006; ISIPE, 2014).

The fact that economics has now been faced with such calls for pluralism for more than four decades without any apparent result[165] may have a number of causes:

- On the one hand, the **ambiguity** over what exactly is meant by pluralism (e.g., disciplinary, theoretical, method, or paradigmatic pluralism, to name just a few possible variations, cf. Dutt 2014, p. 480) may be so great that an attempt to implement the demand in the form of a pluralisation strategy would necessarily run aground due to the lack of a common basis and clearly defined goals (cf. Dutt, 2014; Sent, 2006, p. 179ff.).
- On the other hand, pluralism may also meet with significant **internal resistance** when, from an epistemological perspective, it is equated with relativism, obscurantism,[166] or scientific immaturity.[167]
- Finally, the **diagnosis** of a lack of pluralism might simply be contested.[168]

[165] Recent studies showed that an earlier, quantitatively very limited process of pluralisation during the 1960s and 1970s has long since been reversed through the marginalisation of heterodox economists; cf. Lee (2009); Heise/Thieme (2016); Heise/Sander/Thieme (2016).

[166] As Jean Tirole, the 2014 winner of the Sveriges Riksbank Prize in Economic Sciences in Memory of Alfred Nobel (generally referred to as the 'Nobel Prize' in order to share in the reputation of the 'real' Nobel Prize), wrote in an open letter to the French Education Minister (Tirole, 2014).

[167] Thomas Kuhn's influential theory of scientific progress can be interpreted as stating that, as a science develops, a certain paradigm comes to impose itself as the 'normal science.' The pluralistic coexistence of a number of paradigms would thus imply a low level of development.

[168] For instance the academic responsible for early career researchers at the German Economic Association (*Verein für Socialpolitik – VfS*), Rüdiger Bachmann, states: "In my view, the discipline is indeed very pluralistic. I think it is a shame when some suggest [Bachmann is referring to the students involved in the '*Plurale Ökonomen*' ('Plural Economists') network] that they are the only critical voices [...] since the methods and theories within the mainstream are very diverse. The fields of research include economy and law, family economics, development economics; and then the classics: labour markets, public

In the following, we shall first to examine the concept of pluralism more carefully.[169] We shall also aim to relate the various aspects of scientific pluralism to one another in order to illuminate the apparent paradox of how one can affirm the existence of scientific pluralism and reject it as a norm, and yet still regard the status quo in economics as acceptable—this seems to me the position adopted by Bachmann (2011, p. 263ff), highly representative of the mainstream. Furthermore, a clearer conception of pluralism is also needed to expose those who would illegitimately seek to jump on board the pluralism wagon. These tasks, however, can only be carried out on the basis of a theoretical discussion of the epistemological capacities of economics in its search for 'absolute truth.' Finally, the paper closes with a proposal for conceptualising pluralism and a number of reflections on the politics of scientific enquiry.

2. Preliminary Theoretical Considerations: Truths, Errors, and their Difference

Though economics is generally seen as a strongly methodical and methodological social science, methodological reflection and training is not accorded an especially prominent place within the discipline (cf. Lawson, 1994). This may be because, in the wake of two explicit *'Methodenstreits'* ('method disputes') a consensus has been established that positivism provides us with a solid methodology that does not need to be questioned further. This is a rather recent view, however, and it is surely not possible to say that this broad consensus is the result of an intensive and profound

finance. The methods used include numerical models, traditional statistical methods, and more recently field experiments—I myself like to use surveys to study people's expectations. So there is a great variety" (Bachmann, 2015, p. 87, my translation).

[169] In 2006, Robert Garnett complained that "Pluralism remains an undertheorized topic in economics" (Garnett 2006, p. 527). Though the literature on the topic has grown since then (see the post-2006 literature referenced below), Garnett's analysis is still valid today.

theoretical discussion;[170] it has rather arisen under the influence of attempts to professionalise and legitimise a maturing discipline,[171] in response to the increasing scientific hegemony of the USA,[172] and particularly the standardising power of a few elite US universities.[173]

Changing Conceptions of Economics

Well into the 20th century—and thus long after the historic *'Methodenstreits'* of the late 19th century/early 20th century—economics in most countries was oriented by the idea that scientific enquiry is concerned with the historically and geopolitically rooted 'interpretation' of specific societal developments, and the exertion of political influence on the basis of value judgements. The so-called 'historical school' in Germany, and the American ('Old') institutionalism, for instance, combined these elements to affect social and political change. Moreover, in the German universities, economics was part of the multidisciplinary *Staatswissenschaften*, which also included normatively loaded legal and political sciences. The 'historical school' was certainly not devoid of theory, but it did not aim to arrive at objective, universally valid certainties; it rather sought to influence social processes on the basis of inductively acquired—i.e., empirical—experience and data.

The above methodological disputes did not primarily revolve around whether scientific enquiry should be based upon deduction—i.e., drawing general conclusions from individual or representative derivations by means of certain hypotheses ('theory')—or upon induction—drawing conclusions about a given case on the basis of many empirical observations. They were rather concerned with the appropriate **scientific conception** of

---

[170] Caldwell (1988, p. 233) notes that "(s)ome economists openly disparage methodological work, because they consider it a waste of time."

[171] On this point, cf. Fourcade (2009, p. 125ff.) and Morgan/Rutherford (1998).

[172] Though the '*Methodenstreits*' in the history of economics have taken place within German-language scholarship, similar debates have occurred elsewhere (cf. e.g. Moore, 2003).

[173] On the methodological standardisation of economics cf. Heise (2016). On the standardising power of the elite US universities cf. Graham/Diamond (1997); Lebaron (2006: 92ff.), and Fourcade/Ollion/Algan (2015). Friedman's influential article, 'The Methodology of Positive Economics' (Friedman 1953), played a leading role in this process of methodological standardisation.

a discipline that was just beginning to form and, as in the case of Germany, to break away from the *Staatswissenschaften* and thereby draw a clear distinction between sociology and political science as 'interpretive' disciplines and economics as an 'explanatory' discipline modelled on the natural sciences (cf. Menger, 1985; Schumpeter, 1908).

Rather than being oriented around normative intervention ('advocacy'), economics was to strive for **objective knowledge** of actual economic processes ('objectivity') or, as John Neville Keynes (1891, p. 34) put it, for "a body of systematized knowledge concerning what is." In his famous article, 'The Methodology of Positive Economics,' Milton Friedman added:

> *"Positive economics is in principle independent of any particular ethical position or normative judgement. [...] Its task is to provide a system of generalizations that can be used to make correct predictions about the consequences of any change in circumstances"* (Friedman, 1953, p. 4).

This kind of positivism is not value-free, since it always rests on certain hypotheses and perspectives (including the research questions chosen), selected and shaped by the researchers themselves, and which are not simply given with the object of investigation. Nevertheless, the propositions and conclusions yielded via deductive methods must be intersubjectively verifiable and in this sense free of value judgements.[174]

The Distinction between Knowledge and Non-Knowledge

This transformed conception of economics made it necessary to draw a sharp distinction between 'objective knowledge' ('truth') as the intended and purported result of scientific activity, and the 'opinions,' 'prejudices,' or even 'errors' that result from non-scientific activity. In other words: it demanded basic agreement over which methods produce knowledge that

[174] Referring to the ‚Methodenstreit' implies the concession that there have been (and still are?) different conceptions of the nature of economics as a science. The position taken here is that a split along these conceptual lines between economics and economic sociology cannot be denied. Therefore, schools of thought that deny the scientific claim of economics as put forward by Keynes and Friedman should be regarded as part of economic sociology as proposed by Schumpeter (see Shionoya 1997, p. 193ff.).

can be considered as 'truth' or as scientifically established knowledge (and which methods can be rejected as producing 'errors' or at least dismissed as scientifically untenable). The notion that this distinction between truth and error can always and unambiguously be drawn originates with Francis Bacon (1561 – 1626): "If truth is manifest, truth is there to be seen" (Boland, 1997, p. 98). With Immanuel Kant (1724 – 1804), however, it became clear that empirical experience (induction) and logical derivation (deduction) cannot simply be distinct from one another, since the 'induction problem' (i.e., the possibility that the nth confirmation of an empirical phenomenon might be falsified on its repetition) shows that empirical experience (however well-developed our empirical methods may be) is not sufficient to establish objective knowledge. And 'pure reason' alone, i.e., the deduction of 'synthetic *a priori* knowledge,'[175] as Kant put it, remains an empty category that cannot produce any certainty; the latter is only achieved *a posteriori* (retrospectively, on the basis of empirical experience) by comparing our predictions with empirical experience. Friedman (1953, p. 4) thus observes that:

> *"Its [positive economics'] performance is to be judged by the precision, scope, and conformity with experience of the predictions it yields. In short, positive economics is, or can be, an 'objective' science, in precisely the same sense as any of the physical sciences."*

Open and Closed Systems

Modern economics thus sets itself the task—and here it resembles the natural sciences[176] and departs from the 'interpretive' social sciences—of acquiring knowledge that can be considered 'objective,' that is not based on value judgements, and that therefore **constitutes 'truth**.' In order for this

---

[175] *A priori* = in advance. Kant distinguishes between analytic and synthetic judgements. Analytic judgements are contained within the object in question; they do not bring us any new knowledge (e.g., the 'gray horse' is white); synthetic judgements, by contrast, provide us with new knowledge, since they are not already contained within the object (e.g. 'the horse eats grass'). This distinction between analytic and synthetic judgements would later take on crucial significance in epistemology.

[176] Jack Reardon brought to my attention that even quantum physics has disproved the notion of objectivity. Yet, still the natural sciences stand emblematic for the search for ‚thruth'.

to be possible, it must of course be assumed that such truth exists in the first place—i.e., that there is only one correct explanation of our social and economic phenomena, which is independent of the ideological, religious, or ethnic background of the observer. This in turn implies the singularity of reality as a cognitive and veristic category—or the **'one world, one truth'** principle (cf. Mäki, 2002, p. 124ff.).

However reasonable the idea might seem that all observers are confronted with one and the same reality and that there is therefore only one (correct) 'explanatory' truth of this reality, the 'one world, one truth' principle is contested by relativists and social constructivists. Relativists object that even for 'one world' there may be many possible explanations, since these are always culturally and historically specific. Constructivists, on the other hand, maintain that reality itself (and not only the explanation we give of it)—at least in its social, if not its material, dimensions—is always constructed by the observer (see e.g. Berger/Luckmann 1966).

In calling into question the self-conception of economics as a discipline, the relativist and constructivist rejection of ontological and veristic monism[177] is itself in need of justification. As a meta-theoretical approach, relativism can be contested by turning its own claim ('absolute knowledge is impossible') back against it. The constructivist position, on the other hand, needs to be considered in a little more detail in relation to the philosophy of science. The systems that can be understood to constitute our social reality are comprised of elements (e.g., agents) and their relations or interconnections (actions) (cf. Loasby, 2003).

In closed systems,[178] all of the elements are inter-connected and the development of the system is deterministic (or stochastic, if we admit contingent deviations). Depending on the number of elements and relations it contains, such a system may be extremely complicated (and on account of the

---

[177] The constructivist view is roughly the following: "looked at differently, there are different definitions of problems, different methods for obtaining data, different methods for drawing conclusions from data, different methods for the collation and reconciliation of differing conclusions drawn from data; hence a diversity of ways of conceiving and solving problems, with competing and complementary resolutions and emphases, and with fundamental incompleteness a characteristic of each" (Samuels, 1972, p. 307).
[178] On the difference between closed and open systems cf. also Dow (2004, p. 283).

cognitive limits of the observer, may never be grasped in its entirety), yet it cannot be complex.[179] In such a system, all of the elements can in principle be clearly described, or, in Kant's terminology, they contain within themselves 'analytic *a priori* judgements.' In the literal sense, then, these systems are fully analysable.

In open systems, by contrast, not all of the elements are connected to one another; such systems are thus non-deterministic and not fully analysable. Depending on how many elements they contain and the number of missing links between them, such systems may be both very complicated and very complex. Open systems must then be conceived in terms of 'synthetic *a priori* judgements', i.e., **ontological propositions** that do not rest on empirical experience and that are not already contained within the elements themselves. In order to reduce their complexity, open systems can also be converted into closed systems by invoking certain hypotheses—i.e., what is in reality an open system can be considered in theoretical abstraction a closed system, in the hope that this will not lead one on to the wrong track.

We are now in a position to gain a better understanding of the ontological claims made by the relativist and the constructivist. If our social and economic reality amounts to an open, non-fully analysable (i.e., complex) model, then there cannot be just one (true) theoretical representation of it; rather, all possible representations can and must enter into competition with one another:

> *"Since our representations are always incomplete, innovation is always possible; we can change the set of elements, revise the internal linkages between them or redefine the external connections. [...] since the discovery of better alternatives is necessarily a matter of trial and error, there are clear advantages in encouraging many people to use their imagination"* (Loasby, 2003, p. 301).

---

[179] Since this system can only take on one state, we would speak here of a complexity level of one. More complex systems are able to take on a variety of states (cf. Cramer 1993, p. 275ff.). Complexity is often confused with complicatedness, not only in everyday language, but also in scientific communication: "In a broad, general sense, complex merely means complicated" (Dequech, 2001, p. 913).

In other words: the ontological (and veristic) monism underlying the 'one world, one truth' principle can only be defended if the object of investigation is understood as a closed system.[180] And though it is seldom explicitly acknowledged,[181] this is precisely the premise of neoclassical model of economics:

> *"It is indeed the proclaimed virtue of general equilibrium reasoning that it takes into account all the possible interactions between all the elements that are included in the model; therefore, if uncertainty about future possibilities appears to prevent the completion of the set of connections between present decisions and their full set of consequences, then we must agree that the imaginative response of Arrow and Debreu in extending the set of elements to include all future dates and all possible states of the world – which are fully connected to every other element in the model – was methodologically appropriate"* (Loasby, 2003, p. 291).

The systemic closure assumed by neoclassical orthodoxy in the construction of the 'general equilibrium theory' would thus appear to meet the methodological requirements of positivistic model construction.

Verificationism, Fallibilism, and the Duhem-Quine Thesis

'Positive economics' thus calls for a methodology capable of endowing propositions with a level of scientific knowledge that would generally be interpreted as 'truth.' As we have seen, in order to assume that there is such a singular truth at all, we need to impose certain **ontological restrictions** on our object of investigation. And neoclassical mainstream economics does indeed impose such restrictions: "The mechanistic

[180] To put this as clearly as possible: it is not enough here that the relevant economic and social reality *can* be taken as a closed system; it *must* ***unequivocally*** be taken as such a system. As we saw above, we can treat any system—whether closed or open—as a closed system in order to reduce its complexity; in such cases, however, the representation of a closed system would only be one **possible representation, not its one 'true'** representation.

[181] Neither in Blaug's influential book on economic methodology (Blaug, 1980) nor in the textbooks on macroeconomics noted above is there any reference to the difference between open and closed systems.

worldview of classical economics implies that there is a basically fixed, discernible economic structure that can be used to make predictions" (Roos , 2015, 384; my translation). The 'discernibility' of such a structure implies the possibility of theoretical analysis here.

On this approach, theoretical deduction delivers 'analytic *a priori* judgements' that are on the one hand consistently derivable and thus intersubjectively verifiable, and on the other have to be reconciled with the empirically experienceable reality. Such a methodology is often thought to bring together the human and natural sciences (cf. e.g., Popper, 1957, p. 130). In light of the induction problem, however, empirical tests—contrary to the individual practice of the majority of scientists (cf. Blaug, 1980, p. xiii, ff.)—can neither verify nor confirm the predictions and the underlying model in question, but can at best serve to falsify them.

According to one of the best-known proponents of neo-positivist fallibilism, Karl Popper, while the truth of things may be singular (given the ontological restrictions discussed above), there can be no certain knowledge of this truth, but at best only '**conjectural knowledge**.' Science is thus not in a position to reveal the truth but only to limit error. And any intersubjectively verifiable claim can be considered as conjectural knowledge until an empirical proof is given to the contrary. Science is therefore always 'critical' insofar as every scientist ought to critically examine—i.e., seek to falsify—his results through empirical testing. And even if the scientist as a 'knowledge producer,' should be little inclined to subject his own results to an overly critical regard, the scientific community will test any proposed conjectural knowledge before temporarily accepting it—until it is refuted on the basis of new data or better measuring techniques (see e.g., Hands (2001) for 'Popperism' in economics).

Here we might again recall that this process of trial and error ultimately has the task of discriminating between competing explanatory approaches in the search for the 'one' truth of things. The criteria invoked may include the accuracy of fit, predictive capacities, simplicity (following 'Ockham's razor'), and robustness of these models and theories. According to the fallibilists, at the end of this process (which may involve a long period of competition between various theories), the best conjectural knowledge will prevail (cf. Spinner, 1974, p. 74), thus minimising the likelihood of error through the greatest possible approximation to the 'truth.' An interminable competition between a number of incompatible theories[182] could then only be due to the refusal of part of the scientific community to acknowledge the superiority of another, better explanation of reality. This refusal, however, would have to be rejected as either ideologically motivated or irrational.

And yet, there is a catch: this process of rationally choosing between different propositions of course only works if there is no disagreement or doubt about whether a theory has really been falsified or has to be replaced by another proposition with greater explanatory power. Yet this demands unequivocal measuring techniques and unambiguous 'experimental designs.' The propositions that are to be falsified must then be capable, along with all of their conditions, of being unambiguously described and tested. In non-experimental contexts, however, this is simply not possible, since theories always consist of interlinked axioms and hypotheses or, in Imre Lakatos' terms, of a hard core of assumptions and a 'protective belt of auxiliary hypotheses.'

The claim that only individual hypotheses (normally *ceteris paribus* propositions, which are supposed to provide stable boundary conditions in the construction of economic models) can be falsified, rather than entire theories, has been attributed to Pierre Duhem (1861 – 1916) and Willard Van Orman Quine (1908 – 2000). By changing certain background hypotheses in the protective belt, it is at least possible to escape an *ex post* falsification even if an *ex ante* predictive test has failed. The hope that fallibilism[183] might then provide a reliable method for rationally deciding between theories falls apart in the face of the Duhem-Quine thesis (cf. Blaug, 1980, p. 26).

---

[182] (Kuhn 1962, pp. 66). The coexistence of competing theories or paradigms is indicative of the 'immaturity' of a scientific discipline, either in the sense that the falsification process has not yet come to an end, or in the Kuhnian sense that a 'scientific revolution' is underway.

[183] Fallibilism intends to explain social (or natural) phenomena objectively (‚erklären') while historicism and phenomenalism restrict themselves to describe and understand social phenomena in its historical context.

Economics thus cannot consistently meet the high scientific standards it sets itself, but this does not mean that we are then reduced to a form of 'anything goes' nihilism.[184] For it would clearly be a mistake to conclude that, since purely rational discrimination between competing theories is impossible, any hypothesis, however it might have been arrived at, can be regarded as 'conjectural knowledge.' Positivistic fallibilism—whether in the form of critical rationalism, critical realism, or dialectical materialism (cf. Porstmann, 2002)—sets standards for the logical rigour of the deduction of model-based predictions and their empirical falsifiability (cf. Davis, 2012, p. 13) that pure empiricism, historicism, and phenomenalism (as alternative methodologies; (cf. Blaug, 1980, p. 10; Krabbe 1996) cannot and indeed do not wish to meet (since they subscribe to a very different conception of science).

3. Scientific Pluralism: Conceptual Clarification and Application to Economics

Before we can consider the consequences of the preceding theoretical reflections for our conception of science and scientific practice within economics, we first need to clarify the concept of pluralism and its theoretical foundations. To this end we shall first consider the following statement:

> *"Since no theory can take into account all factors there is scope for pluralism in economic theory. Theories may be discriminated according to which factors they take into consideration in explaining a certain phenomenon. However, even if two theories were to take into account the same set of factors there would still be scope for pluralism: the importance attributed to each of these factors and their interaction may be conceptualized differently. [...] In both cases discussed it could be argued that the alternative theories are not really alternative but complementary, that is, each of them contributes to a better understanding of the phenomenon under discussion. To seek dominance for one theory over the others with the possible result that all rival theories are extinguished amounts to advocating scientific regress. To paraphrase Voltaire: In a*

[184] Langmuir (1989), a Nobel prize laureat in Chemistry, speaks of 'pathological science' in this context which can clearly be distinguished from acceptable conjectural knowledge.

> *subject as difficult as economics a state of doubt may not be very comfortable, but a state of certainty would be ridiculous* (Kurz/Salvatori, 1997, p. 234).

This citation was chosen because it serves to illustrate a range of problems that arise in the pluralism debate: Firstly, it is unclear what kind of pluralism is in question here. In the literature, various kinds of pluralism are discussed, including ontological, epistemological, paradigmatic, methodological, theoretical, all of which might be intended here. Secondly, it is not clear what underlies this call for pluralism: is it the complicatedness or complexity of the object of investigation, or is it the particular epistemological challenges of the discipline ('a subject as difficult as economics') that makes a plurality of theories, methods, or paradigms necessary? Furthermore, the conclusion that the reduction of the various theoretical alternatives to one dominant theory (or is 'paradigm' intended here?) would amount to a scientific regress can neither be reconciled with the notion of the pursuit of (unambiguous) truth nor with the standardising demands and the specific qualities of the 'market for economic ideas' (cf. Heise, 2016). And it is in such terms that Mariyani-Squire/Mossa (2015, p. 200) offer:

> *"...a thumbnail sketch of what a genuine science of economics would amount to: it would ideally be a discipline that sought a complete, objective account of the 'laws of motion' which would causally explain the 'characteristics' and 'function(ing)' of the investigator-independent economic 'system' in its parts and as a whole. Although this conception of an economic science does not deny ontological complexity and diversity and does not deny human fallibility, it does lend itself to an ultimately monistic paradigmatic vision of the future of the economics discipline."*

Sheila Dow (2004, p. 282) describes the monistic impetus of the economic sciences in a very similar, though qualified manner: "Were it defensible, a monist approach would be more satisfactory." Pluralism thus cannot be derived in the form of an ethical norm (e.g., of tolerance) that might be accepted or rejected depending on one's standpoint, but must rather be presented as the only acceptable model of enquiry in light of the rejection of the possibility of monism ('were it defensible'). Yet this first of all requires a clearer delineation of the concept of pluralism.

Plurality, Pluralisation, Pluralism

While the term 'plurality' simply describes a certain state, independently of its desirability as a norm, 'pluralisation' refers to the process of transition from a state of singularity to one of plurality. Both terms are derived from the Latin *pluralis*, which means 'multitude' or 'belonging to more than one.' 'Pluralism,' by contrast, is a **philosophical doctrine** based on a norm that goes beyond the simple defence of a multitude of possibilities. 'Pluralism' thus does not simply refer, in a quantitative manner, to a multitude of elements; these elements must also contain within themselves the qualitative possibility of being opposed (i.e., incompatible) or being incomparable (incommensurable) with one another. In this sense, then, 'pluralisation' does not simply describe the process of transition from a state of singularity to a state of simple multiplicity, but rather to a state of plurality, which involves incompatibilities and incommensurabilities. Where these properties are lacking, we would speak rather of 'variation' or 'differentiation,' and the resultant state would not be a plurality, but a 'variety' or a 'multitude.'

Forms of Scientific Pluralism

In the literature (cf. e.g., Dow 1997; Mäki 1997; Mariyani-Squire/Moussa 2015) a number of forms pluralism are discussed, including:

- Ontological
- Methodological
- Epistemological
- Method
- Theoretical
- Paradigmatic

First, it is to enquire into the essence of the object of economic enquiry—its **ontology**. If we can be absolutely certain that our social reality is singular (i.e., that there are no material or socially constructed parallel worlds) and that it can thus be regarded as a closed system and is in principle fully analysable, then an ontological monism would be justified and ontological pluralism (as a description of a state of affairs, not as a scientific norm) would at best have to be seen as indicative of the discipline's immaturity. If we do not have such certainty, then an ontological scepticism or relativism (where we are confronted with a number of parallel worlds) or an ontological pluralism (where we are confronted with open systems) is the necessary consequence.[185]

Scepticism and relativism deny the existence of 'absolute truths'; pluralism, on the other hand, does not deny their existence, but rather the scientist's capacity to establish these beyond any doubt. The ontological pluralist thus does not have to reject the claim that our social reality is a closed system at the epistemological level (an assumption that serves to reduce complexity); but she/he cannot grant it the status of an axiom.

At this **epistemological level**, concerned with the axiomatic dimensions of a research programme (in Lakatos' terminology; or a 'paradigm' for Kuhn), a monistic position equally requires the analytic *a priori* certainty of a closed system in which the relations between the various elements can be unambiguously specified. If, however, it is not possible to unequivocally and impartially determine all relations between the elements of the social system, the resultant *a priori* synthesis of the object of investigation will call for an epistemological pluralism. An axiomatic explanation of social reality as a **system of symmetrical exchange relations**, for example, cannot then have an *a priori* privilege over other kinds of explanation, such as those which place **hierarchical creditor-debtor relations or relations of subordination** in the foreground. Even an approach that takes **individual rationality** as the basis of relations within a social system in which mechanico-hydraulic dynamic regularities are postulated does not have any *a priori* privilege over a biologistic explanation (such as swarm/collective intelligence and/or rationality; cf. e.g., Bonabeau/Dorigo/Theraulaz 1999), which supposes the existence of **organic relations** between complex, self-regulating systems (cf. e.g., Beinhocker 2013).

---

[185] The claim of 'parallel worlds' denies the 'one world, one truth' principle on the ground that there is not a single reality that needs to be explained but many socially constructed realities. The open system claim does not necessarily deny the existence of a single reality but its certain knowleadgeability due to the very nature of the object of inquiry.

While epistemological pluralism logically follows from ontological pluralism (cf. Dow, 1997, p. 91), ontological monism in no way justifies epistemological monism. In other words: if one defines scientific pluralism in ontological terms, one can defend a form of monism (and thus reject pluralism) even if one grants an epistemological plurality. If one advocates pluralism beyond the epistemological level, however, one must *ipso facto* advocate ontological pluralism and potentially even a form of scepticism/relativism (and thus reject ontological monism).

Table 7: Forms of Scientific Pluralism

Form of Pluralism	Characteristics	Expression	Monism presuppositions
Ontological pluralism	Rejection of the 'one world, one truth' principle.	Acceptance of parallel worlds; Acceptance of reality as an 'open system'	Existence of only one social reality; This social reality constitutes a 'closed system'
Methodological pluralism	Rejection of a universal test of scientific validity	'Anything goes'	Existence of only one social reality
Epistemological pluralism	Rejection of a universal axiomatics in the form of an '*a priori* analysis'	Various axiomatic systems are admitted in the form of an '*a priori* synthesis.'	Social reality fulfils the criteria for '*a priori* analysis'
Method pluralism	Rejection of a universal method	In addition to formal deduction and advanced econometrics, other methods (including abduction, social experiments, narration) are also acknowledged	- (Not justifiable)
Theoretical pluralism	Rejection of an all-encompassing theory	Various complementary theories in different fields of enquiry	Simplicity of social reality, whose simple regularities can be captured through an all-encompassing approach
Paradigmatic pluralism	Rejection of a universal research programme ('paradigm')	Coexistence of various paradigms, which differ in terms of their axiomatics, methods, and heuristics	As a closed system, social reality must be fully analysable

Source: Constructed by author

The methodological and epistemological levels are sometimes seen as corresponding to one another (e.g. Samuels 1997). Yet at issue at the **methodological level**, which is not to be confused with the method level (cf. Sent, 2006, p. 179; Dutt, 2014, p. 482), each doing precisely this[186]), is the process of distinguishing between truth and error. On a naturalistic conception of economics, methods such as historicism and phenomenalism are incapable of establishing 'objective' knowledge.

The alternative constituted by positivistic fallibilism acknowledges that the relevant ontological restrictions do not allow 'truths' to be affirmatively demonstrated, but do allow errors to be excluded. Nevertheless, as we saw above, the limitations of test procedures in non-experimental surroundings (the Duhem-Quine thesis) mean that the 'conjectural knowledge' arrived at in this way cannot necessarily be reduced to a single piece of conjectural knowledge. The dubiousness of such scientific knowledge, however, only justifies a departure from monism if the singularity of social reality is rejected at the ontological level. In such a case, when even the existence of 'objective truth' is challenged and thus no procedure for distinguishing between different claims is required, there is also no justification for the rational restriction of such a procedure. The methodological 'anything goes' position that is defended on these grounds therefore differs from a methodological pluralism that cannot be theoretically justified.[187]

---

[186] Dutt (2014, p. 482), for instance, writes: "The methodological dimension refers to the form in which the analysis is conducted and presented, and to the method by which the analysis is related to the empirical world to examine its suitability or to understand specific real-world situations. The form of analysis refers to whether the analysis is done mathematically (…), whether it involves computer simulation, and the use of verbal analysis and what is sometimes called a broad political economy method. Empirical methods refer to how data are compiled and analyzed…". At best, this statement intermingles, at worst it confounds methods with methodology.

[187] If methodological pluralism is nonetheless advocated (e.g. Dow, 1997; Dow, 2004; Samuels 1997), this is either due to a failure to clearly distinguish between methodological, ontological, and method pluralism (for instance, Dow (2004, p. 275) defines methodological pluralism very broadly "as the advocacy of plurality"); or to the characterisation of an 'anything goes' position in terms of 'radical pluralism'—a characterisation that I would reject for the reasons given above.

In contrast to the methodological level, the **method level** is concerned with the techniques that allow us to present intersubjectively verifiable results. As we have seen, positivistic fallibilism requires a combination of deductive and inductive methods. And since a wide range of techniques are found among the inductive methods of the quantitative and qualitative social sciences in particular, we can speak here of method pluralism as a norm in modern economics, and of method plurality as representing the current state of the discipline. The choice and combination of methods used in any given case has to depend on the relevant research question and must ensure argumentative rigour while also testing the fallibility of the 'conjectural knowledge' acquired. A method monism that made use of only one technique could not be theoretically justified.

'Method monism,' however, might be conceived more narrowly as the exclusive acceptance of a specific form of deduction, such as formal-mathematical reductionism, which is an essential feature of the neoclassical mainstream (cf. Dutt, 2014, p. 482; Lawson, 2013), and which prompted Frank Hahn (1992) to advise his colleagues "to avoid discussions of 'mathematical economics' like a plague." In this case, we would be dealing with a highly controversial[188] yet successful standardisation of the notion of science, one that equates argumentative rigour and neutrality with mathematisation and brands any other form of argument as inferior (cf. Schmidt/aus dem Moore, 2010). The rejection of narrative techniques within deductive approaches, along with alternative methods such as abduction (cf. Mabsoud, 2015), cannot be plausibly justified in this manner, and at best this rejection amounts to an unfortunate 'method-absolutism' (cf. Funk 2009, p. 82). To defend such an absolutism on the grounds that the use of non-formal procedures would constitute a "regression to an obsolete *status quo ante*" (Schmidt/aus dem Moore 2010, 174; my translation, my emphasis), is to fail to see that method pluralism precisely does not allow for the one-sided privileging of certain methods.

[188] What is controversial here is not formalisation in general, but rather the notion that it is a necessary condition of scientific validity. This notion is not only criticised by mathematics-averse economists, but also by (mainstream) economists with a very strong mathematical orientation, such as Robert Solow (2005).

Epistemological pluralism also needs to be distinguished from **theoretical pluralism**. At the epistemological level, at issue is whether competing explanatory systems have to be accepted (pluralism) or rejected (monism). At the theory level, however, what is in question is whether our social reality can be explained by means of an all-encompassing model (monism) or whether a number of approaches (pluralism) are required in order to capture all of the facets of our object of investigation. A central feature of a mature science is that it differentiates this object and develops a range of custom-fit theories, each of which is rooted in a pre-given epistemology, paradigm, or research programme. Examples include adding dynamic elements to basic static models or devoting independent theories (that are nonetheless compatible with basic epistemological models) to individual objects of investigation (e.g., cross-border trade relations in the field of 'international economics' or deeper considerations of the labour market beyond quantitative employment determination in macro models within the field of 'labour economics,' etc.).[189]

Since such a multiplicity of theories would lack the opposition that, on our reading at least, is inherent to the concept of 'pluralism,'[190] we would do better to speak of 'theoretical multiplicity' or 'theoretical differentiation,' rather than 'theoretical pluralism' here. However that may be, it can hardly be seriously disputed that an object of enquiry as complicated as that of economic interaction calls for a variety of theoretical approaches—regardless of whether one subscribes to ontological, epistemological, or methodological monism, pluralism, or scepticism/relativi fallibilism intends to explain social (or natural) phenomena objectively (‚erklären') while historicism and phenomenalism restrict themselves to describe and understand

[189] If this is still too abstract to comprehend, the reader should simply visit the curriculum of an ordinary economics bachelor or master programme. This will comprise different theoretical foundations such as 'monetary theory', 'trade theory', macroeconomic theory', 'microeconomic theory', 'growth theory', etc. Thus economics is made up of a plurality of theories which, nonetheless, in most bachelor and master programmes share the same epistemological grounds (i.e., are based on epistemological monism).

[190] As Helmut Spinner (1974, p. 238; my translation) writes: "Theory pluralism is given if and only if there is a plurality of theories that stand in a mutually critical relation to one another."

social phenomena in its historical context. sm. On the other hand, ontological and epistemological pluralism necessarily requires a 'true' theoretical pluralism, rather than a mere multitude of theoretical approaches.

What remains to be discussed is the **paradigmatic level**, which has been touched on above a number of times. Though the term 'paradigm' is derived from Kuhn's theory of scientific revolutions, the paradigmatic level can best be described in terms of the different dimensions of Lakatos' 'scientific research programmes' (cf. Lakatos, 1976). Alongside the epistemological and method-related dimensions already discussed, there is also a heuristic dimension, which is a defining feature of a paradigm (cf. Homann 1988, p. 88ff.; Heise/Thieme 2015, p. 250). Here it is a question of postulates, 'model predictions' (Graf 1978), or 'ideal types' (cf. Kapeller 2012, p. 124ff.) that anyone who subscribes to a given paradigm would have to share ('positive heuristics') or at least not call into question ('negative heuristics'). The paradigm thus brings together the epistemological level and the method level and, in addition, introduces a further level which makes it possible to introduce a distinction between a true 'paradigmatic pluralism' and simple 'paradigm variation.'[191]

Paradigm **variation** allows for alternative axiomatic explanatory systems at the epistemological level and/or alternative deductive or inductive approaches at the method level, all of which share the same heuristic, whereas paradigmatic **pluralism** involves the adoption of different heuristics, which must be based on an epistemological difference, but not necessarily on method pluralism. If, on the one hand, method monism cannot be theoretically justified, and, on the other, method pluralism does not constitute a necessary condition of paradigmatic pluralism, then the heuristic and epistemic dimensions sufficiently allow us to make consistent statements concerning paradigmatic variation and paradigmatic pluralism (cf. Table 8).

[191] This distinction is sometimes captured in terms of 'intraparadigmatic pluralism' versus 'interparadigmatic pluralism.' In light of the above qualification concerning the concept of pluralism, however, I shall speak of paradigm variation rather than intraparadigmatic pluralism.

Table 8: Paradigmatic monism, paradigm variation, and paradigmatic pluralism

		EPISTEMOLOGICAL LEVEL	
		Pluralism	**Monism**
HEURISTIC LEVEL	**Monism**	Paradigm variation (intraparadigmatic pluralism)	Paradigm monism
	Pluralism	Paradigm pluralism (interparadigmatic pluralism)	-

Source: Constructed by author

While paradigmatic monism necessarily entails the extremely restrictive assumption of an epistemological and heuristic monism, the acceptance of competing explanatory systems at the epistemological level does not necessarily entail paradigmatic pluralism if a uniform (positive or at least negative) heuristic is adopted. Such a form of paradigm variation has to be distinguished from true paradigmatic pluralism, which only arises when axiomatic variation is accompanied by heuristic openness.

Tables 9 and 10 show the internal connections between the various forms of monism and pluralism we have discussed. It is evident here that paradigmatic monism entails ontological monism, but also that it is compatible with method and theoretical pluralism. Epistemological pluralism is also conceivable within a paradigmatic monism, and this combination is characteristic of the positions sometimes described as the 'Colander edge', or 'dissenters' within a paradigm,[192] and which we referred to above in terms of (mere) 'paradigm variation.'

[192] These terms were introduced into the literature by Dobusch/Kapeller (2012, pp. 1036-

Table 9: Forms of Scientific Monism

	Para-digma-tic Monism	Ontologi-cal Mon-ism	Epistemo-logical Monism	Methodo-logical Monism	Method Monism	Theoreti-cal Monism**
Paradig-matic Mon-ism		yes	no	yes	no	no
Ontologi-cal Mon-ism	Yes		no	yes	no	no
Epistemo-logical Monism	Yes	yes		yes	no	no
Methodo-logical Monism	No	No	no		no	no
Method Monism*	-	-	-	-		-
Theoretical Monism	Yes	yes	yes	yes	no	

Notes: * not theoretically justifiable; ** theory monism also includes theory variation/differentiation among object-specific but compatible theories. The table is to be read across the rows: monism x corresponds to/presupposes/is compatible with monism y.

The theoretical assumptions of paradigmatic monism contained within ontological monism—i.e., the endorsement of the 'one world, one truth' hypothesis and the claim that social reality is a closed system—are nevertheless so rigid and unjustifiable that ontological pluralism becomes irrefutable as a theoretical norm. This gives rise to a domino effect, which runs from epistemological pluralism, through method and theoretical pluralism,

7). Colander/Holt/Rosser (2004) speak of the 'cutting edge' or the 'edge of economics.' What is meant here is that scientific progress often takes place through the transformation of certain core assumptions at the epistemological level, while a given (negative) heuristic is maintained, so that novelty is produced through paradigm variation. Behavioural economics offers one example of such variation, since it limits the assumption of the rationality of actors without calling into question the market clearing heuristic. In the wake of the recent global financial crisis, such behavioural approaches are often used to model financial markets. This is regarded as the 'cutting edge' of economics (cf. e.g., McDonald, 2009), illustrated by the awarding of the Nobel Prize to the behavioural economist Robert Shiller — jointly with the more traditional economists Eugene Fama and Lars Hansen – for his work on financial markets. For more on the 'Colander edge' or the 'cutting edge', see below.

and up to **paradigmatic pluralism as the only adequate model of economic enquiry**—any restriction of this pluralism would have to be rejected as a violation of scientificity and academic freedom.

Table 10: Forms of Scientific Pluralism

	Paradigmatic Pluralism	Ontological Pluralism	Epistemological Pluralism	Methodological Pluralism**	Method Pluralism	Theoretical Pluralism
Paradigmatic Pluralism		yes	yes	No	yes	yes
Ontological Pluralism	Yes		yes	No	yes	yes
Epistemological Pluralism	No	yes		No	yes	yes
Methodological Pluralism*	-	-	-		-	-
Method Pluralism	No	no	No	No		no
Theoretical Pluralism	No	no	No	No	no	

Notes: * not theoretically justifiable; ** methodological pluralism explicitly does not include a methodological 'anything goes' (see above). The table is to be read across the rows: pluralism x corresponds to/presupposes/is compatible with pluralism y.

Nevertheless, a thoroughgoing notion of pluralism derived in this way does not by itself justify methodological pluralism or even an 'anything goes' position. These positions depend on the repudiation of the 'one world, one truth' hypothesis advocated by the sceptic and the relativist. In other words: one does not have to be a rigid sceptic or relativist to accept thoroughgoing scientific pluralism as a model of economic enquiry; on the other hand, one must accept inadmissibly restrictive premises in order to reject such scientific pluralism as a model of enquiry.

4. On the (Dire) State of Contemporary Economics

The criticism of economics introduced at the beginning of this paper tends to lament the fact that the current state of the discipline is less plural than a thoroughgoing scientific pluralism would require. At the same time, however, the description of the discipline in these terms is also regarded as a cognitive misjudgement (i.e., some mainstream economists simply denounce the lack of pluralism by misguidedly indicating a variety of theories); and the establishment of a monistic paradigm is celebrated as an indication of a mature (i.e. highly developed, high-performing) 'normal science.'

How might we assess these apparently conflicting appraisals on the basis of the above analysis? Here it is necessary to introduce a conceptual opposition that paradigmatically underpins the notion of pluralism, namely that between heterodoxy and orthodoxy. Orthodoxy refers to the paradigm that uses the dominant heuristic in a discipline; heterodoxy, by contrast, refers to all of the paradigms that reject this heuristic. The relative dominance[193] of a given heuristic is of course time and context dependent, and can therefore change over the course of time. In the sociology and history of science, many studies have addressed the formation of dominant paradigms.[194] For our purposes, however, what is particularly important is the relation between heterodoxy and orthodoxy: paradigmatic pluralism requires the mutual acceptance of and conflict between propositions and methods, along with access to all of the forms of capital (economic, social, symbolic, and cultural) that allow a position to be established in the scientific field. Crucial is that a 'true' paradigmatic pluralism be established, and not merely a form of paradigm variation that, in combining epistemological pluralism with heuristic monism (cf. Table 8), only serves to expand the orthodoxy and transform it into the 'mainstream.' A paradigm monism, by contrast, is characterised by the elevation of the orthodoxy to the status of a 'normal science,' which at best might still tolerate other mainstream paradigms and thus allow for paradigm variation. Heterodox paradigms, however, would be dismissed as non-scientific or at least as not properly belonging to the discipline, and would therefore be excluded from access to resources.

[193] 'Dominance' here means no more than that a relative majority of scientists feel obliged to use the orthodox epistemology, methods, and heuristics. The term 'orthodoxy' often seems to imply not just a quantitative majority, but also the disparagement of other approaches as heretical. Even if this may seem to be the case—particularly in the eyes of heterodox scientists—orthodoxy refers here only to the truth claim that is also shared by pluralists.

[194] Cf. e.g. Heise/Sander/Thiele (2016); Heise (2014); Hesse (2010); Fourcade (2009).

It is rat1Oer uncontroversial to say that neoclassical economics[195] constitutes the dominant contemporary orthodoxy within economics.[196] Since its application in treating economic questions does not need to be explicitly justified, since the neoclassical model of resource allocation determines the historically uncontested canon in textbooks on economics,[197] and since the vast majority of research articles (if they have any theoretical basis at all) employ theories and models rooted in neoclassical economics, the latter can be considered to enjoy the monistic status of a 'normal science.'

This is all the more true insofar as the heterodoxy is largely ignored by the orthodoxy (cf. Colander, 2010, p. 45; Kapeller, 2010; Lee, 2011 p. 575); is excluded from the most prominent economics journals (King, 2002, p. 133ff.); and is largely blocked from significant (non-academic) positions ('symbolic capital') and funding sources (cf. Heise/Sander/Thieme, 2016; Lee 2004; Mata 2009). Finally, the fact that certain crucial 'dissenters' within the mainstream have pledged their allegiance to the dominant heuristic paradigm has served to cement the monistic position of the orthodoxy.[198]

In light of the above theoretical discussion, we would then have to speak of the dire current state of economics insofar as it is bound to a paradigmatic monism. Here it does not help to point to the theory and method **variety** (sometimes unreflectively presented as method **pluralism**) within

---

[195] Under the heading, 'neoclassical economics,' we include both dynamic stochastic general equilibrium modelling (DSGE) and Neo-Keynesianism; on this and the classification of other theories with respect to the orthodoxy-heterodoxy opposition cf. Heise/Thieme (2015). Cf. also Lawson (2013); Blaug (1980, p. 137ff.).

[196] Studies by Colander/Klamer (1987); Klamer (2007); Frey/Humbert/Schneider (2007) and Heise/Sander/Thieme (2016) not only indicate this contemporary dominance, but also show that it has increased in the last three decades.

[197] In sharp contrast to textbooks on sociology, in which various schools of thought or paradigms are quite naturally presented alongside one another without prejudicing a 'mainstream.' Recently, a number of heterodox/pluralist textbooks in economics have been published.

[198] These include e.g. Vernon Smith (2003, p. 505) for behavioural economics; Kenneth Arrow (1988, p. 275ff.) and Blume/Durlauf (2001) for complexity economics. The heuristic characterising the contemporary mainstream is the market-clearing logic manifested in Walras' law as a model solution, which neither excludes disequilibria as temporary phenomena nor disequilibrium as its investigative and methodological basis.

the economic sciences, since, as Table 9 shows, such forms of pluralism can easily be reconciled with an unjustifiable paradigm monism. This now allows us to better understand the position advocated by the representative of the *Verein für Socialpolitik* that we noted at the outset: On the one hand, this position seeks to justify the repression of heterodox approaches on the grounds that they have lost the battle of ideas;[199] on the other, it celebrates a theoretical and method pluralism (Bachmann, 2015a; Bachmann, 2015b; Erlei, 2015).

Since paradigmatic monism is compatible with a plurality of methods and theories, nothing logically prevents such a combination—particularly when 'plurality' in fact solely means variation or differentiation. If we also allow that method pluralism (i.e. acknowledging that inductive and deductive methods must always be combined within fallibilistic positivism) may be compatible with method absolutism (i.e. conceiving formal-mathematical deduction as the implicit standard of scientificity) then we gain a clearer understanding of a frequently voiced intra-paradigmatic criticism. It is particularly the '*Ordnungsökonomen*' and the members of the 'Austrian school'—whose members reject formal-deductive analysis as being based on a 'pretence of knowledge' (cf. Hayek, 1975, p. 441)—who have called for greater acceptance of non-formal approaches or even for a method pluralism that would also allow narrative approaches to be considered scientifically defensible:

"In my view, one can agree with the pluralists that there is currently very little acceptance of non-mathematical approaches and that there is probably a selective distortion which disadvantages non-formal theories. Mathematics undoubtedly allows certain thoughts to be formulated more clearly and unambiguously; yet there is no good reason why one should not be able to gain new and important insights in other ways too" (Erlei, 2015; my translation).

---

[199] It might be noted here that such arguments never are burdened to verify such claims by means of logical or empirical falsification; in a circular manner, they rather take the quantitatively weak position of such heterodoxies within the scientific field as sufficient proof of their failure.

Though this criticism is certainly justified, and though the **means of discriminating** against such 'dissenters' (the 'selective distortion') may be very similar to those encountered by heterodox economists, it should be noted that the **basis** for the discrimination is quite different in each case: the ordoliberal[200] dissenters constitute the 'collateral damage' produced by a standardisation process that emphasises professionalisation, but not by a lack of method or theoretical pluralism. Heterodox economists, on the other hand, see themselves as being excluded from a field governed by a paradigmatic monism, on account of their rejection of the 'mainstream heuristic.'

Finally, our analysis also sheds further light on the meaning of the 'Colander edge': David Colander (2000) is one of the most prominent advocates of the view that the 'normal science' of neoclassical economics has long since given way to a theoretical pluralism, and thus feels justified in speaking of the 'death of neoclassical economics.' On this view, the call for pluralism which suggests that monism represents the current state of the discipline (on account of the narrow-mindedness of its adherents) would then have to be rejected both in substance and on strategic grounds.[201] As Tables 9 and 10 show, however, theory pluralism and epistemological pluralism by no means entail paradigm pluralism. When Colander, in a later work co-written with Richard Holt and Barkley Rosser Jr., speaks of the 'changing face of mainstream economics,' it is clear he has in mind an epistemological pluralism (cf. Table 8), which provides a basis for paradigmatic **variation** (i.e. theories at the 'Colander edge' which contain a number of axiomatic or method-specific innovations) within the mainstream, but not necessarily for a paradigmatic **pluralism** that would spell the 'dissolution of the mainstream' or an 'opening up of the mainstream.'

---

[200] Ordoliberalism or *Ordnungsökonomik* is a German variant of classical liberalism which emphasizes the state's obligation to provide a secure regulatory (e.g. property rights, competition legislation) and social (i.e. welfare state regulations) frame (Ordnung or in latin: ordo) for the market actor's to freely and efficiently do their business. Ordoliberalism is closely entangled with the German economic policy of Western Germany's post-WWII 'economic miracle'.

[201] "Seeing the mainstream's rejection of their ideas as due to the mainstream's closed-mindedness may make heterodox economists feel better, but it is not a way to open up dialogue between mainstream and heterodoxy" (Colander, 2010, p. 36).

5. Conclusion: The Necessity for a Pluralisation of Economics

The essence of the foregoing reflections is simple: the only appropriate model of enquiry in the economic sciences is a thoroughgoing scientific pluralism that culminates in ontological and paradigmatic pluralism. This should not be misconceived as an ethically motivated norm of fairness or tolerance, but is rather a **scientific imperative.**[202] Furthermore, a more extensive methodological pluralism or 'anything goes' position, which denies the ontology of the 'one world, one truth' principle in the manner of the sceptic or the relativist, is not to be categorically excluded, but is also not a logical consequence of ontological and paradigmatic pluralism (cf. Figure 3).

If one regards the historical '*Methodenstreits*' essentially as a conflict over the unifying conception of a scientific discipline, one will also see in the call for methodological pluralism a historical rupture between economics and economic sociology, which has its own disciplinary and academic orientation and representation. It is, therefore, not inappropriate to consider the pluralisation of the economic sciences in terms of the relation between the orthodoxy, the mainstream, and the heterodoxy.

[202] One referee was afraid that the confrontation of an ethical norm with an imperative may be misleading because an imperative can be associated with an ethical norm. Being neither a linguist nor a philosopher, I cannot evaluate this claim. However, what is meant in substance is that an ethical norm can be rejected on no other grounds than simple and unmotivated disagreement. An imperative, however, is a compulsory guidance principle which can be based on moral or ethical values or, as in the case of a scientific imperative, on reason only. Therefore, one cannot reasonably reject a scientific imperative but one could easily reject an ethical norm.

Figure 3: Pluralism and Paradigms

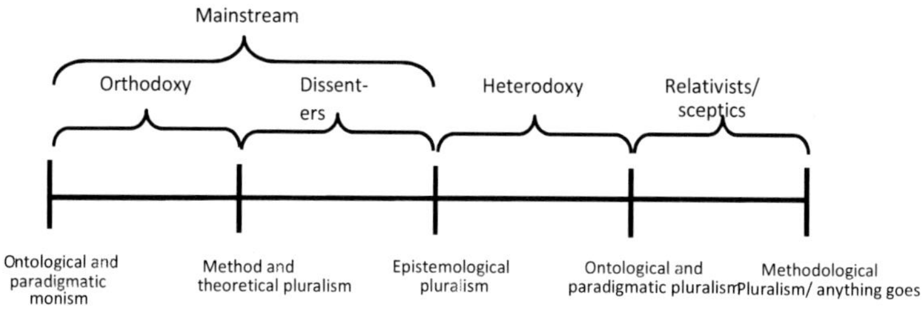

Here we can see (cf. Figure 3) that economics is characterised by an ontological and paradigmatic monism in which neoclassical economics constitutes the 'normal science.' Though the latter allows for method and theoretical pluralism, and comes to form a 'mainstream' (i.e., facilitates epistemological pluralism and paradigm variation) through the inclusion of 'dissenting' schools of thought or paradigms, including information economics, complexity economics, and behavioural and evolutionary economics, it nevertheless excludes heterodox paradigms such as Post-Keynesianism, Neo-Ricardianism, Marxism and other heterodox school such as old-institutionalism or socio-economics[203] on the basis of heuristic differences. The interpretative pre-eminence of the mainstream is so great that even mainstream paradigms that do not adopt a formal-mathematical, deductive approach (such as the *Ordnungsökonomik* tradition and the 'Austrian school') are discriminated against. This not only results in the loss of economics' legitimacy, but also of its academic freedom and capacity for critical reflection—the very resources that determine the progressive character of a discipline.

[203] For an explanation of this classification and a discussion of the potential ambiguities of these paradigms, cf. Heise/Thieme (2016).

A healthy form of economics would not then be marked by an adherence to a 'normal scientific' paradigmatic monism, but rather by a state of competition between a wide range of heuristics[204], all of which would potentially be subject to empirical falsification. Within the sphere of economics so conceived, it would be taken as given that advocates of the various different paradigms should mutually acknowledge, communicate with, and criticise one another; and, as a necessary precondition of such engagement, would allow one another access to those resources which make it possible to maintain a position within the scientific field.

Pluralism entails neither relativism nor nihilism, nor the application of an eclectic approach or the elaboration of 'pluralistic paradigms'; it merely entails the absence of discrimination against ontologies, paradigms, and methods subject to scientific critique and an acceptance of the limitations of the economic sciences (and the social sciences in general): namely that there is no certain, universally accepted knowledge ('truth'), but rather only 'conjectural knowledge' that could potentially be falsified at any time.

In light of the criticism of economics discussed at the outset, we can surely doubt that such a modest form of economics would lose social and scientific legitimacy. And yet a vague hope of legitimacy of course cannot provide a sure theoretical foundation for an academic discipline in any event. Finally, on such a scenario, economics would no longer be able to elevate itself above other disciplines of the social sciences in which a wide-ranging pluralism is taken for granted.

In a number of prior studies (cf. Heise, 2014; Heise/Sander/Thieme, 2016), doubts have been raised whether economics can achieve the necessary pluralisation from within its own scientific community.[205] Put in the language

---

[204] One referee argued that there should be some discussion of what Kuhn and Lakatos say on the questions of pluralism. Although this must be left to experts of Kuhnian and Lakatosian philosophy of science, I believe it fair to say that for Thomas Kuhn paradigmatic pluralism is merely a state of transition while for Imre Lakatos it is the obvious state of any serious science.

[205] The reasons include: the wholly unequal endowment of the mainstream and the heterodoxy with economic, social, cultural, and symbolic capital; the resultant strength of the mainstream within the scientific field; path dependence; and the prevalent formal and

and logic of the discipline itself, it would seem that the 'market for economic ideas' has experienced a **market failure**, which can only be rectified via external intervention. This is not the place, however, to elaborate the precise form that such a 'regulated pluralism' would have to take, nor the mode of its implementation—this task will need to be left to further studies.

---

informal incentive structures. The mainstream is also able to bolster its position by placing itself at the head of, and seeking to guide, a reform movement under the motto 're-thinking economics.' At the international level, this role has been taken on by the 'Institute for New Economic Thinking' founded by the financial speculator George Soros (cf. Häring 2014).

Reference List

Arrow, K.J. (1988) 'Workshop on the Economy as an Evolving Complex System: Summary,' Anderson, P.W., Arrow, K.J., Pines, D. (Eds.); *The Economy As An Evolving Complex System*, Addison- Wesley, Redwood

Bachmann, R. (2011) 'Zum Neueren Methodenstreit – Rückblick und Ausblick' Caspari, V., Schefold, B. (Eds.); *Wohin steuert die ökonomische Wissenschaft*?, Campus, Frankfurt, pp. 259 – 268.

Bachmann, R. (2015) *Erkennen, was Quatsch ist*; in: brand eins, 17.Jg., H.11, pp. 86 – 89.

Berger, P.L., Luckmann, T. (1966) *The Social Construction of Reality. A Treatise in the Sociology of Knowledge*, Anchor Books, Garden City, NY.

Beinhocker, E.D. (2013) 'Reflexivity, complexity, and the nature of social science', *Journal of Economic Methodology*, Vol. 20, No.4, pp. 330 – 342.

Besley, T., Hennessey, P. (2009) 'Letter in response to a question of Queen Elisabeth', British Academy of Science, London.

Blaug, M. (1980) *The Methodology in Economics*, Cambridge University Press, Cambridge, UK

Blume, L., Durlauf, S. (2001) 'The Interaction-Based Approach to Socioeconomic Behavior', Durlauf, S., Young, P. (Eds.) *Social Dynamics*, Cambridge University Press, Cambridge, Mass.

Boland, L.A. (1997) *Critical economic methodology. A Personal Odyssey*, Routledge, London.

Bonabeau, E., Dorigo, M., Theraulaz, G. (1999) *Swarm Intelligence. From Natural to Artificial System*, Oxford University Press, Oxford, UK.

Caldwell, B.J. (1988) 'The case for pluralism',N. de Marchi (Ed.) *The Popperian Legacy in Economics*, Cambridge University Press, Cambridge, UK, pp. 231 – 244.

Cassidy, J. (2009) *How Markets Fail. The Logic of Economic Calamities*, Picador, New York.

Colander, D. (2000) 'The death of neoclassical economics,' *Journal of the History of Economic Thought,* Vol. 22, No.2, pp. 129 – 143.

Colander, D. (2010) 'Moving beyond the rhetoric of pluralism. Suggestions for an 'inside-the-mainstream' heterodoxy; in: Garnett, R., Olsen, E.K., Starr, M. (Eds.) *Economic Pluralism*, Routledge, Abingdon, pp. 36 – 47.

Colander, D., Holt, R.P., Barkley Rosser Jr., J. (2004) 'The Changing Face of Mainstream Economics,' *Review of Political Economy*, Vol. 16, No. 4, pp. 485 – 499.

Colander, D., Klamer, A. (1987) 'The Making of an Economist,' *Journal of Economic Perspectives*, Vol. 1, No.2, pp. 95 – 111.

Cramer, F. (1993) *Chaos und Ordnung – Die komplexe Struktur des Lebendigen*, Insel Publ., Frankfurt/Leipzig.

Davis, J. (2012) 'Samuels on Methodological Pluralism in Economics; Department of Economic Working Paper 2012-01, Marquette University, Milwaukee.

Dequech, D. (2001) 'Bounded Rationality, Institutions, and Uncertainty,' *Journal of Economic Issues,* Vol. 25, No. 4, pp. 911 – 929.

Dobusch, L., Kapeller, J. (2012) 'Heterodox United vs. Mainstream City? Sketching a Framework for Interested Pluralism in Economics,' *Journal of Economic Issues*, Vol. XLVI, No.4, pp. 1035 - 1057

Dow, S. C. (1997) 'Methodological Pluralism and pluralism of methods,' Salanti/Screpanti *Pluralism in Economics. New Perspectives in History and Methodology*, Edward Elgar, Cheltenham, pp. 89 – 99.

Dow, S. C. (2004) 'Structured Pluralism,' *Journal of Economic Methodology*, Vol. 11, No.3, pp. 275 – 290.

Dutt, A.K. (2014) 'Dimensions of Pluralism in Economics,' *Review of Political Economy,* Vol. 26, No.4, pp. 479 – 494.

Erlei, M. (2015) ‚Was ist richtig an der Kritik heterodoxer Ökonomen?' Wirtschaftliche Freiheit. Das ordnungspolitische Journal. 23rd September 2015 (available at: http://wirtschaftlichefreiheit.de/wordpress/?p=18020, accessed 15, February 2016).

Fourcade, M. (2009) *Economists and Societies. Discipline and Profession in the United States, Britain and France, 1890s to 1990s*, Princeton University Press, Princeton New Jersey.

Fourcade, M., Ollion, E., Algan, Y. (2015) 'The Superiority of Economists,' *Journal of Economic Perspectives*, Vol. 29, No.1, pp. 89 – 114.

Frey, B.S., Humbert, S., Schneider, F. (2007) ‚Was denken deutsche Ökonomen. Eine empirische Auswertung einer Internetbefragung unter den Mitgliedern des Vereins für Socialpolitik', *Perspektiven der Wirtschaftspolitik*, Vol. 8, No.4, pp. 359 – 377.

Friedman, M. (1953) '*The Methodology of Positive Economics,'* Friedman, M. (Ed.) *Essays in Positive Economics*, University of Chicago Press, Chicago. pp. 3 – 43

Funk, L. (2009); Kontroverse volkswirtschaftliche Interpretationen zur Finanzmarktkrise – einige kritische Anmerkungen, *Sozialer Fortschritt*, H. 4, pp. 79 – 83.

Garnett, R. F. jr. (2006) 'Paradigms and pluralism in heterodox economics,' *Review of Political Economy*, Vol. 18, No.4, pp. 521 – 546.

Garnett, R., Olsen, E.K., Starr, M. (Eds.) (2010) *Economic Pluralism*, Routledge, Abingdon

Graf, H.-G. (1978); *'Muster-Vorhersagen' und 'Erklärungen des Prinzips' bei F.A. von Hayek*, Mohr Siebeck, Tübingen.

Graham, H.D., Diamond, N. (1997) *The Rise of American Research Universities: Elites and Challengers in the Postwar Era*, John Hopkins University Press, Baltimore.

Häring, N. (2014) 'George Soros' INET: An Institute to Improve the World or a Trojan Horse of the Financial Oligarchy?;' *Real World Economic Review*, No.67, pp. 90 – 96.

Hands, D.W. (2001) *Reflections Without Rules: Economic Methodology and Contemporary Science Theory*, Cambridge University Press, Cambridge.

Hahn, F. (1992) 'Reflections,'*Royal Economics Society Newsletter,* No. 77, April

Hayek, F.A. von (1975) 'The Pretence of Knowledge,' *Swedish Journal of Economics*, Vol. 77, No.4, pp. 433 – 442.

Heise, A. (2014) 'The Future of Economics in a Lakatos-Bourdieu Framework,' *International Journal of Political Economy,* Vol. 43, No.3, pp. 70 – 93.

Heise, A. (2016) 'Why has economics turned out this way? A socio-economic note on the explanation of monism in economics', *Journal of Philosophical Economics*, Vol. 10, No.1, (forthcoming).

Heise, A., Sander, H., Thieme, S. (2016); *Das Ende der Heterodoxie? Entwicklung der Wirtschaftswissenschaften in Deutschland*, Springer VS, Wiesbaden.

Heise, A., Thieme, S. (2016) ‚The short rise and long fall of heterodox economics. Explorations in a scientific field of power and struggle,' *Journal of Economic Issues,* Vol. 50, No.4, pp. 1105 - 1130.

Hesse, J.-O. (2010) *Wirtschaft als Wissenschaft. Die Volkswirtschaftslehre in der frühen Bundesrepublik*, Campus, Frankfurt.

Homann, K. (1988); *Rationalität und Demokratie,* Mohr Siebeck, Tübingen.

ISIPE (2014); Internationaler studentischer Aufruf für eine plurale Ökonomik; (available at: http://www.isipe.net/home-de/, accessed, 22nd February 2016)

Kapeller, J. (2010) 'Some critical notes on citation metrics and heterodox economics,' *Review of Radical Political Economics*, Vol. 42, No. 3, pp. 330-337.

Keynes, J.N. (1891); *The Scope and Method of Political Economy*, Macmillan, London.

King, J. E. (2002) *A History of Post Keynesian Economics since 1936*, Edward Elgar, Cheltenham.

Klamer, A. (2007) 'Does this Have to Be our Future?' Colander, D. (Ed.); *The Making of an Economist, Redux*, Princeton University Press, Princeton, pp. 277 – 233.

Krabbe, J.J. (1996) *Historicism and Organicism in Economics: The Evolution of Thought,* Kluwer, Dordrecht.

Kurz, H.D., Salvatori, N. (1997) 'On critics and protective belts,' in: Salanti, A., Screpanti, E. (Eds.) *Pluralism in Economics. New Perspectives in History and Methodology*, Edward Elgar, Cheltenham, pp. 232 – 255.

Lakatos, I. (1976) 'Falsification and the Methodology of Scientific Research Programmes,' Harding, S.G. (Ed.) *Can Theories be Refuted?,* Kluwer, Dordrecht, pp. 205 – 259.

Langmuir, I. (1989) 'Pathological Science,' transcribed and edited by R.N. Hall; in: Physics today, October, pp. 36 - 48.

Lawson, T. (1994) 'Why Are So Many Economists So Opposed To Methodology?', in: *Journal of Economic Methodology*, Vol.1, No.1, pp. 105 – 133

Lawson, T. (2013) 'What is this 'school' called neoclassical economics?,' *Cambridge Journal of Economics,* Vol. 37, No. 4, pp. 947 – 983.

Lebaron, F. (2006) 'Nobel Economists as Public Intellectuals: The Circulation of Symbolic Capital,' *International Journal of Contemporary Sociology*, Vol.43, No.1, pp. 87–101.

Lee, F.S. (2009) *A History of Heterodox Economics: Challenging the mainstream in the twentieth century*, Routledge, London.

Lee, F. S. (2011) 'Heterodox Economics, Tolerance, and Pluralism: A Reply to Garnett and Mearman,' *Review of Radical Political Economy*, Vol. 43, No.4, pp. 573 – 577.

Loasby, B. (2003) 'Closed Models and Open Systems,' *Journal of Economic Methodology*, Vol. 10, No.3, pp. 285 – 306.

Mabsoud, R. (2015) 'Abduction and economics: the contributions of Charles Pierce and Herbert Simon,' *Journal of Economic Methodology*, Vol. 22, No.4, pp. 491 – 516.

McDonald, I.M. (2009) 'The Global Financial Crisis and Behavioural Economics,' *Economic Papers*, Vol. 28, No.3, pp. 249 – 254.

Mäki, U. (1997) 'The one world and the many theories,' in: Salanti, A., Screpanti, E. (Eds.) *Pluralism in Economics. New Perspectives in History and Methodology*, Edward Elgar, Cheltenham, pp. 37 – 47.

Mariyani-Squire, E., Moussa, M. (2015) 'Fallibilism, Liberalism and Stilwell's Advocacy for Pluralism in Economics,' *Journal of Australian Political Economy*, Vol. 75, pp. 194 – 210.

Mata, Tiago (2009) 'Migrations and Boundary Work: Harvard, Radical Economists, and the Committee on Political Discrimination,' *Science in Context*, Vol. 22, No. 1, pp. 115-143.

Menger, C. (1985) *Investigations into the Method of the Social Sciences with special reference to Economics*, New York University Press, New York

Moore, G. (2003) 'John Neville Keynes's Solution to the English Methodenstreit,' *Journal of the History of Economic Thought*, Vol. 25, No.1, pp. 5 – 38.

Morgan, J. (2015) 'Is Economics Responding to Critique? What do the UK 2015 QAA Subject Benchmarks Indicate?', *Review of Political Economy*, Vol. 27, No. 4, pp. 518-538.

Morgan, M. S., Rutherford, M. (1998) 'American Economics: The Character of the Transformation,' Morgan, M.S, and Rutherford,M. (Eds.), *From Interwar Pluralism to Postwar Neoclassicism*, Duke University Press, Durham, pp. 1 – 26.

Popper, R. (1957) *The Poverty of Historicism*, The Beacon Press, London.

Porstmann, Reiner (2004) Wissenschaftstheoretische Grundfragen in den Wirtschaftswissenschaften; Teil II: Vergleich moderner Wissenschaftsprogramme, Norderstedt: Books on Demand.

Roos, M.W. (2015) ‚Die Komplexitätsökonomik und ihre Implikationen für die Wirtschaftspolitik,' *Perspektiven der Wirtschaftspolitik*, Jg.16, No. 4, pp. 379 – 392.

Salanti, A., Screpanti, E. (Eds.) (1997) *Pluralism in Economics. New Perspectives in History and Methodology*, Edward Elgar, Cheltenham.

Samuels, W. J. (1972) 'The History of Economic Thought as Intellectual History,' *History of Political Economy*, Vol.6, No. 3, pp. 305 – 323.

Samuels, W. J. (1993) 'In (limited but affirmative) defence of nihilism,' *Review of Political Economy,* Vol. 5, No.2, pp. 236 – 244.

Samuels, W. J. (1997) 'The case for methodological pluralism,' Salanti/Screpanti *Pluralism in Economics. New Perspectives in History and Methodology*, Edward Elgar, Cheltenham, pp. 67 – 79.

Schmidt, C.M., aus dem Moore, N. (2010); Die Methodendiskussion in den Wirtschaftswissenschaften vor dem Hintergrund der Finanzkrise; in: Jens, U., Romahn, H. (eds.); *Methodenpluralismus in den Wirtschaftswissenschaften*, Metropolis, Marburg, pp. 143 – 182.

Schumpeter, J. (1908) *Das Wesen und der Hauptinhalt der theoretischen Nationalökonomie*, Duncker & Humplot, Leipzig.

Sent, E.-M. (2006) *Pleas for Pluralism*; Fullbrook, E. (Ed.); *Real World Economics. A Post-Autistic Reader*, Anthem Press, London, pp. 177 – 184

Shionoya, Y. (1997) *Schumpeter and the idea of social science. A Metatheoretical Study,* CambridgeUniversity Press, Cambridge/UK.

Smith, V. L. (2003) 'Constructivist and Ecological Rationality in Economics,' Frängsmayr, F. (Ed.) *The Nobel Prizes 2002*, Nobel Foundation, Stockholm, pp. 502- 561.

Solow, R.W. (2005) 'How Did Economics Get That Way & What Way Did It Get?; *Daedalus*, Vol. 134, No. 4, pp. 87 – 100.

Spinner, H. (1974) *Pluralismus als Erkenntnismodell*, Suhrkamp, Frankfurt.

Tirole, J. (2014); Letter to the French Minister of Education Fioraso. (http://assoeconomiepolitique.org/wp-content/uploads/Lettre-de-jean-Tirole.pdf , accessed 22, February 2016).

Seven
Walras' law in the context of pre-analytic visions: a note*

1. Introduction**

Walras' law is the link between partial microeconomics of goods exchange and the macroeconomics of general equilibrium analysis (see Patinkin 1987: 4f.)[206]. On the one hand, it holds that there can be no *overall* excess supply or excess demand in an economy comprised of n markets where goods, labour, capital, bonds, and money are exchanged freely. On the other hand, it is the basis of general equilibrium as the long-term centre of gravity of a laissez-faire exchange economy, i.e. Walras' law is compatible with temporary disequilibria and long-run equilibrating forces.

The acceptance of Walras' law has become crucial in categorising the economic discipline: For many heterodox economists, it is the watershed between mainstream economics, comprising the orthodox dynamic stochastic general equilibrium model as well as many dissenters from evolutionary, complexity or behavioural economics, and heterodox economics, comprising Post Keynesian, Marxian and some of the evolutionary and complexity economics (see e.g. Heise 2014: 77f.). This paradigmatic fault-line has been adumbrated by John Maynard Keynes in his *General Theory* (Keynes 1936: 18 – 21) and has been put plainly by Robert Clower (1965: 278) as follows: "...either Walras' law is incompatible with Keynesian economics, or Keynes had nothing fundamentally new to add to orthodox

* Originally published: Economic Thought, Vol. 6, No. 1, 2017, 83-96

** I would like to thank Colin Rogers, Bruce Littleboy and Tom Palley for their valuable comments. However, the usual caveats apply.

206 Although the microfoundation of macroeconomics has been successfully critizised by complexity economists with reference to the Sonnenschein-Mantel-Debreu theorem (see e.g. Kirman 1989), there is no doubt that Walras' law holds and, therefore, links lower level analysis (whether complexity microeconomics or neoclassical microeconomics) and higher level analysis (general analysis of unique or multiple equilibria); see Elsner (2012: 117).

economic theory". In contrast to that, for most mainstream economists, the violation of Walras' law only proves the analytical short-comings of heterodox economics (see Sargent 1979: 67ff.) and prompts some heterodox economists to hastily concede that Walras' law holds even in heterodox (or, at least, Keynesian) economics (see e.g. Palley 1998).

The purpose of this short research note is, therefore, to elaborate on the possibilty of a refutation of Walras' law and to inquire into its preconditions. It is organised as follows: In the next section, a short introduction to Walras' law is given and, in section 3, the main theoretical challenges portrayed. As those challenges all share the same pre-analytic vision as the Walrasian general equilibrium theory, the attack was not entirely successful. Therefore, in section 4 an attempt is made to outline yet another assault on Walras' law based on the different pre-analytic vision of a genuine 'monetary economy' as foreshadowed by John Maynard Keynes.

2. Walras' law

In the wake of the interpretational debate on 'What Keynes really meant' (see Coddington 1976), Walras' law became the centre of attention. With the publication of the *General Theory*, Keynes pledged to have revolutionized economic thinking, and thus initiated a scientific revolution (see Keynes 1935) in the Kuhnian sense. That revolution appeared in the idea that an economy can be in equilibrium on every market except for the labour market, i.e. there can be equilibrium with involutary unemployment or, more generally, disequilibrium-equilibrium. This idea, of course, was completely alien to general equilibrium economics and seemed to contradict Walras' law.

For those who took Walras' law as the 'entropy law' of economics, i.e. a simple truism resulting from accounting necessities, the idea was obviously going to be rejected on analytical grounds. For those who took Walras' law as the major obstacle to a more realistic perspective on economic thinking, refuting Walras' law became pivotal, and the refutation needed to be rigorous.

Before we start scrutinizing the arguments put forward in that debate, let us first take a closer look at the meaning and derivation of Walras' law.

Leon Walras' intention was to show (or, rather, to prove mathematically) that there may exist a system of relative prices (a price vector) which will simultanously equilibrate all markets – for consumer goods, capital goods, labour, and money, i.e. to create a general equilibrium. In such an equilibrium state, where supply equals demand, excess demand must necessarily be zero. Although Walras' pre-analytic vision of the economic system was not only one of an exchange economy where initial endowments with goods, factors of production, and money are intertemporally allocated, he also assumed the equilibrium prices to commonly prevail due to a tâtonnement process prior to the actual contract settlement. Yet, even if some prices deviate from their equilibrium values, there still would be no overall, i.e. economy-wide, excess demand, but the excess demand (or excess supply respectively) in some markets would be cancelled out by an excess supply (or excess demand) in some other markets:

> *"The importance of Walras's law ... is that it apparently rules out the possibility of a general glut of commodities. For every excess supply there must be an equal (value) of excess demand, somewhere in the system. Corresponding to an excess supply of labour there must be an excess demand for goods. The former will drive down the level of money wages while the latter raises money prices. The resulting fall in the real wages will increase demand for labour and lead the economy back to full employment"* (Gale 1983: 18).[207]

This symmetrical reaction, which allowed for temporary partial disequilibria within a model of general equilibrium, was the necessary outcome of the application of budgetary constraints that the economic actors – (intertemporal) traders – face. And, therefore, it became a 'plausibility check'

[207] In this citation, Walras' law implies an equalibrating process. Other authors (such as Becker/Baumol 1952) take Walras' law simply to state the definitional equality between total supply and total demand. However, if the latter is meant, I would prefer to call it ‚Walras' equality'. Walras' law, however, epitomizes the self-regulating nature of an exchange economy. Having said this, the refutation of Walras' law does not merely imply the rejection of the stability of the Walrasian equilibrium solution, as provided by Sonnenschein, Mantel and Debreu (see e.g. Kirman 2004) but also the rejection of ‚Walras' equality'. In any case, the stability condition can easily be restored by using the very common gross subsitute assumption (see Gul/Stacchetti 1999).

for economic modelling: if Walras' law does not hold in an economic model, the model should be rejected on analytical grounds[208].

Of course, the mathematical proofs of the existence of a unique 'equilibrium' price vector and the absence of economy-wide excess demand rest on several assumptions: e.g. the homogeneity and continuity of the excess demand both function by building on the acceptance of the gross substitution axiom on the one hand, but also, on the other hand, on the pre-analytic vision[209] of an exchange economy as the basis for the market rhetoric of intertemporally exchanging value-equivalences.

3. Challenging Walras' law

All the modern predators of Walras' law somehow stem from Keynes' work. Either they appear, at least from the distance, to simply violate Walras' law, as in the case of 'hydraulic Keynesianism' of the IS-LM-type, or they try to re-invigorate Keynes' message based on a refutation of Walras' law, as in the case of the 'new microeconomists' of 'reconstituted reductionism'. Or, moreover, they refer to the concepts of a 'monetary economy' as in Keynes' *General Theory* or in preliminary work emphazising the non-accpetance of the axiom of gross substitution with respect to money and the distinction between a 'real exchange economy' and a 'monetary economy' as in the case of 'fundamental Keynesianism'[210].

[208] Davidson (2015: 371) argues that it was Paul Samuelson via his most inflencial 'Foundations of Economic Analysis' who not only established this idea but also maintained that Keynes' *General Theory* must have been based on it: "...Samuelson's view of the foundations of all economic theory, ... had to based on Samuelson's Foundations of Economic Analysis and its classical microeconomic Walrasian foundations. If the microfoundations of macroeconomics was not Walrasian, then it could not be what Keynes meant or any valid theory of macroeconomics".

[209] Immanuel Kant distinguishes between analytic and synthetic *a priori* judgements. Analytic *a priori* judgments describe attributions to objects or systems which are inherent ('the grey horse is white') or tautological, while synthetic *a priori* judgements describe attributions which are attached to objects or systems on a presumptive base ('the horse eats grass') and can be challenged theoretically and empirically (see Kant 1781/1983: 176ff.). Such synthetic *a priori* judgements need to be granted to open systems and can be termed as 'pre-analytic vision'.

[210] 'Hydraulic Keynesianism', 'reconstituted reductionism', and 'fundamental Keynesianism' are the three different categories of Keynes interpretations that Alan Coddington

Hydraulic Keynesianism

The (in)famous 'hydraulic Keynesianism' of the ISLM scheme seemed to contradict Walras' law: the IS curve portrayed various equilibria on the (capital) goods market (in relation to different interest rate (i)-income (Y) settings) while the LM curve depicted various equilibria on the money market (equally in relation to different i-Y settings). At the intersection of the IS and the LM curve, the equilibrium levels of the (real) rate of interest and (real) income were determined, specifying a unique equilibrium on the goods and on the money market. However, equilibrium (real) income – taking the money supply, the nominal wages, the capital stock, and the technology as exogenously given – need not correspond necessarily to full employment as determined on an 'ordinary' labour market. Thus, in this three-market-model, Walras' law appears to be refuted as it combines equilibrium on two markets with disequilibrium on one market. Yet, Walras' law implies in an n-market-model that the n-th market ought to be in equilibrium, if n-1 markets are in equilibrium. Palley (1998) has shown that this judgement rests on a misconception of 'hydraulic Keynesianism': If one takes into account that every demand for labour as much as every supply of labour corresponds to a supply of and demand for money income in a monetary economy, a situation of unemployment (i.e. excess supply of labour) matches an excess demand for money income, re-instating Walras' law again.

Reconstituted Reductionists

At this stage, Robert Clower (1965) and other 'reconstituted reductionists' such als Edmond Malinvaud (1977) and Axel Leijonhufvud (1968) argued that Walras' statement is based on the idea that every market actor – as price taker – can always sell his initial endowment at the ruling market price. The ensuing budgetary constraints underlying Walras' law are dubbed 'notional', i.e. fictitious, by Clower since they only hold good in equilibrium (i.e. when the ruling market price equals its equilibrium value)

(1976) provides in his seminal work. However, Coddington's account of 'fundamental Keynesianism' is rather critical (accusing 'fundamental Keynesians' of theoretical nihilism), while here the more positive interpretation of Davidson (2003) is followed.

but not in a situation when transactions are allowed at prices that are unequal to its equilibrium values (i.e. in disequilibrium or when trading at 'false price' occurs). Such a situation, which is described as 'non-Walrasian' disequilibrium, produces budgetary constraints that are dubbed 'effective'. As the 'short' market side (either the sellers or the buyers) will be rationed once a 'false price' is contracted, the resulting 'effective' budgetary constraint will differ from the 'notional' budget constraint either in 'Walrasian equilibrium' (when contracts are only concluded at equilibrium prices and quantities) or in 'Walrasian disequilibrium' (when contracts are concluded at disequilibrium prices but unrationed quantities). If the budetary constraints differ due to 'false price trading' on one market, so will the effects on other markets ('spill over'), as the economic agents would have to revise their buying decisions accordingly – this is what Clower terms 'dual decision hypothesis'. Moreover, in this he claims to have established the central message of Keynes' *General Theory*: "In short, Keynes either had a dual-decision-hypothesis at the back of his mind, or most of the *General Theory* is theoretical nonsense" (Clower 1965: 290). The point that Clower tries to make is that Walras' law purportedly holds only in Walrasian equilibrium and disequilibrium, but not in non-Walrasian disequilibrium:

> *"...the dual decision hypothesis effectively implies that Walras' law, although valid as usual with reference to notional market excess demands, is in general irrelevant to any but full employment situations. Contrary to the findings of traditional theory, excess demand may fail to appear anywhere in the economy under conditions of less than full employment"* (Clower 1965: 292).

It is one thing to argue about whether Clower has provided a fair interpretation of Keynes' *General Theory* and another to argue whether his rejection of Walras' law is consistent. Although the former is not the centrepiece here, it should be noted that Clower did not challenge the Walrasian pre-analytic vision of economic reality as basically an exchange economy as Keynes had called for in the prelude to writing his *General Theory*[211]. Therefore, the 'revolutionary contents' of Keynes' *General Theory* would

[211] See Keynes (1933a), Keynes (1933b), Keynes (1933c).

have to reside in an 'inconsistency proof' with respect to the claim of Walrasian theory to having established a *general* equilibrium theory. For this, the latter, i.e. the consistency of the refusal of Walras' law, is pivotal. Many post Keynesians with a 'fundamentalist' background (see e.g. Davidson 1984, Edwards 1985, Rhodes 1984) deny that Clower's approach is consistent. As Thomas Palley points out:

> *"Just as for the case of notional demands and supplies, Walras' law will continue to hold for the case of effective demands and supplies. This is because the logic of exchange continues to hold, which implies that a decision to buy involves an offer that is an act of supply, while a decision to supply involves a willingness to accept payment that is an act of demand. Consequently, Walras' law holds for economies in which agents face quantity constraints".* (1998: 335)

Fundamentalist Keynesianism

The last assault on Walras' law came from those 'fundamentalist Keynesians' who promised to take Keynes' reasoning seriously: the particular nature of money – zero (or negligible) elasticities of production and substitution – renders the axiom of gross substitution futile and, as a consequence, violates an assumption necessary to prove the existence of Walrasian general equilibrium (see Arrow/Hahn 1971: 361). The economic intuition is that in a monetary economy where

> *"... 'commodities do not buy commodities' and hence there is always the necessity to transform commodity value into money value to purchase other commodities.... the excess supply of commodities in the goods market might fail to be matched by an excess demand for money. Hence, Walras' Law does not hold and disequilibrium might not be compensatory, ..."* (Tunez Arena 2015: 111).

A 'monetary economy' in this sense appears to be characterized by the existence of a money good which α) separates the act of selling from the act of buying, β) shows peculiar properties and γ) is responsible for the violation of Walras' law[212]. However, several important questions arise: 1) is it really money's function as medium of exchange (as in α) which distinguishes a barter or exchange economy from a monetary economy? 2) It is really the introduction of a medium of exhange which explains the peculiar properties (as in β) as Tunez Arena (2015: 106; my italics) asserts: "Money is, therefore, the only *medium of exchange* to buy commodities. Hence, money buys commodities but commodities do not buy commodities. Therefore, the Gross Substitution Theorem does not apply which is a more realistic abstraction of monetary market economies." Moreover 3), does the introduction of a money good as medium of exchange really entail the refutation of Walras' law (as in γ)? According to Hahn (1977: 31) it is the function of money as store of value ('resting place for savings other than reproducible assets') which explains its properties and which is essential for non-Walrasian results. However, non-Walrasian results based on the considerations of non-homogeneity and discontinuty of excess demand functions imply the questioning of the existence of general equilibrium (i.e. Walrasian equilibrium) but not necessarily of the validity of Walras' law (i.e. non-Walrasian disequilibrium) as demonstrated among others by Palley (1998: 338f.), Rhodes (1984: 121) and Hahn (1987: 12f.). The latter notes: "In brief, a sufficient condition for the validity of Walras' Law is that the individual's demand and supply functions on which it is ultimately based are all derived from the same budget constraint, whether quantity-constrained or not" (Hahn 1987: 13). Moreover, although this non-Walrasian disequilibrium will look different from a Walrasian disequilibrium, it still rests on the pre-analystic vision of an exchange economy (with money) and has to comply with its accounting principles.

---

[212] Several authors (see e.g. Hahn 1973, Rogers 1989, Laidler 1990) crafted out the difference between an ‚exchange economy with money' and a ‚monetary economy': In an ‚exchange economy with money' (termed ‚inessential (sequence) economy' by Hahn), the equilibrium solution is ultimately independent of the existence of money, while in a ‚monetary economy', the use of money as medium of exchange, store of value and unit of account constitute a different ‚monetary equilibrium' as compared to the ‚non-monetary equilibrium' of inessential economies. However, as will be argued below, the relation and causation of monetary non-neutrality and the different functions of money remain, at least, vague and its implications for Walras' law unclear.

4. The non-applicability of Walras' law in a genuine monetary economy

Keynes' *General Theory* was definitely conceived as an assault on Say's law of markets (see Keynes 1936: XXXV and 26; Sweezy 1947: 105), but it can only be inferred that he also had in mind a refutation of Walras' law. Taking this for granted and maintaining that the refutation of Walras' law is central to the revolutionary nature of Keynes' contribution and, thus, marks the demarcation line between orthodox and heterodox epistemology, the meaning of the following statement of Keynes may be crucial for his approach: "For if orthodox economics is at fault, the error is to be found not in the superstructure, which has been erected with great care for logical consistency, but in a lack of clearness and of generality in the premisses" (Keynes 1936: XXI). If the premisses of Walrasian economics is the pre-analytic vision of an exchange economy, his idea of a monetary economy, "in which money plays a part of its own and affects motives and decisions and is, in short, one of the operative factors in the situation, so that the course of events cannot be predicted, either in the long period or in the short, without a knowledge of money between the first state and the last" (Keynes 1933a: 408) must be based on a different pre-analytic vision.

Keynesians of the 'fundamentalist' stripe have come up with just such an alternative pre-analytic vision of a hierarchic relationship of creditors and debtors, substituting the homologous exchange of value-equivalences as basic constituent of economic interaction[213]. Thus a genuine 'monetary economy' is not simply a social construction in which the intertemporal exchange of goods, services, and factors of production is facilitated and, for that matter, sometimes (and only temporarily) interrupted by the use of money, but instead is a social provisioning process based on nominal obligations (denominated in terms of the money good which, therefore, primarily serves as a medium of deferred payments or unit of account) which need to be settled in the future. Money is created *pari passu* with nominal obligations, compelling the debtor to start a money-income-generating

[213] See e.g. Heise (1991), Davidson (1996), Minsky (1996), Baisch/Kuhn (2001), Steiger (2008). It must be confessed, though, that creditor-debtor-relationships are not always emphazised in due form but rather introduced by the side-door, see e.g. Lavoie (2014: 186ff).

process (usually production) and rendering the creditor illiquid for the time being (who is, thus, asking for a compensation in terms of nominal interest payments according to his liquidity preference). The rhetoric of market exchange focusing on allocational issues is replaced by a rhetoric of obligations focusing on issues of resource utilization and nominal income and employment creation[214]. In contrast to orthodox exchange economics, the budgetary constraints in monetary economics are not explained by initial endowments but by the willingness (or necessity) to engage in creditor-debtor-relationships on the part of economic actors. It is, therefore, the operations on the money and credit markets[215] generating nominal income which determine the operations in the commodity and employment markets, taking technology, preferences, the nominal wage rate(s), and the state of confidence as given. Due to simple national accounting principles (assuming, for the sake of simplicity, a closed economy), the nominal income generated as wage and profit income will always be equal to the nominal value of consumption and investment goods supplied at any level of income. Equilibrium in a genuine monetary economy is characterized as much by an equilibrium of supply and demand as by the fulfillment of expectations (about cash flows and the price level in order to 'real'-ize nominal rewards).

---

[214] see Keynes (1936: 245); Keynes (1937a: 209); Keynes (1937b: 219); Keynes (1937c: 119)

[215] I use the term 'credit market' very reluctantly and only for want of a better expression, as it is commonly referred to as the market on which savings (as a supply of unspent income as a flow magnitude or a demand for bonds as stock variable) and investment (as a demand for unspent income as a flow variable or a supply of bonds as stock variable) are equalibrated. In a monetary economy, however, the credit market is made up of 'finance' (i.e. the supply of liquid resources (money) for a specified period of time as a flow magnitude) and 'investment' (i.e. the demand for liquid resources (money) for a specified period of time as a flow magnitude) – income and savings have not yet been generated: "Dr. Herbert Bab has suggested to me that one could regard the rate of interest as being determined by the interplay of the terms on which the public desires to become more or less liquid and those on which the banking system is ready to become more or less illiquid. This is, I think, an illuminating way of expressing the liquidity theory of the rate of interest; but particularly so within the field of 'finance'. (…) In any case, given the state of expectation of the public and the policy of the banks, the rate of interest is that rate at which demand and supply of liquid resources are balanced. Saving does not come into the picture at all" (Keynes 1937b: 219 and 222).

In order to be able to formulate a stable equilibrium, the money good must be either a naturally scarce commodity (such as precious metals) or a good controlled by a public authority (such as a central bank in case of fiat money) because otherwise there would be no check against a (hyper)inflationary increase of nominal income (see e.g. Heise 1992: 290ff.). The zero (or negligible) elastictity of production of the money good is, thus, a precondition for the unit of account not to be stripped of its function as medium of deferred payments. The zero (or negligible) elasticity of substitution of money, on the other hand, is the indication of the peculiar status of the most liquid asset – money – in an economy based on nominal obligations instead of exchange activities.

But how does that relate to the acceptance or refutation of Walras' law in markets? Walras' law is based on the idea of the supply of initial endowments in order to demand a different bundle of commodities according to utility maximisation principles. In a genuine monetary economy based on nominal obligations, however, the (degree of) utilization of initial endowments is determined by the expectations to settle obligations, including pre-fixed interest payments in a future which is fundamentally uncertain. The resulting budgetary constraint allows for equilibrium on the money, credit, and commoditiy markets once expectations are fulfilled and is compatible with partial, compensating disequilibrium if expectations are not met. However, this accountancy truism is not to be confused with Walras' law simply because in a genuine monetary economy, a labour market does not exist as an operating supply and demand mechanism adjusting according to real rewards (i.e. real wages; see e.g. Lavoie 2014: 275, Seccareccia 1991). The existence of such a market would presume that the share of income being rewarded to labour (and, *pari passu*, the share of income being rewarded to capital) could be fixed in advance – such would be the vision of what Keynes termed 'real-wage', 'cooperative', or 'neutral economy' (see Keynes 1933b, Keynes 1933c) corresponding to the pre-analytic vision of an exchange economy. In an 'entrepreneur' or 'money wage economy' "...that we actually live today" (Keynes 1993b: 78), however, employment is not determined by an adjustment of real wages to supply-demand discrepancies as declared by Walras' law, but by the conformity of expected aggregate demand (ultimately depending on the propensity to consume and the liquidity preference of wealth owners) and aggregate supply (ultimately depending on technological conditions) on the one hand and on the other hand the willingness on the part of the labourer to work at the ruling nominal wage rate.[216] The amount of employment provided by companies and the amount of employment supplied by labourers may coincidentally become equal, yet there is no operational mechanism (i.e. no market) based on a re-adjustment of real remuneration rates that would automatically close a potential gap between job offers from companies and employment offers from labourers as implied by Walras' law (see e.g. Stockhammer 2012: 167). A stable position of the economy including cleared money, credit and commodity markets, and excess labour supply[217] (i.e. unemployment) would merely need the assumption of fulfilled revenue expectations on the part of the companies and of price level or inflation expectations on the part of the wealth owners and labourers.

Formal digression

The stylised Post Keynesian model presented here is an elaboration of Setterfield (2006), Heise (2008) and Pusch/Heise (2010). It comprises 10 structural, behavioural and definitional equations. The structural equations depict the Post Keynesian core of the model, the behavioural equations refer to empirically grounded descriptions of behaviour of macroeconomic actors (e.g. the policy rule of the Central Bank) which might be subject to

[216] For a detailed discussion see Davidson (1994: 164ff.); Davidson (2009: 68ff.). Of course, the 'ruling' nominal wage rate needs to be explained. Among other factors, inflation expectations, the actual unemployment rate and the institutional imprint of the collective bargaining system are very likely to play a determining role. However, as the nominal wage rate will be fixed before the production process starts, analytically it can be taken as exogenously given. This is no concession to any 'rigid wage' arguments of unemployment because flexible (i.e. falling in case of unemployment) nominal wages do not causally determine real wages (as would be necessary for the argument). Rather the rigidity of nominal wage rates in the face of unemployment is a necessary feature ('nominal anchor') of a genuine monetary economy in order to guarantee stability (see Herr 2009).

[217] We could also envisage excess labour demand (as during the 1960s in West Germany), but there are good reasons to believe that a situation of excess labour supply is more common in mature economies.

changes and, in any case, does not reflect the paradigmatic core. We start with the demand equation:

$$D_t = \alpha(\bar{w}, I_t, \overline{m}, \overline{G}, L_t), \quad (1)$$

where D is the value of aggregate demand, which evolves depending on (given) nominal wages $\bar{w}$, nominal private investment outlays I, the (given) investment multiplier $\overline{m}$, (given) governmental spending $\overline{G}$ and labour employed L.

The supply relation is:

$$Z_t = \beta(\bar{w}, \overline{T}, L_t). \quad (2)$$

Z is the value of aggregate supply. $\overline{T}$ denotes (given) technology. The next equation is an equilibrium condition:

$$D_t \equiv Z_t. \quad (3)$$

The price level p depends on the nominal (given) wage rate $\bar{w}$, given technology and a given mark-up $\bar{\pi}$:

$$p_t = \gamma(\bar{w}, \overline{T}, \bar{\pi}). \quad (4)$$

The model also includes a relation for the output gap:

$$Y_t^{gap} = Y_t - Y_{Trend}, \quad (5)$$

where Y is real income and Y_{Trend} is (given) trend income. Real income

$$Y_t = \theta(\overline{K}, L_t, \overline{T}) \quad (6)$$

is depending on production factors and technology. L is the level of employment determined by eq. (3), K is the (given) stock of real capital. The next equation describes nominal private investment outlays:

$$I_t = \lambda(i_t, \overline{E}) \qquad (7)$$

which depends on a (given) schedule of expected profit rates $\overline{E}$ and the long-term interest rate i. The latter is determined by the following:

$$i_t = \mu(i_t^{CB}, \overline{LP}). \qquad (8)$$

Here the Central Bank's instrument variable i_t^{CB} comes in as well as the (given) schedule of liquidity preferences $\overline{LP}$.

Lastly we give a behavioural equation for the CB's interest rate:

$$i_t^{CB} = \phi(p_t^{gap}, Y_t^{gap}) \qquad (9)$$

which depends on the price gap p^{gap} and the output gap. The price gap is defined by

$$p_t^{gap} = p_t - p^*, \qquad (10)$$

where p stands for the actual price level and p^* is the (given) targeted price level[218].

The model comprises an aggregate demand-aggregate supply section (eq. 1–3) determining the equilibrium employment level, an ordinary production function (eq. 6), mark-up pricing (eq. 4), a (Taylor-rule) monetary reaction function (eq. 9–10 and 5) portraying the money and credit market and endogenously (and only implictly) determining the quantity of money and a Keynesian investment function (eq. 7). The model is distinctly Post Keynesian in nature, as the employment level depends on the propensity

[218] Commonly, eq. (4) and (10) are expressed in rates of change (i.e. inflation rates and rates of change of wages). For the sake of simplicity, levels (i.e. price levels and wage rates) are used here.

to consume, the incentive to invest, the nature of long-term expectations and liquidity preference considerations (see Keynes (1936: 250)), money is endogenously created and nominal investment outlays ('finance'; see footnote 215) generate the nominal obligations on which a monetary economy is based.

As the model comprises 10 unkowns and 10 equations, it is strictly solvable. However, we need to realize that equilibrium employment L_t determined in the aggregate demand-aggregate supply section merely explains the aggregate employment demand by firms given their demand expectations are met. In order to understand whether such equilibrium employment demand matches the supply of labour provided by households, we either have to assume a given amount of labour brought forward at the ruling nominal wage rate (irrespective of what the real wage rate will turn out to be) or, as will be done here, we assume a behavioural function of labour supply L_S dependend on the given wage rate and an expected price level p_e:

$$L_S = \lambda(p_e, \overline{w}) \tag{11}$$

In order to satisfy the conditions of expectational equilibrium and the conditions of Walras's law, we need to extend the model by two more equations:

$$p_e = p_t \tag{12}$$

and

$$L_S = L_t \tag{13}$$

Now, our model comprises 12 unkowns and 13 equations and is, hence, over-determined. However, that means – assuming expectational equilibrium (i.e. the fullfillment of eq. (12) and the fullfillment of profit expectations in eq. (7)) as stability criterium – that Walras' law (eq. (13)) cannot hold in an economy as depicted by the above described model[219].

---

[219] It should be clear that eq. (13) may be fullfilled accidentally, if the profit expectations

5. Conclusion

It has been argued that the validity of Walras' law rests on the pre-analytic vision of the economic system being an exchange economy. Taking for granted the intertemporal exchange of initial endowments as a basic constituent, the ensuing budgetary constraints and accounting truism render a situation of dis-equilibrium-equilibrium impossible. Walras' law is inescapable, general equilibrium (i.e. a simultaneous equilibrium on every market) is the necessary long-run centre of gravity in an exchange economy[220]; partial disequilibrium on single markets, while possible (and very likely), is compensated by partial disequilibrium in other markets.

Any refutation of Walras' law has, thus, to rely on a different pre-analytic vision. We presetend such an alternative based on creditor-debtor-relationships as a basic constituent. In this vision, the decision to part with liquid means for a specified period of time (i.e. creating credit) explains the degree of factor utilization in order to generate (nominal) income sufficient to repay interest-bearing obligations. The ensuing budgetary constraints and accounting truism maintain the general rule ('law') that money, credit and commodity markets will simultaneously clear once expectations are fulfilled. To turn this statement into a re-affirmation of Walras' law would assume that expectations are not merely fulfilled but take a magnitude that is compatible with the exact absorbtion of the labour supplied at the ruling nominal wage rate (i.e. full employment). Though this may coincidentally be the case, there is no operative mechanism in a monetary economy to bring it about automatically as Walras' law would require – therefore, a Walrasian general equilibrium[221] can only be the random outcome in a genuine monetary economy, but is inapplicable as a generally binding budgetary constraint and accountancy truism.

---

of firms and price expectations by labourers are such that the derived equilibrium employment L_t and labour supply L_s happen to turn out identical. However such an equality cannot be a necessary conditional constraint to our model.

[220] This is not to deny stability and uniqueness problems as demonstrated by complexity economics and the Sonnenschein-Mantel-Debreu theorem; see e.g. Kirman (2004).

[221] It may be arguable whether this would constitute a 'Walrasian' general equilibrium as it would still not be based on an exchange economy vision.

Walras' law epitomizes a theoretical understanding of economic activity which does not allow for a 'general glut' of commodities and 'involuntary unemployment' as equilibrium outcomes. Any economic paradigm which attempts to challenge this heuristic dimension must reject Walras' law. The refutation of Walras' law, therefore, lies at the root of heterodox scientific research programmes and, as demonstrated, must replace the common pre-analytic vision of an exchange economy. Keynes' vision of a genuine monetary economy, as proposed here, is an adeuqate candidate.

References

Arrow, K.J., Hahn, F.H. (1971); General Competitive Analysis, San Francisco (: Holden-Day)

Baisch, H., Kuhn, W. (2001); Risikowirtschaft. Eigen- und Fremdfinanzierung im gesamtwirtschaftlichen Kontext, Berlin (: Duncker und Humblodt)

Becker, G. S., Baumol, W.J. (1952); The Classical Monetary Theory: The Outcome of the Discussion; in: Economica, Vol. 19, No.76, pp. 355 - 376

Clower, R. W. (1965); The Keynesian Counter-Revolution: A Theoretical Appraisal; in: Hahn, F.H., Brechling, F.P.R. (eds.); The Theory of Interest Rates, London (: Macmillan), pp. 103 – 125

Coddington, A. (1976); Keynesian Economics: The Search for First Principles; Journal of Economic Literature, Vol. 14, pp. 1258 – 1273

Davidson, P. (1984); Reviving Keynes's revolution; in: Journal of Post Keynesian Economics, Vol. 6, No. 4, pp. 561 – 575

Davidson, P. (1994); Post Keynesian Macroeconomic Theory; Aldershot (: Edward Elgar)

Davidson, P. (1996); What are the Essential Elements of Post Keynesian Monetary Theory? in: Deleplace, G., Nell, E.J. (eds.); Money in Motion. The Post Keynesian and Circulation Approaches, Houndsmill (: Macmillan), pp. 48 - 69

Davidson, P. (2003); Setting the record straight on *A History of Post Keynesian Economics*; in: Journal of Post Keynesian Economics, Vol. 26, No.2, pp. 245 - 272

Davidson, P. (2009); John Maynard Keynes, Houndsmill (: Palgrave Macmillan)

Davidson, P. (2015); What was the primary factor encouraging mainstream economiststo marginalize post Keynesian theory?; in: Journal of Post Keynesian Economics, Vol. 37, No.3, pp. 369 - 383

Edwards, J.R. (1985); Effective Demand Failure: Critique of an Anti-Monetary Theory; in: South African Journal of Economics, Vol. 53, No. 2, pp. 124 – 140

Elsner, W. (2012); Microeconomics of Interactive Economies, Cheltenham (: Edward Elgar)

Gale, D. (1983); Money: in disequilibrium, Cambridge (: University Press)

Gul, F., Stacchetti, E. (1999); Walrasian Equilibrium with Gross Substitutes; in: Journal of Economic Theory, Vol. 87, pp. 95 - 124

Hahn, F.H. (1973); On transaction costs, inessential economies and money; in: Review of Economic Studies, Vol. 40, pp. 449 - 461

Hahn, F.H. (1977); Keynesian Economics and General Equilibrium Theory: Reflections on Some Current Debates; in: Harcourt, G.C. (ed.); The Microeconomic Foundations of Macroeconomics, London (:Palgrave Macmillan), pp. 25 – 40

Heise, A. (1991); Tauschwirtschaft und Geldökonomie. Historiographie, Dogmengeschichte und positive Theorie der monetären Produktion, Frankfurt (: Peter Lang)

Heise, A. (1992); Commercial banks in macroeconomic theory, in: Journal of Post Keynesian Economics, Vol. 14, No. 3, pp. 285 – 296

Heise, A. (2008); Economic Governance and Employment : Policy, Polity and Politics of Economic Rise and Decline, Münster: Lit Verlag

Heise, A. (2014); The Future of Economics in a Lakatos-Bourdieu Framework; in: International Journal of Political Economy, Vol. 43, No. 3, pp. 70 - 93

Herr, H. (2009); The labour market in a Keynesian economic regime: theoretical debate and empirical findings; in: Cambridge Journal of Economics, Vol. 33, No.1, pp. 949 – 965

Kant, I. (1781/1983); Kritik der reinen Vernunft, Vol.1, Darmstadt (:Wissenschaftliche Buchgesellschaft)

Keynes, J.M. (1933a); A Monetary Theory of Production; in: Der Stand und die nächste Zukunft der Konjunkturforschung: Festschrift für Arthur Spiethoff, München; citied after: Collected Writings of John Maynard Keynes ed. by Donald Moggridge, Vol. XIII, London (: Macmillan) 1973, pp. 408 – 411

Keynes, J.M. (1933b); The Distinction between a Co-operative Economy and an Entrepreneur Economy (1933); in: Collected Writings of John Maynard Keynes ed. by Donald Moggridge, Vol. XXIX, London (: Macmillan) 1979, pp. 76 – 87

Keynes, J.M. (1933c); The Charactereistics of an Entrepreneur Economy (1933); in: Collected Writings of John Maynard Keynes ed. by Donald Moggridge, Vol. XXIX, London (: Macmillan) 1979, pp. 87 - 101

Keynes, J.M. (1935); Letter to George Bernard Shaw of 1st of January 1935; in: Collected Writings of John Maynard Keynes ed. by Donald Moggridge, Vol. XIII, London (: Macmillan) 1973, pp. 492 – 493

Keynes, J.M. (1936); General Theory of Employment, Interest and Money, London

Keynes, J.M. (1937a); Alternative Theories of the Rate of Interest; in: Economic Journal, Vol. 47, No. 2; cited after: Collected Writings of John Maynard Keynes ed. by Donald Moggridge, Vol. XIV, London (: Macmillan) 1973, pp. 201 - 215

Keynes, J.M. (1937b); The ‚Ex Ante' Theory of the Rate of Interest; in: Economic Journal, Vol. 47, No. 4; cited after: Collected Writings of John Maynard Keynes ed. by Donald Moggridge, Vol. XIV, London (: Macmillan) 1973, pp. 215 – 223

Keynes, J.M. (1937c); The General Theory of Employment; in: Quarterly Journal of Economics, Vol. 51; cited after: Collected Writings of

John Maynard Keynes ed. by Donald Moggridge, Vol. XIV, London (: Macmillan) 1973, pp. 109 – 123

Kirman, A. (1989); The Intrinsic Limits of Modern Economic Theory: The Emperor has No Clothes; in: Economic Journal, Vol. 91, Issue 325, pp. 126 - 139

Kirman, A. (2004); Economics and Complexity; in: Advances in Complex Systems, Vol. 7, pp. 139 – 155

Laidler, D. (1990); Taking Money Seriously and Other Essays, Cambridge,MA (:MIT Press)

Lavoie, M. (2014); Post-Keynesian Economics. New Foundations, Cheltenham (: Edward Elgar)

Leijonhufvud, A. (1968); On Keynesian Economics and the Economics of Keynes, Oxford (:University Press)

Malinvaud, E. (1977); The Theory of Unemployment Reconsidered, Oxford (:University Press)

Minsky, H.P. (1996); The Essential Characteristics of Post Keynesian Economics; in: Deleplace, G., Nell, E.J. (eds.); Money in Motion. The Post Keynesian and Circulation Approaches, Houndsmill (: Macmillan), pp. 70 - 88

Palley, T. (1998); Walras' Law and Keynesian Macroeconomics; in: Australian Economics Papers, Vol. 37, No.3, pp. 330 – 340

Patinkin, D. (1987); Walras' Law, WIDER Working Paper No.13, Helsinki

Pusch, T., Heise, A. (2010); Central banks, trade unions, and reputation - is there room for an expansionist maneuver in the European Union?, in: Journal of Post Keynesian Economics, Vol. 33, No. 1, pp. 105-126

Rhodes, J.R. (1984); Walras' Law and Clower's Inequality; in: Australian Economic Papers, Vol. 23, pp. 112 – 122

Rogers, C. (1989); Money, Interest and Capital: A Study in the Foundations of Monetary Theory, Cambridge (:University Press)

Sargent, T.J. (1979); Macroeconomic Theory, New York (: Academic Press)

Seccareccia, M. (1991); An alternative to labour-market orthodoxy: the post-Keynesian/institutionalist view; in: Review of Political Economy, Vol. 3. No.1, pp. 43 – 61

Setterfield, M (2006). Effective demand and endogeneous money in a pathdependent economy: towards a "Moorian" credit supply curve – and a reconciliation between horizontalists and structuralists?, in: Setterfield, M.; Complexity, Endogenous Money And Macroeconomic Theory : essays in honour of Basil J. Moore, Cheltenham (: Edward Elgar), pp.

Steiger, O. (ed.) (2008); Property Economics. Property Rights, Creditor's Money and the Foundation of the Economy, Marburg (: Metropolis)

Stockhammer, E. (2012); Entry: Employment; in: The Elgar Companion to Post Keynesian Economics ed. by J.E. King, Cheltenham (: Edward Elgar), pp. 166 - 170

Sweezy, P.M. (1947); John Maynard Keynes; in: Harris, S.E. (ed.); The New Economics, London, pp.

Tunez Area, N. (2015); The Validity of Walras' Law in a Monetary Exchange Economy: Money, Prices and the Integration of Monetary and Value Theory; in: Iberian Journal of the History of Economic Thought, Vol. 2, No.2, pp. 101 – 114

Eight

Whither economic complexity? A new heterodox economic paradigm or just another variation within the mainstream?*

1. Introduction

Economics is in considerable disarray. Neoclassical orthodoxy still remains the 'normal science' providing the foundation for economic education, yet many economists have claimed that its scientific research programme as a problem-solving tool is no longer at the cutting-edge (see e.g., Colander,Holt and Rosser 2004; Holt,Rosser,and Colander 2011; Arthur 2013).

After the recent global financial crisis, the time seemed right for a scientific overhaul of economics under the heading of 'new economic thinking', an idea promoted as much by economists unhappy with the state of the discipline as by economics students unwilling to learn something irrelevant for the real world; and by economic and business practitioners (and patrons) who sponsored research that, in the past, few were willing to support financially.

It seems obvious that heterodox economics—the scientific community long critical of the state of the discipline and persisently demanding a 'new economic thinking—was a natural candidate for a scientific research programme or paradigm to assume the spotlight. However, heterodox economics is a blurred description of a scientific paradigm comprising quite different thought collectives, and is based on very shaky analytical grounds (see e.g. Mearman 2012).

* Originally published: Int. J. Pluralism and Economics Education, Vol. 8, No. 2, 2017, 115 – 129(https://www.inderscience.com/jhome.php?jcode=ijpee)

In this paper we will closely examine a scientific research programme often cited as one whose time has come: complexity economics (see e.g., Buchanan 2004; Colander 2003; Beinhocker 2006; Davis 2008; Roos 2015). Before we describe the paradigmatic foundations of complexity economics and arrange them in the context of the orthodox/heterodox divide, we need to explain our understanding of the concept of a paradigm and clarify what makes a paradigm orthodox or heterodox and why it is important to so classify it. The paper will conclude with a statement about the paradigmatical position of complexity economics and its significance for the future of the economic discipline.

2. Why should we care about the orthodoxy/heterodoxy divide?

When Thomas Kuhn's *The Structure of Scientific Revolutions* was first published in 1962 (Kuhn 1962), it was met with great interest by many economists who believed that Piero Sraffa's *Production of Commodities by Means of Commodities* (Sraffa 1960) heralded the advent of a paradigmatic shift in economics, along with renewed interest in John Maynard Keynes's writings and the sudden discussion about 'what Keynes really meant' (see e.g. Clower 1965, Coddington 1974).[222] Although this 'Keynesian revolution' never occured, the late 1960s and early 1970s saw, at least, the rise of paradigmatic approaches considering themselves clearly in opposition to the neoclassical mainstream (Fine 1997, p. 148, Lee 2009, Heise, Thieme 2016). While the label 'heterodoxy' became popular only later, this oppositional perspective taken by, among others, Marxian, Sraffian, Post Keynesian and Radical economists established the dualistic divide between orthodox or mainstream economists on one side and heterodox or non-mainstream economists on the other. Despite being criticized for ignoring too many shades in between—e.g. dissenters within the mainstream or mainstream heterodoxy, new heterodoxy and traditional heterodoxy (see Lavoie 2014, p. 8f.; Davis 2008)—or for being too static,

[222] According to Kuhn, a scientific revolution can be triggered either by the proof of internal theoretical inconsistencies within the mainstream or by empirical falsification. Yet, it will lose its dominant position only if an alternative is available to replace it. The Sraffian critique was considered just such a proof of internal theoretical inconsistencies and the (post) Keynesian theory as the necessary alternative.

this dualistic division is useful in order to distinguish between a meaningful pluralism which builds on clear paradigmatic oppostion and less meaningful variation, multitude or specialisation which can be achieved within paradigmatic monism (see Heise 2017a).

The distinction between orthodoxy and heterodoxy and the classification of paradigms as belonging either to the one or the other is not only interesting from a philosophical point of view, but it is also important in order to understand the development of a discipline: if in the course of events a heterodox paradigm becomes dominant (and, thus, assumes a position that would be called 'orthodoxy' or 'mainstream' henceforth), this would truly mark a paradigmatic revolution—something the history of the economics discipline has yet to experience despite assertions to the contrary.[223] Moreover, if the pluralism campaign finally gains momentum and results, for example, in institutional support for otherwise neglected or downplayed heterodox paradigms, then in order to prevent free-rider behaviour it must be clear which paradigms can rightly claim to be heterodox and which cannot.[224]

3. Scientific Paradigm – weasel word or concept of substance?

The orthodoxy/heterodoxy divide rests on the distinction between different scientific paradigms which themsevles are based on inherent incompatibilities and incommensurabilities framing the oppositional perspective of the dualism. Taking Kuhn's (1962, p. 10) definition of a scientific paradigm as "universally recognized scientific achievements that, for a time, provide model problems and solutions for a community of practitioners", one is left without clear orientation or concise delineation. While the

[223] Best known, of course, is the 'marginalist revolution' which marked a radical methodical shift, but involved no clear rejection of the 'classical' ontology— more on this in the next section. And the 'Keynesian revolution', as another contender, never really was (see e.g. Blaug 1991; Laidler 1999; Hutton 2001).

[224] One referee criticized this as a 'Jacobinian statement', insinuating the repressive orientation of the 'Jacobin Club' during the French Revolution; however, from a pluralistic perspective it means to secure the effectiveness of pluralisation of a discipline which is characterized by a monistic mainstream rather than to argue in favor of a 'reign of terror' of the heterodox.

openess and flexibilty of the concept may, on the one hand, have been crucial for its career in the philosophy of science, they make it difficult, on the other hand, to apply it distinctively. Therefore, in order to avoid rendering it a scientific weasel word[225], we will borrow substance from a related concept which, moreover, appears better suited to the social sciences: Imre Lakatos's scientific research programmes (see Lakatos 1976).

Using Lakatos' concept of scientific research programmes (SRP) as a framework, we can identify the dimensions that constitute a scientific paradigm: (1) **methodical:** i.e. a methodology, and related research methods considered acceptable, or 'scientific', and that direct the research perspective (e.g. static-equilibrium or dynamic-disequilibrium oriented); (2) **epistemological:** which centres around a series of core assumptions (axioms) that underlie the models or theories comprising a paradigm. This core is surrounded by a protective belt of auxiliary assumptions which, if they are varied, are responsible for an epistemological variation within a paradigm; and, most importantly, the (3) **heuristic (or ontological),** which builds on ('ex ante' synthetic[226]) pre-analytic visions, 'model-solution' or 'ideal types'. They form postulates correlating with the core assumptions of the epistemological dimension, that must be accepted ('positive heuristics') or, at least, not called into question ('negative heuristics') if allegiance to a paradigm is to be maintained.

The heuristic dimension is critical as it frames a shared belief of the adherents of a paradigm about the nature of the subject under investigation. The nature of the subject is to be distinguished from the perspective from which the subject will be investigated. More concretely: if the economic system is onotologically understood as primarily involving intertemporal exchange relations ('market economy'), this does not exclude the possibility of different perspectives which will be addressed in the epistemological or

---

[225] As Hayek (1988: 116) wrote: „As a weasel is alleged to be able to empty an egg without leaving a visible sign, so can these words deprive of content any term to which they are prefixed while seemingly leaving them untouched."

[226] Immanuel Kant, the German philosopher, distinguishes between analytic and synthetic judgements. Analytic judgements are contained within the object in question; they do not bring us any new knowledge (e.g. the 'gray horse' is white); synthetic judgements, by contrast, provide us with new knowledge, since they are not already contained within the object (e.g. 'the horse eats grass').

methodical dimensions: The assumption of either strictly rational or 'bounded rational' choices at an epistemological level is not inconsistent with a common heuristic, nor is the focus on either static or dynamic properties of a complex, evolving system at a methodological level.

Table 11: Orthodoxy and Heterodoxy

<table>
<tr><th colspan="3">Heuristic B, C, D</th><th colspan="2">Heuristic A</th></tr>
<tr><th colspan="3">Non-Mainstream</th><th colspan="2">Mainstream</th></tr>
<tr><td rowspan="3">Theory J</td><td rowspan="3">Theory I</td><td>Theory F</td><td>Theory D</td><td>Theory A</td></tr>
<tr><td>Theory G</td><td rowspan="2">Theory E</td><td>Theory B</td></tr>
<tr><td>Theory H</td><td>Theory C</td></tr>
<tr><th colspan="3">Heterodoxy</th><th>Dissenter</th><th>Orthodoxy</th></tr>
</table>

Note: Capital letters A – J represent different heuristics or theories such as 'intertemporal exchange' or 'nominal obligations based relations' for different heuristics or 'neo-Keynesian theory', 'post-Keynesian theory' or 'neo-Ricaridanism' for different theories.

Theories and models that share the same methodical, epistemological and heuristic dimensions can, thus, be said to form a common paradigm ; theories and models that differ in one or more of these dimensions can be regarded as forming different paradigms. Yet, however fierce the intellectual competition may be between paradigms that differ in the epistemological and methodical dimensions, as long as they share the same (at least negative) heuristic, i.e. as long as they are based on the same pre-analytic vision, they could be seen as compatible and commensurable. In terms of the previously mentioned orthodoxy/heterodoxy divide, all paradigms that are based on the same pre-analytic vision as the dominant paradigm constituting the 'normal science' of a discipline would be part of the wider mainstream, although regarded perhaps as 'dissenters' from the orthodoxy (see Table 11).

Sometimes, the broader conjunction of paradigms sharing the same heuristic dimension as the dominant one is called 'orthodoxy' and the narrower one 'mainstream' (see e.g. Lavoie 2014, p. 8f, refering to Backhouse). I have opted for the opposite naming because it better complies with the common usage of 'orthodoxy' as the pure doctrine to be found, for instance, in textbooks, while 'mainstream' commonly indicates a broader current (see Dequech 2012, p. 354)[227].

Let's put some flesh on the bones by considering a variety of theoretical thought collectives: it appears safe to say that the Dynamic Stochastic General Equilibrium (DSGE) constitutes the macro-economic orthodoxy (see Table 11). It is an amalgam of New Classical Economics and neo-Keynesianism which is based on the same core assumptions of rationality, ergodicity, and substitutionality exhibiting the hallmarks of social exchange theory (see e.g. Davidson 1984; Davidson 2007) at the epistemological level. In addition, the DSGE relies exclusively on formal-mathematical, positivist deductive reductionism (see Lawson 2006) at the methodical level. Over the course of the so-called 'empirical turn' during the past three decades, this constellation of elements has been combined with sophisticated systems of micro and macroeconometrics, as well as experimental designs that harness approaches used in the natural sciences, such as physics and chemistry (see Schmidt/aus dem Moore 2010).

The postulates of (long-term) stability, optimality and neutrality (Walras's Law, monetary neutrality, policy inefficiency), which are operational *a priori* in the core assumptions of DSGE theory, guide the 'ideal solution' (*Musterlösungen*) at the ontological level, thus functioning as a metric for negative heuristics, i.e. the research approaches not to be called into question. Methodically, DSGE models can be said to occupy an allocational perspective ('constrained optimisation'). The ostensibly large differences

[227] There exists some cognitive disagreement about the present state of economics. While most claim a strong dominance of the neoclassical orthodoxy (e.g. Miller 2012; Marglin 2010), others argue a changing face of mainstream economics towards a multi-varied mainstream including the neoclassical orthodxy aside a multitude of dissenters (see e.g. Colander, Holt and Rosser 2004; Davis 2006; Coyle 2007). However, there appears to be no doubt about the marginalisation of heterodox economics over the past two to three decades (see e.g. Heise and Thieme 2016; Rochon and Docherty 2012).

in forecasts delivered by the hyperstable equilibrium models of New Classical Economics compared with the dis-equilibrium models of standard Keynesianism and neo-Keynesianism (i.e. Theories A, B and C in Table 11) are attributable to modified assumptions within the 'protective belt' (e.g. concerning adjustment speeds, price and quantity rigidities, expectation formation, etc.), yet these differences are not(!) evidence of divergent paradigmatic origins[228].

Behavioural economics, assuming that this rather new approach is given the status of a paradigm of its own, discloses little about its ontological basis. The fact that prominent protagonists for this paradigm hasten to claim alliance with and allegiance to the DSGE orthodoxy[229] suggests that they share (positive heuristic) or, at least, do not oppose (negative heuristic) the real exchange ontology of the DSGE paradigm. If one still maintains a paradigmatic distinction from the orthodoxy, differences must be found either at the methodical or epistemological levels. Indeed, the experimental character of behavioural economics and the rejection of the rationality axiom (as an outcome of the experiments as much as a behav-

---

[228] Accordingly, both approaches are found in modern textbooks, where a distinction is made between short-term forecasts (the neo-Keynesian model) and long-term forecasts (the neoclassical model). For more, see Abel/Bernanke (2005); and Blanchard (2006).

[229] See e.g. Smith (2003, p. 505); Cartwright (2011, p. 4). Sometimes, behavioural economics has been rated among the heterodox paradigms (e.g. Lavoie 2014, p. 8; Earl and Peng 2012, p. 454), either due to a very loose definition of heterodoxy or hints of two possible factions of behavioural economists – 'old' and 'new'. Earl and Peng (2012, p. 454) describe how 'new' behavioural economics "has been accepted purely because it does not violate the hard core of the mainstream research program, unlike the earlier approach for which Herbert Simon was awarded the 1978 Nobel Prize in Economics. Instead of following Simon by emphasizing the challenges of complex decision-making environments and advocating a view of choice based upon aspiration levels, decision rules and satisficing, new behavioural economics focuses largely on using mainstream tools, modified by incorporating empirically-grounded 'heuristics and biases' to deal with behavioural anomalies that mainstream economists otherwise found hard to admit." It is in this vein that Jefferson and King (2010, p. 215) state: "Thus, there is some ongoing tension as to whether behavioral economics is a challenge to mainstream economics or a set of Lakatosian 'anomalies' waiting to be synthesized into mainstream analysis." This is what appears to have happens particularily to behavioural macroeconomics (see Jefferson and King 2010, p. 216ff.)

ioural assumption) can be seen as methodically and epistemologically different enough to grant it a paradigmatic status on its own—however, not one in opposition to the orthodoxy but rather a dissenter as in Table 11.

Post Keynesianism, as a third example, comprises different Kaleckian, Sraffian and Fundamentalist approaches (i.e. Theories F,G and H in Table 11). These all, by and large, share the methodical dimension with the orthodoxy, yet reject the rationality, substitutionality and ergodicity axioms at the epistemological level and, crucially, draw on a different pre-analytic vision: the economic system is not primarily understood as a network of (real and symmetric) exchange relations but as a system based on (asymmetric and nominal) obligations or power relations (see Heise 2017b). Ontologically, Post Keynesianism claims a social provisioning perspective[230]. Therefore, it surely forms not only a distinct paradigm, but also one that clearly opposes the orthodoxy and must be rated as heterodox (see Table 11).[231]

4. Complexity economics – its paradigmatical substance

Although economics is often lamented to be a colonizing, imperial discipline particularily with respect to other social sciences, it has throughout its existence always borrowed from other disciplines: from history, physics, biology and informatics. Basing its methods, methodology and epistemology solidly on other sciences was usually meant to import authority and professionality. What was acceptable in the highly reputed sciences seemed good enough for economics. While the neoclassical mainstream emulates the concepts of hydraulic physics[232], complexity economics is

---

[230] "...the theory of output and employment *as a whole*..." as Keynes (1936: 293) wrote in the *General Theory*. For more on the heterodox concept of social provisioning see Jo (2011).

[231] Sometimes the vehemence by which leading Post Keynesians try to set themselves apart from standard or neo-Keynesians (e.g. Davidson 1992, Lavoie 2014) appears abstruse and difficult to convey—our claim that they are not only part of different paradigms but on opposing sides of the orthodoxy/heterodoxy divide might help understand this behaviour.

[232] This is probably best illustrated by the 'Monetary National Income Analogue Computer' (MONIAC) constructed by Alban W. Phillips and displayed at the University of Cambridge.

part of an transdisciplinary project of complexity sciences covering physics, biology, chemistry and informatics[233]; some already talk of this as a revolution in science from the predominant **reductionist** approach of the past to **emergentism** as the future of science (see Fromm 2004, p. 4ff).

'Complexity' and 'complex systems' are ill-defined terms; Perona (2007), accordingly, speaks of 'the confused state of complexity economics'. Despite that some ingredients seem to be uncontroversial, the ontological and epistemological character of complexity economics is anything but clear and uniform. Let's start with the less controversial ingredients (see e.g. Durlauf 2012; Arthur 2013; Roos 2015):

- a large number of heterogenous interacting agents
- self-organisation, self-adaptability
- non-linear dynamics
- non-equilibrium

These ingredients form the system properties of emergence and (theoretical) unpredicatability, which again, appear uncontroversial[234]. 'Emergence' means a system property which combines determinacy (due to the assumed existence of interconnections between all system elements) with downward causation (i.e. the assumption that macro-level outcomes restrict micro-level behaviour and, thus, cannot be deduced entirely from micro-level properties), which therefore, gives rise to unpredictability (e.g. Christen and Franklin 2002).

However, two distinct approaches can be broadly identified in the literature which differ in focus and accentuation (e.g. Bronk 2011, p. 1) **'Epistemological complexity'** concentrates on the non-linear interconnections of heterogenous interacting agents resulting in emergent macro-outcomes

---

[233] A major cornerstone in the development of complexity science was the foundation of the Santa Fe Institute (SFI) in 1984 which brought together a number of leading scientists from the natural sciences as well as the social sciences and humanities. The research agenda was about 'complex adaptive systems' in which systems could be economic, biological, physical, chemical or social.

[234] Theoretical, as opposed to inductive unpredictability (for the difference see Christen and Franklin 2002), simply means that from the bare axiomatic (micro) structure of a theory, no unique macro outcome can be predicted.

at the epistemological level. As the system is assumed to be closed and (macro)determinate at the ontological level, complexity translates in 'complicatedness':

> *"It is a vision that sees the economy as so complicated that simple analytical models of the aggregate economy—models that can be specified in a set of analytically solvable equations— are not likely to be helpful in understanding many of the issues that economists want to address"* (Holt, Rosser and Colander 2011, p. 358).

In contrast to neoclassical orthodoxy, this school of complexity economics rejects reductionist constraint optimisation at the methodical level as too simplistic and replaces it with an emergentism[235] that relies on algorithmic computation rather than linear optimisation. As science is based on a reduction of the complexities of reality, epistemological complexity economists praise neoclassical economics for their historical merits in the formation of the discipline (see Foster 2005, p. 881) but claim that deductive reductionism has eliminated too many essential features of economic reality to still be of use: Ockham's razor has simply been too sharp. Although, as far as I am aware, this has never been stated explicitly; there seems no reason why complexity economics of this kind would—at the macroeconomic level – reject Walras' law[236] since it shares the same pre-analytic vision with the orthodoxy as a heuristic device.

2) **'Ontological complexity', as the second distinct approach,** blows up the monistic vision of economic reality as a closed system in favour of an open system ontology which enhances emergence towards contingency[237]. Contingency relates to a representation of reality which is non-deterministic and non-ergodic in the sense that the future occurrence of a variable

---

[235] Emergentism entails the methodical proposition that a system is "exhibiting wholes that are in some way greater than the sum of their parts" (Rosser 2012, p. 122).
[236] Vela Velupillai (2007, p. 287) asserts: "As a consequence of the S-D-M (Sonnenschein-Debreu-Mantel, A.H.) theorem, the only structural properties that have to be preserved when, say, introducing ad hoc price dynamics for a general equilibrium exchange economy, are Walras's Law and continuity."
[237] The concept of contingency originated in Niklas Luhmann's systems theory; see Provost (1986).

cannot be traced by its past developments and, thus, cannot be fully analysed and rationally expected using probability calculus because it is fundamentally uncertain. Fundamental uncertainty is not to be confused with non-predictability: As Davidson (1993; 1996) has shown, fundamental uncertainty does not need to rely on non-linear dynamics (as non-predictability), while Rosser (2006, p. 89) argues that non-predictability, unlike fundamental uncertainty, also occurs in ergodic environments—leaving it open which of the two conceptions is the more general one.

Epistemologically and methodically, both complexity conceptions follow similar routes: algorithmic, non-equilibrium modelling based on bounded rational, heterogenous and socially interacting agents engaged in intertemporal exchanges in network structures[238]. Again, it has never been made explicit how complexity economics of the ontological kind positions itself regarding the validity of Walras' law. Yet, in open, non-ergodic systems Walras' law does not necessarily hold if the pre-analytic vision is different from a real-exchange economy (see Heise 2017b; Keynes 1933a; Keynes 1933b). In this domain, the ontological kind of complexity economics remains unclear and inaccessible.

By way of summary, it should be pointed out that complexity economics forms two different paradigms that show a close 'family resemblance' (Arthur et al. 1997, p. 2) with respect to the epistemological and methodical dimensions of their respective scientific research programmes, yet do not share the same ontological basis. The two paradigms called complexity economics I and complexity economics II, for want of better names at this point[239], may have more in common (non-equilibirum orientation, algorithmic formalisation, bounded rational operation) than separating them (closed versus open, emergent versus contingent, deterministic-ergodic versus non-deterministic-non-ergodic); yet the distinction should not be

[238] Foster (2005, p. 884) highlights the importance of the network structure of the connections for complexity economics as distinct from the neoclassical orthodoxy which focuses on actors. Taking into account his belief that networks must always be seen as open systems, the complexity economics he has in mind refers to 'ontological complexity'.
[239] Rosser (2006, p. 76) also distinguishes two approaches to complexity science: broad tent and small tent complexity. However, as his distinction does not entirely conform with my distinction, I refrain from using these labels.

overlooked and may be important with respect to the orthodoxy/heterodoxy divide.

5. Complexity economics: on which side of the orthodoxy/ heterodoxy divide?

The majority of complexity economists group around the epistemological notion used, for example, by the renowned and influential Santa Fe Institute (SFI; see Peroni (2007, p. 41ff.). Authors such as Steven Durlauf, Lawrence Blume and Brian Arthur are confident about the new opportunities that complexity economics brings to economics, in addition to orthodox neoclassical economics. Nevertheless, they clearly do not see their paradigm in opposition to and, therefore, as a challenge to neoclassical economics but rather as a modernized, probably more general version of it or, perhaps more appropriately, an addition to it. As Steven Durlauf (2012, p. 45f.), longtime project leader at SFI, puts it:

> *". . . I argue that complexity thinking can enrich the way in which economists conceptualize various phenomena, but that this enrichment is complementary to current economic methodology. The claim is justified by considering a range of definitions of compelxity in order to highlight the features of complex systems that differ from conventional economic reasoning. In doing this, I reject suggestions that complexity represents a new paradigm for the social sciences".*

And Brian Arthur (2013, p. 17ff; italics in the original), one of the founders of the economics programme at SFI, focuses on the different, yet compatible perspectives of neoclassical and complexity economics (of the epistemological kind):

> *"There are two great problems in economics. One is allocation within the economy: how quantities of goods and services and their prices are determined within and across markets. This is represented by the great theories of general equilibrium, international trade, and game-theoretic analysis. The other is formation within the economy: how an economy emerges in the first place, and grows and changes structurally*

> *over time. This is represented by ideas about innovation, economic development, stuctural change, and the role of history, institutions, and governance in the economy . . . It is now clear to economists that the mathematical analysis of allocation far from covers all of economics and operates poorly with questions of formation, exploration, adaptation, and qualitative change . . . Complexity economics by contrast is very much about these questions of creation and formation of structure, and it studies the mechanisms by which these operate."*

And he adds: "Complexity economics is not a special case of neoclassical economics. On the contrary, equilibrium economics is a special case of nonequilibrium and hence complexity economics" (Arthur 2013, p. 19). A third problem, that of social provisioning, which is addressed particularly by Post Keynesian and Marxian economists and gives rise to an alternative pre-analystic vision, is neglected[240].

This appraisal goes along very well with the paradigmatical categorisation given above (see Table 2): Complexity economics I – which we will call 'mainstream complexity economics' (MCE) henceforth – is based on different epistemological and methodical foundations than neoclassical (DSGE) economics but shares by and large the same ontology. And even here, as with the differences in the epistemological and methodical dimensions, the distinction is one of perspective, not of substance. It, therefore, appears appropriate to categorise MCE as part of the mainstream, albeit as a dissenting part. This assessment is reinforced by the fact that proponents of MCE (are allowed to) publish in the most highly reputed economics journals (such as the American Economic Review, Journal of Political

[240] One referee asked why 'formation' cannot be seen as a different pre-analytic vision—making any approach which particularly adresses problems of formation heterodox. However, the problem of 'formation' as defined by Brian Arthur addresses the methodical dimension of a scientific research programme emphasizing change and adaptation focusing on dynamics and innovation, while 'allocation' emphasizes stability and equilibrium focusing on statism and optimisation. 'Formation' and 'allocation' are related to each other complementary rather than oppositionally. This is different from and unrelated to its ontological dimension pertaining to the object of inquiry. The 'complex adaptive system' of a dynamic methodical approach and the 'equilibrium system' of a static methodical approach may still be based on the same pre-analytic vision of a 'market economy' as a social exchange system as appears to be the case, at least with MCE (see Table 2).

Economy, European Economic Review, Economic Journal) which are usually not open to heterodox contributions.

Table 12: Classification of paradigms

Paradigm	Epistemological dimension (Axioms)	Methodical dimension	Ontological dimension (heuristics/ postulates)	Status
Neoclassical economics (DSGE)	• Rationality • Ergodicity • Substitutionality	• Reductionism • Linear optimization • Static-equilibrium • Empiricism • Allocational perspective	• Symmetric exchange • Closed system • Acceptance of Walras' law	Orthodox
Complexity economics I (mainstream complexity economics MCE)	• Bounded rationality • Substitutionality • Ergodicity • Heterogeneity • Non-Linearity	• Emergentism • Non-linear algorithmic computation • Non-equilibrium • Simulation • Formational perspective	• Symmetric exchange • Closed system • Acceptance of Walras' law	Dissenter within the mainstream
Complexity economics II (heterodox complexity economics HCE)	• Bounded rationality • Substitutionality • Non-Ergodicity • Heterogeneity • Non-Linearity	• Contingentism • Non-linear algorithmic computation • Non-equilibrium • Simulation • Formational perspective	• Symmetric exchange • Open system • Rejection of Walras' law	Heterodox
Post Keynesianism	• Bounded rationality • Non-substitutionality • Non-ergodicity	• Reductionism • Linear modelling • Static-equilibrium • Narrative reasoning • Empiricism • Allocational perspective	• Asymmetric obligations/ Social provisioning • Open System • Rejection of Walras' law	Heterodox

Source: Author

Complexity economics of the ontological camp shares neither the epistemological and methodical dimensions nor the ontological dimension with neoclassical economics. Whether this distinction is of substance depends primarily on the judgement whether or not the open systems claim is based on a different pre-analytic vision (including the rejection of Walras' law). As noted earlier, in this respect complexity economists of this camp remain vague and unclear[241]. However, major proponents of the ontological camp, such as Barkley Rosser Jr., Herbert Gintis and Alan Kirman, openly display their esteem for heterodox economics by engaging in academic exchanges with them, and discussing the compatibility of complexity economics with heterodox schools of thought such as Post Keynesian Economics (see e.g. Rosser 1998; Rosser 2006)[242]. Therefore, it seems appropriate to rate the ontological camp of complexity economics as heterodox and labelling them heterodox complexity economics (HCE; see Table 12). This assessment is supported by the fact that HCE proponents (are only allowed to) publish—except for particular journals specializing in features of economic formation such as the *Journal of Economic Dynamics and Control*— mainly in heterodox journals such as the *Journal of Post Keynesian Economics; the Review of Political Economy;* and the *Cambridge Journal of Economics*[243].

6. MCE, HCE and the future of economics

David Colander and Roland Kupers (2014) use the picture of the one or two mountains to tackle the question about the novelty of complexity economics: either complexity economists climb the same mountain as orthodox neoclassical economists but take a different route or, alternatively, they abandon the mountain the neoclassical economists try to climb and turn instead towards another mountain which appears more appropriate. This picture fits our analysis well: the proponents of MCE climb the neoclassical mountain (yet use a different methodical route), while the HCE

---

[241] Kirman (2016, p. 544ff.) argues that Walras did not establish a coherent mechanism to bring an out-of-equilibrium economy back into general-equilibrium. Yet, it remains unclear whether this involves the rejection of Walras' law or, merely, that Walras' law may be compatible with lasting partial disequilibria.

[242] Herbert Gintis even started off his academic career as a heterodox (radical) economist (see Katzner 2011, p. 12ff).

[243] Whether the distinctly different publication patterns of HCE proponents are voluntarily chosen or non-voluntarily enforced by the non-admission into core mainstream journals can only be revealed by the respective authors— however, the point is that HCE proponents obviously target a different epistemic community than MCE proponents.

proponents turn towards another mountain. So, as with the Keynesians, there is a mainstream and a heterodox camp of complexity economists.

How does this assessment impact on the future of the economics discipline? Primarily, one may argue that complexity economics stands a good chance of having a considerable effect: One, calls for a 'new economic thinking' are today louder than ever—certainly the recent global financial crisis can be understood as the empirical anomaly which pushed neoclassical economics into a state of crisis, and complexity economics can be seen as a potential alternative (see e.g. Colander et al. 2009; Kirman 2010; Arthur 2006); two, complexity economics is a 'sister science' to complexity theories in other disciplines including the natural sciences, lending considerable 'natural authority' to this approach; three, during the advancement of a scientific discipline, the degree of complexity (in common parlance) becomes higher—complexity science seems to be the next step in this direction in the domain of economics (but not only economics); and four, complexity economics is a highly formalized approach satisfying demands for accuracy and professionality. Moreover, since the bigger and more influential camp—MCE—does not claim to oppose neoclassical economics[244], resistance from the ranks of the orthodoxy with respect to access to economic, social and cultural capital in the field— i.e., professorships, grants, journal space, respected positions outside academia etc.—will be low.

But what does this imply for HCE and heterodox economics in general? On the one hand, it appears most likely that HCE will not succeed in truly kicking off a paradigmatic revolution in economics. At best, it will not be strictly separated from MCE and, therefore, may also secure access to the aforementioned kinds of capital. 'Family resemblance' may be as helpful in this respect as the professional cooperation of proponents of both complexity economics camps[245]. On the other hand, from the perspective of

[244] Fontana (2008) rates the methodical impact of complexity economics as revolutionary—yet, this does not make for a paradigmatic revolution ('climbing no other mountain') as long as there is no ontological opposition to orthodox neoclassical economics.
[245] Proponents of MCE and HCE, for example, often co-author articles or co-edit books. In this respect, both complexity economics camps alongside the orthodoxy/heterodoxy

heterodox economics, not much can be hoped for[246]: even if complexity economics were to rise to the state of a 'normal science' in economics, this would only pluralise the paradigmatic pathways with respect to the ontological dimension, once the formation perspective of complexity economics and the allocation perspective of neoclassical economics is broadened by a social provisioning perspective of heterodox economics. After all, there are some indications (e.g., Colander, Holt and Rosser 2010; Roos 2015) that HCE (and, to a lesser extent even MCE) is tolerant and open-minded in this repect.

---

divide are much more friendly than the two Keynesian camps on that divide (neo-Keynesianism and Post Keynesianism), which either ignore or outrightly combat each other.

[246] Keynesianism and behavioural economics may be seen as evidence of how potentially revolutionary new approaches became absorbed into the mainstream by emphasizing (and, maybe, mis-interpreting) the complementary parts and aspects of the new approach with the mainstream and by de-emphasizing its oppositional (heterodox) parts and aspects (see e.g. Rochon and Docherty 2012, p. 504ff; Fontana and Gerrard 2006). This may even have been aggrevated by using a 'stealth strategy' of not openly combating the mainstream, yet did not result in a 'Trojan Horse' victory of the heterodox (as advocated by Earl and Peng 2012) but the marginalization of the heterodox faction of the paradigm and a claim for sole representation by the mainstream faction.

References

Abel, A.B., Bernanke, B.S. (2005) *Macroeconomics*, Pearson, Boston.

Arthur, W.B. (2006) 'Out-of-Equilibrium Economics and Agent-Based-Modeling' in Tesfatsion, L., Judd, K. L. (Eds.); *Handbook of Computational Economics*, Vol.2, North Holland, Amsterdam.

Arthur, W.B. (2013) 'Complexity Economics: A Different Framework for Economic Thought,' Santa Fe Institute Working Paper No. 2013-04-012.

Backhouse, R. (2004) 'A Suggestion for Clarifying the Study of Dissent in Economics,' *Journal of the History of Economic Thought,* Vol. 26, No.2, pp. 261 – 271.

Beinhocker,E.D. (2006) *The Origin of Wealth: Evolution, Complexity, and the Radical Remaking of Economics*, Harvard Business School Press, Boston.

Blanchard, O. (2006) *Macroeconomics*, Prentice Hall, New York.

Blaug, M. (1991) 'Second Thoughts on the Keynesian Revolution' *History of Political Economy*, Vol. 23, No.2, pp. 171 – 192.

Bronk, Richard (2011) 'Epistemological Difficulties with Neoclassical Economics,' Paper presented at the Southern Economic Conference, November 20, 2011, Washington D.C.. Available at http://eprints.lse.ac.uk/39423/. Accessed: August 18, 2016.

Buchanan, M. (2004) 'It's the economy, stupid,' *New Scientist*, No. 182, pp. 34 – 37

Cartwright, E. (2011) *Behavioral Economics*, Routledge, Abingdon.

Christen, M., Franklin, L.R. (2002) 'The Concept of Emergence in Complexity Science: Finding Coherence between Theory and Practice,' *Proceedings of the Complex Systems Summer School*, SFI, Santa Fe.

Clower, R. (1965) 'The Keynesian Counter-Revolution: A Theoretical Appraisal,' in, Hahn, F.H., Brechling, F.P.R. (Eds.) *The Theory of Interest Rates*, MacMillan, London, pp. 103 – 125.

Coddington, A. (1974) What Did Keynes Really Mean? *Challenge*, Vol. 17, No.5, pp. 13 – 19.

Colander, D., Goldberg, M., Haas, A., Juselius, K., Kirman, A., Lux, T., and Sloth, B. (2009) 'The Financial Crisis and the Systematic Failure of the Economics Profession,' *Critical Review,* Vol. 21, Issue 2-3, pp. 249 – 267.

Colander, D., Holt, R.P., and Barkley Rosser Jr., J. (2004) 'The Changing Face of Mainstream Economics,' *Review of Political Economy*, Vol. 16, No. 4, pp. 485 – 499.

Colander, D., Holt, R.C.F., and Rosser, J.B. Jr. (2010) 'How to win friends and (possibly) influence mainstream economists,' *Journal of Post Keynesian Economics,* Vol. 32, No.3, pp. 397 – 408.

Coyle, D. (2007) *The Soulful Science: What Economists Really Do and Why It Matters,* Princeton University Press, Princeton.

Davidson, P. (1984) 'Reviving Keynes' Revolution,' *Journal of Post Keynesian Economics*, Vol. 6, No.4, pp. 561-575.

Davidson, P. (1992) 'Would Keynes be a New Keynesian?,' *Eastern Economic Review*, Vol. 18, No. 4, pp. 449 – 463.

Davidson, P. (1993) 'The Elephant and the Butterfly: Or Hyterisis and Post Keynesian Economics,' *Journal of Post Keynesian Economics,* Vol. 15, No.3, pp. 309 – 322.

Davidson, P. (1996) 'Reality and Economic Theory,' *Journal of Post Keynesian Economics,* Vol. 18, No.4, pp. 479 – 508.

Davidson, P. (2007) *John Maynard Keynes*, Palgrave MacMillan, Basingstoke.

Davis, J. B. (2006) 'The Turn in Economics: Neoclassical Dominance to Mainstream Pluralism?', *Journal of Institutional Economics*, vol. 2, issue. 1, pp. 1-20.

Davis, J.B. (2008) 'The turn in recent economics and return of orthodoxy,' *Cambridge Journal of Economics*, Vol. 32, No.3, pp. 349 – 366.

Dequech, D. (2012) 'Post Keynesianism, Heterodoxy and Mainstream Economics,' *Review of Political Economy*,Vol. 24, No. 2, pp. 353–368.

Durlauf, S.N. (2012) 'Complexity, economics, and public policy,' *Politics, Philosophy and Economics,* Vol. 11, No. 1, pp. 45 – 75.

Earl, P. E., and Peng, T.C. (2012) 'Brands of Economics and the Trojan Horse of Pluralism,' *Review of Political Economy*, Vol. 24, No.3, pp. 451 – 467.

Fine, B. (1997) 'The New Revolution in Economics,' *Capital & Class*, No. 21, No.1, pp. 143 – 148.

Fontana, M. (2008) 'The Complexity Approach to Economis: a Paradigm Shift,' CESMEP Working Paper Series No. 01/2008, University of Torino, Torino.

Fontana, G., Gerrard, B. (2006) 'The Future of Post Keynesian economics,' *BNL Quarterly Review*, Vol. 59, No. 236, pp. 49 – 80.

Foster, J. (2005) 'From simplistic to complex systems in economics,' *Cambridge Journal of Economics*, Vol. 29, No. 4, pp. 873 – 892.

Fromm, J. (2004) *The Emergence of Complexity*, Kassel University Press, Kassel.

Hayek, F.A. (1988) The Fatal Conceit. The Errors of Socialism, in Bartley, W.W. (ed.); *The Collected Works of Friedrich August Hayek*, Vol. I, London, Routledge

Heise, A. (2017a) 'Defining Economic Pluralism: Ethical Norm or Scientific Imperative,' *International Journal of Pluralism and Economic Education* (forthcoming).

Heise, A. (2017b) 'Walras' law in the context of pre-analytic visions, in Economic Thought, Vol.6, No.1, pp. 83 - 96

Heise, A., Thieme, S. (2016) 'The Short Rise and Long Fall of Heterodox Economics in Germany after the 1970s: Explorations in a Scientific Field of Power and Struggle,' *Journal of Economic Issues*, Vol. 50, No.4, pp. 1106 – 1130.

Holt, R.P.F., Rosser Jr, J.B., and Colander, D. (2011) 'The Complexity Era in Economics,' *Review of Political Economy*, Vol. 23, No.3, pp. 357 – 369.

Hutton, W. (2001) *The revolution that never was. An assessment of Keynesian economics*, Penguin Books, London.

Jefferson, T., and King, J.E. (2010) 'Can Post Keynesians make better use of behavioral economics?', *Journal of Post Keynesian Economics*, Vol. 33, No. 2, pp. 211-234.

Jo, T.-H. (2011) 'Social Provisioning Process and Socio-Economic Modelling,' *American Journal of Economics and Sociology*, Vol. 70, Issue 5, pp. 1094 -1116.

Katzner, D. (2011) *At the Edge of Camelot. Debating Economics in Turbulent Times*, Oxford University Press, Oxford.

Keynes, J.M. (1933a) 'The Distinction between a Co-operative Economy and an Entrepreneur Economy, in *Collected Writings of John Maynard Keynes*, Moggridge, D. (Ed.),Vol. 29, Macmillan, London, 1979, pp. 76 – 87.

Keynes, J.M. (1933b) 'The Characteristics of an Entrepreneur Economy,' in: *Collected Writings of John Maynard Keynes,* Moggridge, D.(Ed.), Vol. 29, Macmillan, London, 1979, pp. 87 – 101.

Keynes, J.M, (1936) *The General Theoy of Employment, Interest and Money,* MacMillan, London.

Kirman, A. (2010) 'The Economic Crisis is a Crisis for Economic Theory,' *CESIfo Economic Studies*, Vol. 56, No. 4, pp. 498 – 535.

Kirman, A. (2016) 'Complexity and Economic Policy: A Paradigm Shift or a Change in Perspective? A Review Essay on David Colander and Roland Kupers's Complexity and the Art of Public Policy,' *Journal of Economic Literature,* Vol. 52, No. 2, pp. 534 – 572.

Kuhn, T.S. (1962) *The Structure of Scientific Revolutions*, Unviersity of Chicago Press, Chicago.

Laidler, D. (1999) *Fabricating the Keynesian Revolution: Studies of the Inter-War Literature on Money, the Cycle, and Unemployment*, Cambridge University Press, Cambridge.

Lakatos, I. (1976) 'Falsification and the Methodology of Scientific Research Programmes,' in Harding, S.G. (Ed.) *Can Theories be Refuted?,* Kluwer, Dordrecht, pp. 205 – 259.

Lavoie, M. (2014) *Post Keynesian Economics: New Foundations*, Edward Elgar, Cheltenham, UK.

Lawson, T.(2006) 'The Nature of Heterodox Economics,' *Cambridge Journal of Economics*, Vol. 30, No.4, pp. 483 – 507.

Lee, Fred S. (2009) *A History of Heterodox Economics: Challenging the Mainstream in the Twentieh Century*, Routledge, London.

Marglin, S. A. (2010) *The Dismal Science. How Thinking like an Economist Undermines Community,* Harvard University Press, Boston.

Mearman, A. (2012) 'Heterodox Economics' and the problems of classification,' *Journal of Economic Methodology*, Vol. 19, No.4, pp. 407 – 424.

Miller, J. (2012) 'The dismal state of the dismal science,' *Critical Quarterly*, Vol. 54, No.2, pp. 16 – 21.

Perona, E. (2007) 'The Confused State of Complexity Economcs: An Ontological Explanation,' in Salzano, M., and Colander, D. (Eds.) *Complexity Hints for Economic Policy*, Springer, Milano , pp. 33 – 53.

Provost, W.H. Jr. (1986) 'Contingency and Complexity in the Social Theory of Niklas Luhmann,' *International Journal of General Systems*, Vol. 12, No.1, pp. 39 – 53.

Rochon, L-P., Docherty, P. (2012) 'Engagement with the Mainstream in the Future of Post Keynesian Economics,' *Review of Political Economy*, Vol. 24, No.3, pp. 503-518.

Roos, Michael W. M. (2015) 'The macroeconomics of radical uncertainty,' Ruhr Economic Papers, No. 592.

Rosser, J.B. Jr. (1998) 'Complex Dynamics in New Keynesian and Post Keynesian Models,' in: Rotheim, R.J. (Ed.) *New Keynesian Economics/Post Keynesian Alternatives*, Routledge, London, pp. 288 – 302.

Rosser, J.B. Jr. (2006) 'Complex dynamics and Post Keynesian economics,' in Setterfield, M. (Ed.) *Complexity, Endogenous Money and Macroeconomic Theory: Essays in Honour of Basil J. Moore*, Edward Elgar, Cheltenham, pp. 74 – 98.

Rosser, J.B. Jr. (2012) ′Emergence and Complexity in Austrian Economics,‘ *Journal of Economic Behavior and Organization*, Vol. 81, No. 1, pp. 122 – 128

Schmidt, C. M.,aus dem Moore, N. (2010) 'Die Methodendiskussion in den Wirtschafstwissenschaften vor dem Hintergrund der Finanzkrise,‘ in Jens, U., Romahn, H. (Eds.) *Methodenpluralismus in den Wirtschaftswissenschaften,* Metropolis, Marburg, pp. 143-182.

Smith, V. L. (2003) 'Constructivist and Ecological Rationality,' *in Economics*: Frängsmayr, F. (Ed.) *The Nobel Prizes 2002*, Nobel Foundation, Stockholm, pp. 502- 561.

Sraffa, P. (1960) *Production of Commodities by Means of Commodities*, Cambridge University Press, Cambridge.

Vela Velupillai, K. (2007) 'The Impossibility of an Effective Theory of Policy in a Complex Economy,' Salzano, M., and Colander, D. (Eds.) *Complexity hints for economic policy,* Springer, New York.

Nine

The Resilience of Modern Neoclassical Economics – a case study in the light of Ludwik Fleck's 'harmony of deception'*

1. Introduction

Ludwik Fleck's contribution to the sociology and philosophy of science has gone almost unnoticed to the present day (see Sady 2017). Although his ideas about the development of scientific knowledge as a collective effort organised in 'thought collectives' ('*Denkkollektive*') based on shared 'thought styles' ('*Denkstile*') may have been elaborated and honed in Thomas S. Kuhn's works on scientific revolutions and paradigm shifts and those of Imre Lakatos on scientific research programs (srp), Fleck's work is still insightful beyond Kuhn's and Lakatos' contributions, not so much with respect to what triggers scientific progress but rather what impedes the correction of scientific deceptions.

While Kuhn and Lakatos built on the rationality of the scientific community not to follow paradigmatic lines or adhere to scientific research programs defeated by empirical falsification or the proof of logical inconsistency or having entered the 'state of degeneration', Fleck was more concerned with the sociological forces that explain the resilience of ideas and what today we would call 'fake knowledge' even in the face of mounting evidence that does not fit the established wisdom.

In the following, Fleck's philosophy and sociology of science will be briefly outlined in order to establish a 'theory of the resilience of scientific misapprehension'. This theory will be tested against the development of modern neoclassical economics by singling out a case of extreme deviation

* Originally published: Journal of Philosophical Economics, Vol. 13, No.1, 2019

of theoretical prediction from empirical evidence: minimum wages' impact on employment.

2. Ludwik Fleck and the 'harmony of deception'

Ludwik Fleck was convinced that there are no such things as 'objective knowledge' or only 'facts' which constitute a true understandig of the real world. Rather, facts, like knowledge, are always socially constructed in the sense that what we see (as a fact) or know (as 'truth') depends on the way we look at it. And in order to be plainly able to see something when we look at it, we need a 'pre- or proto-idea' ('*Prä- oder Ur-Idee*') which is neither wrong nor false but merely a devise with which to construct reality. Observations and reflections under the influence of such pre- or proto-ideas develop into a 'thought style' (,*Denkstil*') which then can be defined

> *"as (the readiness for) directed perception, with corresponding mental and objective assimilation of what has been so perceived" (Fleck 1979: 99).*

As distinct from the social constructivists, Fleck must not necessarily reject the existence of a unique social reality independent of the observer, but the way the observer sees and explains such a unique social reality always depends on the particular heuristic devices and hermeneutics that constitute a 'thought style'. A social element comes in because a certain 'thought style' can produce 'facts' and 'knowledge' in any meaningful way only if such 'facts' and 'knowledge' are accepted by more than one individual, i.e. a group of people or, more generally, a collective which shares the same way of seeing and explaining: a 'thought collective' ('*Denkkollektiv*').

In order to attribute to a certain 'thought style' the power of generating and developing facts and knowledge that assume scientific status, it must not only be shared by a collective of scientists (which Fleck calls the 'esoteric circle') and laymen accepting the outcome as scientific wisdom (the 'exoteric circle') but must also be stable or last some time. Therefore, the thought collective must develop a certain solidarity to the thought style Fleck calls the 'collective mood' and which can be described as *"an intellectual taste and a notion of what counts as a good result and appropriate path to it"* (von Sass 2016: 75).

The stronger such bonds of solidarity, the stronger the 'thought compulsion' (*'stilgemäßer Denkzwang'*) emanating from it, the more stable a thought style will be. Its flipside is the neglect and rejection of everything – from facts to ideas or theories originating from alternative 'pre- or proto-ideas' – that does not conform to the thought style of the thought collective. This kind of group pressure may be harmless as long as membership of a thought collective is entirely voluntarily (i.e. independent of any social or institutional inducement or pressure) and there are different thought collectives entertaining different thought styles. Yet if a scientific discipline does not allow a plurality of different thought styles but enforces a unitarian-monistic approach de-legitimizing every thought style but one, the likelihood of what Fleck calls ',a harmony of deception' (*'Harmonie der Täuschungen'*)[247] is high.

If tenacity is a necessary pre-condition for thought styles to become powerful in the sense that it creates explanations and narratives which are regarded as scientific truth by both the esoteric and exoteric circles and, indeed, as common knowledge, collective mood and thought compulsion must be effective. Although the collective mood may have very different origins and modes of operation, thought compulsion is similar regardless of thought style:

> *"Once a structurally complete and closed system of opinions consisting of many details and relations has been formed, it offers enduring resistance to anything that contradicts it:[...] (1) A contradiction to the system appears unthinkable. (2) What does not fit into the system remains unseen; (3) alternatively, if it is noticed either it is kept secret or (4) laborious efforts are made to explain an excep-*

[247] Thomas S. Kuhn in his foreword to the English edition of Fleck's *Entstehung und Entwicklung einer wissenschaftlichen Tatsache* (Genesis and Development of a Scientific Fact) calls it "a damaging metaphor, for it reinforces the impression that, in the absence of social pressure, illusion might have been avoided" (Kuhn 1979: X). Actually, if 'absence of social pressure' refers not to the 'thought compulsion' necessary for any thought collective but to the inadmissibility of more than one thought style at a time, the impression appears to be well founded.

> *tion in terms that do not contradict the system. (5) Despite the legitimate claims of contradictory views, one tends to see, describe, or even illustrate those circumstances which corroborate current views and thereby give them substance".* (Fleck 1979: 27)

The more pervasive the collective mood is, the stronger the thought compulsion will be, resulting in a strong resilience of the thought style and, possibly, scientific misapprehention or a 'harmony of deception'. In the following section, the economic discipline will be explored with respect to its collective mood and its thought compulsion by referring to a field in which 'exceptions' or 'anomalies', in Kuhn's terminology, appear to be devastating for the dominant thought style (mainstream neoclassical economics), yet do not trigger a 'thought style transformation' (*Denkstilumwandlungen*) but, if anything, merely 'thought style supplementations' (*Denkstilergänzungen*) or 'thought style extensions' (*Denkstilerweiterung*): labour market economics in general and the introduction of minimum wages in particular.

3. The impact of minimum wages on employment and the dominant 'thought style'

The dominant neoclassical labour market theory is based on the premise that the labour market can basically be analysed in the same way as any other commodity market. That is to say that supply of and demand for labour (services) follow the same utility maximisation prinicples as on any other market: households provide labour (services) according to the optimisation principle of exchanging leisure time (which provides utility, and thus any offer of labour services reducing leisure time implies disutility) for income (which compensates for the loss of utility) up to the point where the disutility of an extra unit of sacrificed leisure time is merely compensated for by the utility of the extra unit of income gained; i.e. marginal disutility of labour supply simply equals the real wage rate as the price of the extra unit of labour supply. In a similar fashion, the microeconomics of firms' demand for labour align the utility of an extra unit of labour with the cost of that extra unit; i.e. the marginal productivity simply equals the real wage rate as the price of the extra unit of labour demand. As the marginal disutility of labour supply is assumed to increase with each unit of labour supplied, the ordinary labour supply curve rises with the real wage rate. And since the labour demand curve falls as the marginal productivity of labour is assumed to fall under the conditions of a 'well-behaved' production function, both curves will intersect at the real wage rate which equalises the marginal productivity of the last unit of labour demanded with the marginal disutility of the last unit of labour supplied – hence we get a cleared labour market at the 'equilibrium wage rate' and full employment in the sense that every unit of labour supplied at the equilibrium wage rate will find employment. Unemployment can only be 'voluntary' in the sense that households may ask a price (real wage rate) for their labour supply which lies above the market-clearing level (i.e. above the marginal productivity of the unit of labour if it were employed additionally) and cannot, therefore, be paid by the firms unless they accept losses (in the short term and bankruptcy in the long run).

This rather technical approach to a very social mechanism follows the dominant thought style ('mainstream economics') of translating any social process in the economic sphere into an exchange procedure in a market place – *the 'pre- or proto-idea' of mainstream economics is thus market exchange in order to increase the welfare of the market participants involved* by using advantages of specialisation ('economies of scope') and by exploiting favourable exchange opportunities based on initial endowments. But 'the market', i.e. market exchange, is not only seen technically as a coordination mechanism (harmonising diverging interests) but also ideologically as a superior device for creating a 'spontaneous order' which reduces social power to symmetrical exchange relations and provides (pareto-)optimal outcomes which can be accepted without the need to determine collective objectives such as a 'common good' or general welfare – here superiority refers to allocative and productive efficiency in comparison to an alternative coordination mechanism such as a central plan. 'The market' and its defence against other coordination mechanisms therefore becomes a constitutive element of mainstream economics not only because it promises superior economic outcomes but also because it is based on the preservation and defence of property rights and, implicitly, a given distribution of wealth (initial endowments). How much the idea of market exchange as the constituent of economic activity analysed by the economics profession permeates the dominant thought style – and thus creates a collective mood of the thought collective – is illustrated by the fact that the object of inquiry is widely dubbed 'market economy'. The classical political economists of the eighteenth and nineteenth centuries used the term 'capitalism' instead, which does not yet convey the message of market exchange as central and definitive to their object of inquiry. Moreover, the centrality of market exchange for analysing and modelling economic activities is strengthened and reinforced by society's attitude towards markets and market outcomes: the more 'market conforming' or 'market oriented' a society and its cultural norms, the stronger the collective mood of the thought collective of scientists in general and of economists in particular – thus establishing a strong thought compulsion which excludes the possibility of any other basic constituent such as power relations (as in Marxian economics) or nominal obligations (as in post-Keynesian economics).[248]

The mandatory tenacity of a thought style based on its 'thought compulsion' may turn it into a 'harmony of deception' if the scientific discipline involved does not allow a plurality of thought styles to coexist. This, again, may be the case when the scientific claim of the discipline is to provide 'truth' in a singular form (and to reject pluralism as relativism) and when thought collectives are in a position to set the methodological, epistemological and, particularily importantly, the ontological standards for the discipline as a whole. This appears to be exactly the case in economics, where a handful of US elite university departments are bestowed with a level of economic, social, institutional and cultural capital (in a Bourdieuian sense) which puts them in a position to play key roles in offering the standards which the peculiar 'market for economic ideas' requests (see Heise 2016). Fourcade/Ollion/Algan (2015: 91) therefore conclude:

[248] Marion Fourcade shows that a market-oriented collective mood is particularily strong in the USA, while in other countries (such as the UK or France) the collective mood is (or, rather, has been) more state-oriented or public-minded: "The American political distrust of centralized political power has a natural corollary in the celebration of the market. [...] The Sherman Act implied that markets are not simply the *structure* of the American economy: they are its *law* (Fourcade 2009: 35 ff.; italics in original).

> *"Economics occupies a unique position among academic disciplines. It is characterized by far-reaching scientific claims linked to the use of formal methods; the tight management of the discipline from the top down; high market demand for services, particularly from powerful and wealthy parties".*

Through institutionalised incentive systems (rankings, journal hierarchies, third-party funding as 'objective' quality measurements), the US market-oriented collective mood has turned into a worldwide thought compulsion which leaves almost no room for other thought styles to flourish (see e.g. Heise/Thieme 2016, Chavance/Labrousse 2018, Corsi/D'Ippoliti/Zacchia 2018).

Notwithstanding the glorification of markets in mainstream economics, its smooth functioning rests on some assumptions which may not necessarily hold in the real world: perfect competition, perfect information and foresight, absence of transaction cost and the absence of political interference. With respect to the labour market, myriads of theories have been put forward on how the real-world refutation of any of these assumptions can explain what appears to be – contrary to the prediction of perfect markets – a common feature of highly developed economies: lasting mass unemployment. Monopoly union, right-to-manage, insider-outsider and NAIRU[249] theories reject the assumption of perfect competition in labour markets, and efficiency wage theories point to the fact that wage contracts are incomplete in the face of imperfect knowledge and information. Job search and menu cost theories refer to positive transaction costs involved in real-world labour markets. The result is always a deviation of the market outcome from market clearing at full employment level due to restrictions either on the demand or on the supply side of the labour market. Moreover, once social policies or legal restrictions render the assumption of the 'absence of political interference' futile, reservation or minimum wages will provide the same explanation for unemployment: the real wage rate turns out to be too high for full employment. In terms of Ludwik Fleck's philosophy, all such 'theories of unemployment' can be seen as thought style supplementations and extensions to the initial 'theory of the non-existence

[249] NAIRU stand for *N*on-*A*ccelerating *I*nflation *R*ate of *U*nemployment.

of involuntary unemployment', yet they remain compatible and commensurable with it[250] and thus rather stabilise the initial thought collective than spark a veritable thought style transformation.

It is in this sense that the minimum wage has become part of almost every textbook on macroeconomics: if it is set at a level above the 'equilibrium wage rate' – and a minimum wage below that level would clearly make no sense – it will cause unemployment (see e.g. Blanchard/Illing 2017: 339; Bofinger 2015: 340; Altmann 2009: 373f.).[251] The obviousness of this result – merely the exact quantity of unemployment remains to be empirically settled – is illustrated by the fact that unemployment on this theoretical basis is typically termed 'minimum wage unemployment' irrespective of what or who determines the minimum wage: it could as much be initiated by the trade unions via encompassing collective bargaining agreements as simply being statutorily set by the law maker.

4. Empirical minimum wage research and the introduction of minimum wages in Germany

Academic economics considers itself to be a 'positive science'; i.e. it claims to theoretically explain what 'is', not what 'should be'. Therefore, theoretical modelling in economics always has to face the reality test of empirical falsificationism: theoretical statements can be accepted as establishing 'truth' as long as they are not rejected by rigorous empirical testing. There is a long tradition in Labour Market Economics of doing exactly this: testing the effects of minimum wages on sectoral and overall employment, (wage) income distribution, and collective bargaining, among other things. With respect to the employment effect of minimum wages, the picture remains perplexing:

[250] As a mainstream referee to a paper of mine once wrote: 'No matter how you look at it, unemployment ultimately always turns out to be a problem of excessively high real wages' – mainstream heuristics does not allow for any other interpretation.

[251] I will concentrate on the German literature – textbooks in this case – only because Germany and the introduction of minimum wages in Germany in 2015 form the case studied in this paper. However, the same is true for the more influential American textbooks; see Dolar (2013).

> *"Economists have conducted hundreds of studies of the employment impact of the minimum wage. Summarizing those studies is a daunting task, but two recent meta-studies analyzing the research conducted since the early 1990s concludes that the minimum wage has little or no discernible effect on the employment prospects of low-wage workers".* (Schmitt 2013: 22)

These findings are in stark contrast to mainstream neoclassical labour market theory exposed above. How does the thought collective (of mainstream economists) react to such an apparent falsification of its thought style? Will we experience a transformation of thought style which brings the ideas back in line with the facts? Or how will the thought compulsion serve to keep the thought style intact? The introduction of statutory minimum wages in Germany in 2015 provides an interesting basis for study. However, before we examine the German case, let us extract potential reactions from a review of the international literature: 1) a common reaction, of course, is simply to ignore contradicting empirical evidence altogether. 2) Many studies avoid addressing the question of overall, economy-wide employment effects by merely focussing on sectoral, i.e. partial impacts. In doing so, they can demonstrate the expected negative employment effects in the very sectors in which sectorial minimum wages were introduced and thus avoid conceding 'exceptions' or 'anomalies'. 3) With the seminal papers of Card/Krueger (1995) and Manning (2003), the common assumption of perfect competition in labour markets has been replaced by the assumption of monopsonistic labour markets, i.e. the idea that regionally, employers may not be faced with competing employers for labour (the 'industry town') or the idea that transaction cost (job search cost, moving cost, loss of firm-specific human capital, etc.) may give employers wage-setting power (pseudo-monopsony) even in the face of complete competition. As smartish as this thought style supplementation is, it is not without problems: truly monopsonistic competition appears to be rather rare in modern advanced economies and, therefore, of only marginal importance. Moreover, to take the argument seriously, the introduction of minimum wages will curtail the wage-setting power of monopsonistic firms and, if we assume ordinary labour supply behaviour, increase employment compared to a situation without a minimum wage. This, again, would not be consonant with empirical evidence. And although the introduction of transaction cost definitely renders the theoretical approach more realistic and explains some limited the wage-setting power of firms, negative employment effects can only be avoided if the minimum wage is set very low indeed: once the minimum wage exceeds the equilibrium wage rate of the least qualified worker by more than the margin given by transaction cost, employment losses would have to be expected. To summarise, the artificiality of the arguments put forward are a clear indicator of the working of thought compulsion: stabilising a thought style confronted with empirical evidence to the contrary.

For long time, minimum wages sparked little attention in German academic economics: the principle of the autonomy of collective bargaining granted to the social partners evoked negative responses on the part of employers' organisations to the same degree as trade unions whenever the topic of introducing minimum wages arose on the political agenda. It was only from the early 2000s onwards, when it became ever more apparent that collective bargaining agreements no longer covered most employees at the lower end of the wage scale and (wage) income inequality and poverty rates increased markedly, that minimum wages became more topical. The discussion was fuelled mainly by the big policy-oriented German think tanks such as the *ifo-Institut* or the *Deutsche Institut für Wirtschaftsforschung (DIW)* and official counselling institutions such as the *Institut für Arbeitsmarkt- und Berufsforschung (IAB)* of the German Labour Agency and the *Sachverständigenrat* (SVR – Council of Economic Experts).

The latter adressed the question of minimum wages as early as 2006, when the mainstream majority of experts[252] clearly rejected the introduction of a minimum wage in Germany on the basis of expected negative employment effects as predicted by the ordinary neoclassical labour market theory. They did mention empirical evidence to the contrary, yet refused to accept such evidence was of guiding importance for Germany, since it was

---

[252] The German council of economic experts (SVR) comprises 5 'economic experts' (mainly economics professors). 3 of them are nominated by the German government, one is nominated by the German employers' organisation and one is nominated by the German trade unions. In most cases, 3 + 1 experts are from a mainstream neoclassical background while 1 (the trade union's nominee) has a more Keynesian background.

allegedly based on economies (mainly the USA and the UK) which are different from the German economy and where labour markets are more flexible than in Germany (see Sachverständigenrat 2006: 401ff.). However, they failed to explain why these qualifications matter, but mention labour market monopsony as a potential argument in favour of minimum wages. Again, they rejected this approach due to the argument outlined above: only very low minimum wages (much lower than the mooted hourly minimum wage of €7.50) could claim neutral or even positive employment effects. Interestingly, in a minority votum, one expert pointed to empirical evidence to the contrary in order to back his pro-minimum wage position. Yet he made no effort to fortify his adversarial position with a theoretical argument. In the editorial revision of his textbook on macroeconomics (Bofinger 2015: 159ff.), this expert added the monopsony model of labour markets to justify minimum wages – the earlier editions only mentioned mainstream minimum wage unemployment. Unfortunately, he neither bothered to explain the difference between theoretical prediction (increase in employment) and empirical evidence (neutral employment effect) nor did he make any effort to prove the existence of monopsonistic labour markets in Germany. When the government finally decided to introduce a minimum wage in 2015, the Council of Economic Experts simply replicated its earlier judgment in its 2013 and 2014 annual reports (see Sachverständigenrat 2013; Sachverständigenrat 2014).

The *ifo-Institut* was even more explicit in its compliance to the ordinary mainstream labour market approach by resorting to citing the alleged analogy between apple and car markets on the one hand and labour markets on the other (see Ragnitz/Thum 2008): if the price is too high, there will be a quantity reaction, i.e. if the minium wage is set above the equilibrium wage rate, employment will fall and unemployment will rise – merely the strength of this reaction may be questionable. The higher the employment elasticity of the (real) wage rate, the higher the negative impact will be. According to the estimates used by the *ifo-Institut*, even low minimum wages will cause considerable employment losses in Germany. The study mentions conflicting empirical evidence only in passing and rejects it outright by simply claiming a lack of suitable accuracy for Germany.

In a common declaration of the six publicly financed economic think tanks[253] and the research institut of the German employers' organisation *Institut der deutschen Wirtschaft (IW)* and the privately funded *Institut für die Zukunft der Arbeit* (*IZA*) (see DIW et al. 2008), the introduction of a minimum wage is rejected on the grounds that it will damage employment to a considerable extent. Again, empirical evidence to the contrary is played down and other theoretical constructions such as the monopsonistic labour market even entirely ignored.

The *Institut für Arbeitsmarkt- und Berufsforschung (IAB)* of the German Labour Agency is the only major research institute in Germany that was slightly less critical of the introduction of a statutory minimum wage (see Möller/König 2008). However, this was not due to different theoretical reasoning but simply to a different weighting of empirical evidence against theoretical prediction – highlighting the applied research focus of the institute. The trick was to point to the inconclusive empirical evidence and to claim that the theoretical prediction is also inconclusive once the ordinary neoclassical (competitive) labour market model is supplemented by a monopsonistic labour market model.[254] Moreover, it was argued that as long as the minimum wage is kept low – close to the bottom end of the wage scale – negative employment effects can be contained. Clearly, in substance there is not much difference to the lines of argument pursued by the critics of a minimum wage.

After the political debate culminated – despite the strong resistance from German academic economics – in the resolution to finally introduce a statutory minimum wage in Germany in 2015, Knabe et al. (2014) provided probably the most comprehensive study on the potential employment effects. They conclude:

> *"The introduction of a comprehensive, statutory minimum wage of € 8.50is a big experiment which entails high social*

[253] *Deutsches Institut für Wirtschaftsforschung (DIW), ifo-Institut, Hamburger Weltwirtschaftsarchiv (HWWA), Rheinisch-Westfälisches Institut für Wirtschaftsforschung (RWI), Institut für Weltwirtschaft (IfW) and Institut für Wirtschaftsforschung Halle (IWH).*

[254] Of course, conflicting theoretical predictions are translated into inconclusiveness of theoretical prediction – which is clearly not the same thing.

risks. The objective of this review article is to evaluate these risks on the basis of existing theoretical and empirical literature. The result is that neither theoretical research nor empirical work from other countries provide the all-clear.

Arguments for a neglible effect on employment all rest without exception on theoretical and empirical work on moderate minimum wage increases. Up to 2015, for example, presumably 1.1 million employees will earn less than 5 euros per hour. For these people, the introduction of a minimum wage will cause their wages to incease by 70 percent and more and thus these arguments cannot be applied". (Knabe 2014: my translation)

They estimate considerable job losses in Germany of 910,717 on the basis of a standard neoclassical model and, interestingly, an only marginally lower figure of 425,676 if a monopsonistic labour market is assumed.[255] The former result is entirely in line with exactly the same theoretical reasoning which empirical evidence has not supported. The latter result appears to contradict the monopsony model; however, the monopsony model's prediction of an overall gain in employment rests on the assumption of very low minimum wages. Once this assumption is dropped, job losses – although lower in number – are inevitable even under (pseudo-)monopsonistic conditions. And it is precisely this argumentative turn – that the minimum wage of € 8.50 to be introduced statutorily in Germany in 2015 is far too high for positive or neutral employment effects – which is also directed against the empirical literature: the wage increase in many sectors is far higher than has ever been empirically tested and therefore empirical evidence to the contrary is considered inappropriate for the German case.

Summarising the debate, we find all the elements of "enduring resistance" (Fleck 1979: 27) predicted by Ludwik Fleck to anything that contradicts the considerable negative effects of such a regulatory step: (1) For most studies and their authors, a contradiction of the outcome of mainstream

[255] Other studies suggest quite similar negative employment effects: Henzel/Engelhardt (2014) expect job losses of 857,000, Arni et al. (2014) estimate a decline in employment of 570,000 – differences are basically due to different assumptions about the wage elasticity of labour demand.

neoclassical labour market theory with respect to wage setting above the equilibrium wage rate is simply unthinkable! (2) Although scientific credibility and integrity precludes ignoring conflicting theoretical and empirical evidence outright ('not see or keep secret' as Fleck puts it),[256] (3) in most cases it is either played down or rejected as not appropriate for the case under investigation, i.e. "laborious efforts are made to explain an exception" (Fleck 1979: 27). (4) Finally, even those studies that appear not to be in line with the predictions of the mainstream thought collective – i.e. those that favour minimum wages – do not refute the dominant thought style altogether but, rather, add ideas to or change assumptions of that dominant thought style, thereby triggering 'thought style supplementations' or 'thought style extensions'. It should be noted that such 'supplementations' and 'extensions' have been easily re-integrated into the original 'thought style' by claiming their limited validity and commensurability with it[257].

5. 'Thought compulsion' and scientific misapprehension – a conclusion

It has been argued in this paper that – on the basis of the sociology and philosophy of science of Ludwik Fleck – every thought collective needs to create a certain thought compulsion in order to (temporarily) stabilise. However, there is a trade-off between the stability of a thought collective and the apprehensiveness of a thought style in that the inherent rebuttal of theoretical and empirical evidence to the contrary may eventually become a 'harmony in deception' and thus may harm scientific progress.

The introduction of a statutory minimum wage in Germany in 2015 and the preceding academic discussion reveal the resilience of mainstream la-

---

[256] Nevertheless, the joint appeal of the presidents and directors of the important German economic think tanks, admittedly not a scientific document, does not even bother to mention the construction of a monopsonistic labour market as a potential theoretical counterargument; see DIW et al. (2008).

[257] It should also be noted that there were (and are) alternative approaches available which would constitute veritable ‚thought style transformations‘ (see e.g.Herr/Kazandziska 2011; Herr/Kazandziska/Mahnkopf-Praprotnik 2009) – however, they did not receive any attention and remained entirely marginalised.

bour market theory based on a thought compulsion of the thought collective: although there was abundant empirical evidence demonstrating that neither the standard (competitive) labour market model nor the peculiar approach of a (pseudo)monopsontistic labour market can be brought in line with real-world labour market outcomes in the face of minimum wages, the mainstream academic community in Germany adhered to those models and, at least in its vast majority, fervently rejected minimum wages as being economically harmful. Only a small minority supported minimum wage legislation – however this was not based on a rejection of the dominant 'thought style' but on a rather unconvincing bias towards empirical evidence (and, possibly, on ideological motivations).

The political actors in Germany did not follow the recommendations of the majority position and thus allowed an economic (and, of course, social) experiment: will Germany suffer a heavy blow to employment (the standard labour market model and monopsony labour market model in the interpretation of the majority of mainstream economists) or will employment even rise (as in the interpretation of the monopsony model by a minority of mainstream economists)? Or will the effect be rather negligible, as international empirical evidence suggests – putting the accuracy of the dominant thought style in doubt?

Without exception, all studies on the effects of the introduction of a statutory minimum wage on employment in Germany with their different methods – the minimum wage act codified research to be conducted concomitantly – conclude that overall employment effects are negligible (and more reliably so the more time has elapsed since the introduction of minimum wages; see e.g. Mindestlohnkommission 2018, Bossler/Möller 2018, Caliendo et al. 2017, Bonin et al. 2018, Heise/Pusch 2018; Zilius/Bruttel 2018).[258] There appears to be a negative impact on so-called 'mini-jobs'[259] and more so in those branches that are more exposed to the minimum wage than the average, but this seems to be almost entirely compensated for by an increase in regular jobs ('*sozialversicherungspflichtige Arbeitsplätze*').

[258] Interestingly, most of these studies are provided by the very economic think tanks that rigorously opposed a minimum wage upon the advent of such legislation.

[259] These are jobs in which employees do not earn more than € 450 per month and are exempt from social insurance contributions.

Certainly, unemployment has not increased due to minimum wages but there have been a slight (and desired) shift of jobs from precarious to 'normal' and a slight sectoral change.

Taking these results seriously, we must consider not only neoclassical labour market theory to be 'in crisis' (to borrow Kuhn's terminology) but also neoclassical (market) theory in general, since most neoclassical economists claim labour markets and other commodity and factor markets to be similar with respect to their 'laws of motion'. Therefore, if the ordinary price–quantity correlations and causalities in labour markets appear not to work, why should they nevertheless work in other markets? It will be interesting to see whether and how[260] mainstream neoclassical (labour) market theory manages to survive this blow to its very foundations as the dominant thought style.

---

[260] One line of defence appears to be to point to other 'adjustment channels' of firms rather than quantity reactions: e.g. price or productivity changes (see e.g. Zilius/Bruttel 2018: 716 f., Schmitt 2013: 11ff.). However, the dubious nature of the logical rigour of such 'adjustment channels' suggests another set of 'laborious efforts to explain an exception'.

References

Altmann, J. (2009); Volkswirtschaftslehre (7th edition), Stuttgart

Arni, P. et al. (2014); Der gesetzliche Mindestlohn in Deutschland: Einsichten und Handlungsempfehlungen aus der Evaluationsforschung; in: Schmollers Jahrbuch, Vol. 134, No. 2, pp. 149–182

Blanchard, O., Illing, G. (2017); Makroökonomie (7th edition), Hallbergmoos

Bofinger, P. (2015); Grundzüge der Volkswirtschaftslehre. Eine Einführung in die Wissenschaft von Märkten (4th edition), Hallbergmoos

Bonin, H. et al. (2018); Auswirkungen des gesetzlichen Mindestlohns auf Beschäftigung, Arbeitszeit und Arbeitslosigkeit. Studie im Auftrag der Mindestlohnkommission, Bonn/Potsdam/Berlin

Bossler, M., Möller, J. (2018); Auswirkungen des gesetzlichen Mindestlohns, IAB-Stellungnahme 1/2018, Nürnberg

Caliendo, M. et al. (2017); The Short-Run Effects of the German Minimum Wage Reform, SOEP Papers 950, Berlin

Card, D.E., Krueger, Alan B. (1995); Myth and Measurment: The New Economics of the Minimum Wage, Princeton

Chavance, B., Labrousse, A. (2018): Institutions and 'Science': The Contest about Pluralism in Economics in France; in: Review of Political Economy, forthcoming

Corsi, M., D'Ippoliti, C., Zacchia, G. (2018): A Case Study of Pluralism in Economics: The Heterodox Glass Ceiling in Italy, in: Review of Political Economy, forthcoming

DIW et al. (2008); Gemeinsamer Aufruf der Präsidenten und Direktoren der Wirtschaftsforschungsinstitute vom 12. März 2008; in: ifo Schnelldienst, Vol. 61, No.6, pp. 3–4

Dolar, V. (2013); The treatment of minimum wages in undergratuate economic textbooks revisited; in: International Journal of Pluralism and Economic education; Vol. 4, No.2, pp. 157 - 182

Fleck, L. (1979); Genesis and Development of a Scientific Fact, Chicago

Fourcade, M. (2009); Economists and Societies. Discipline and Profession in the United States, Britain and France, 1890s to 1990s, Princeton

Fourcade, M., Ollion, E., Algan, Y. (2015); The Superiority of Economists; in: Journal of Economic Perspectives, Vol. 29, No.1, pp. 89–114

Heise, A. (2016); Why has economics turned out this way? A socio-economic note on the explanation of monism in economics; in: The Journal of Philosophical Economics, Vol. X, Issue 1, pp. 81–101

Heise, A., Thieme, S. (2016); The Short Rise and Long Fall of Heterodox Economics in Germany After the 1970s: Explorations in a Scientific Field of Power and Struggle; in: Journal of Economic Issues, Vol. 50, No. 4, pp. 1105–1130

Heise, A., Pusch, T. (2018); Introducing Minimum Wages in Germany Employment Effects in a Post Keynesian Perspective; ZÖSS Discussion Paper No. 68, University of Hamburg

Henzel, S.R., Engelhardt, K. (2014): Arbeitsmarkteffekte des flächendeckenden Mindestlohns in Deutschland– eine Sensitivitätsanalyse,in: ifo Schnelldienst Vol. 67, No. 10, pp. 23–29

Herr, H., Kazandziska, M. (2011): Principles of minimum wage policy : economics, institutions and recommendations; Global Labour University working papers ; No.11

Herr, H., Kazandziska, M., Mahnkopf-Praprotnik (2009): The theoretical debate about minimum wages; Global Labor University working papers No. 6

Knabe, A., Schöb, R., Thum, M. (2014); Der flächendeckende Mindestlohn; in: Perspektiven der Wirtschaftspolitik, Vol. 15, No.2, pp. 133–157

Kuhn, T.S. (1979); Foreword; in: Fleck, L.; Genesis and Development of a Scienfic Fact; edited by Trenn, T.J., Merton, R.K., Chicago/London

Manning, A. (2003); Monopsony in Motion. Imperfect Competition in Labor Markets, Princeton

Möller, J., König, M. (2008); Ein Plädoyer für Mindestlöhne mit Augenmaß; in: ifo Schnelldienst, Vol. 61, No.6, pp. 13–16

Ragnitz, J., Thum, M. (2008); Beschäftigungswirkungen von Mindestlöhnen – eine Erläuterung zu den Berechnungen des ifo-Instituts; in: ifo Schnelldienst, 61. Jg., No.1, pp. 16–20

Sachverständigenrat (2006); Widerstreitende Interessen - ungenutzte Chance, Jahresgutachten 2006/07, Wiesbaden

Sachverständigenrat (2013); Gegen eine rückwärtsgewandte Wirtschaftspolitik, Jahresgutachten 2013/14, Wiesbaden

Sachverständigenrat (2014); Mehr Vertrauen in Marktprozesse, Jahresgutachten 2014/15, Wiesbaden

Sady, W. (2017); 'Ludwik Fleck'; in: Zalta, E.N. (ed.); The Standard Encyclopedia of Philosophy; URL=https://plato.stanford.edu/archives/fall2017/entries/fleck/

Schmitt, J. (2013); Why Does the Minimum Wage Have No Discernible Effect on Employment?, CEPR Reports and Issue Briefs No.4, Washington

von Sass, H. (2016); For your eyes only: Transcendental pragmatism in Ludwik Fleck; in: Transversal – International Journal for the Historiography of Science, Vol. 1, pp. 72–78

Zilius, J., Bruttel, O. (2018); Auwirkungen des gesetzlichen Mindestlohns – Bilanz nach fast 4 Jahren; in: Wirtschaftsdienst, Vol. 98, No.10, pp. 711–717

In der Reihe ‚Studien zur Staatswissenschaft – Studies in Economic Governance' sind bisher erschienen:

Band 1: Arne Heise; Economic Governance and Employment. Policy, Polity and Politics of Economic Rise and Decline, 2008

Band 2: Matthias Kroll; Monetäre Stabilität und die Finanzierung von Staatsdefiziten durch Zentralbankkredite bei endogener Geldmenge, 2008

Band 3: Toralf Pusch; Policy Games. Die Interaktion von Lohn-, Geld- und Fiskalpolitik im Lichte unkooperativer Spieltheorie, 2009

Band 4: Arne Heise, Einführung in die Wirtdschaftspolitik. Grundlagen, Institutionen, Paradigmen, 2010

Band 5: Arne Heise; Das Ende der SPD … …und ihr Neuanfang, 2012

Band 6: Martin, Sauber; Komparativer Vorteil, Währungskonkurrenz und Entwicklung: Eine monetärkeynesianische Perspektive, 2012

Band 7: Selda Ulutas Aydogan; Tirkish Science, Technology and Inovation Policy for Economic Development within the Context of European Integration, 2015

Band 8: Arne Heise; Europa. Gut. Gestalten. Die europäische Wirtschaftsarchitektur – Realitäten und Alternativen, 2015

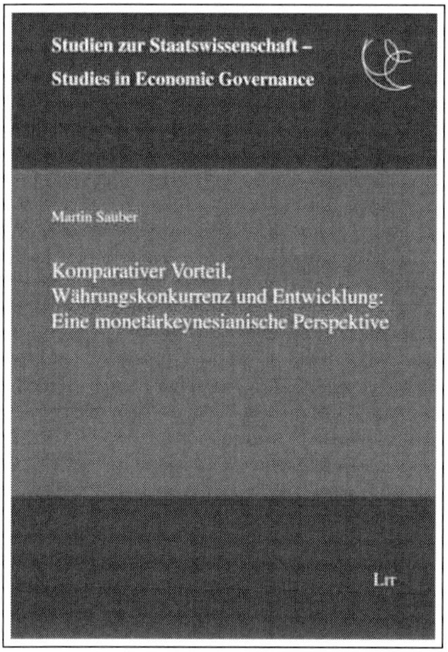

Martin Sauber
Komparativer Vorteil, Währungskonkurrenz und Entwicklung: Eine monetärkeynesianische Perspektive
Der dem Buch zugrundeliegende Forschungsbedarf ergibt sich aus der allgemeinen entwicklungstheoretischen Fragestellung und dem Theorem der komparativen Vorteile in der Außenhandelstheorie. Mit einer vermögensmarkttheoretischen Perspektive auf den komparativen Vorteil, und der monetären Integration von Struktur in eine makroökonomische, (monetär-) keynesianische Entwicklungstheorie für offene, geldwirtschaftliche Länder schließt das hier vorgestellte Projekt eine Forschungslücke und leistet einen Beitrag für die notwendige Debatte um die Relevanz des Agrarsektors für die Entwicklung.
Bd. 6, 2012, 376 S., 29,90 €, br., ISBN 978-3-643-11524-9

Arne Heise
Das Ende der SPD...
... und ihr Neuanfang
Die Sozialdemokratische Partei Deutschlands steht gewiss vor ihrer größten Herausforderung zumindest seit Bestehen der Bundesrepublik: Wird sie als „linke" Volkspartei weiterhin in der Lage sein, breite Bevölkerungskreise anzusprechen und dazu bewegen können, ihr die Stimme zu geben? Oder muss sich die SPD daran gewöhnen, die allenfalls größte der kleinen Sparten- oder Sonderinteressenparteien zu sein, die auf Dauer kaum mehr als ein Viertel der jeweils abgegebenen Stimmen auf sich vereinen kann und deren Machtperspektive allenfalls als gleichberechtigter Partner in einer Mehrparteien-Konstellation zu sehen wäre.
Bd. 5, 2012, 176 S., 14,90 €, br., ISBN 978-3-643-11515-7

Arne Heise
Einführung in die Wirtschaftspolitik
Grundlagen, Institutionen, Paradigmen
Bd. 4, 2010, 560 S., 29,90 €, br., ISBN 978-3-643-10638-4

LIT Verlag Berlin – Münster – Wien – Zürich – London
Auslieferung Deutschland / Österreich / Schweiz: siehe Impressumsseite

Toralf Pusch
Policy games
Die Interaktion von Lohn-, Geld- und Fiskalpolitik im Lichte der unkooperativen Spieltheorie

In der Wirtschaftswissenschaft gewinnt die Erkenntnis zunehmend an Bedeutung, dass wirtschaftspolitische Akteure zum eigenen Vorteil kooperieren sollten, dies aus Eigenrationalität aber nicht tun werden. Mit dem postkeynesianischen Marktkonstellationsansatz als Grundlage lassen sich spieltheoretische Untersuchungen über die Voraussetzungen und das Aussehen derartiger (Nicht-) Kooperationskonstellationen vornehmen. Nach dem sich abzeichnenden Ende der „Nach-Keynes-Dominanz" der „Neuen Klassischen Makroökonomie" greift die Arbeit daher ein ungemein wichtiges Thema auf.

Bd. 3, 2009, 192 S., 24,90 €, br., ISBN 978-3-643-90005-0

Matthias Kroll
Monetäre Stabilität und die Finanzierung von Staatsdefiziten durch Zentralbankkredite bei endogener Geldmenge

Die Frage, ob ein Staat bei seiner eigenen Zentralbank Mittel zur Haushaltsfinanzierung aufnehmen sollte, galt lange als negativ beantwortet. Zu groß schien das inflationäre Risiko zusätzlicher Geldschöpfung. In Anbetracht, der aus den Finanzierungsnöten resultierenden Glaubwürdigkeitsverluste der meisten demokratisch legitimierten Regierungen, ist die Frage aber erneut zu untersuchen. In dieser Arbeit soll gezeigt werden, dass unter den Bedingungen der real existierenden Geldschöpfungsprozesse aus einem Zentralbankkredit an den Staat weder eine überschüssige Geldmenge noch Inflation drohen muss.

Bd. 2, 2008, 184 S., 24,90 €, br., ISBN 978-3-8258-1256-0

Arne Heise
Economic Governance and Employment
Policy, Polity and Politics of Economic Rise and Decline

vol. 1, 2008, 240 pp., 24,90 €, pb., ISBN 978-3-8258-0974-4

LIT Verlag Berlin – Münster – Wien – Zürich – London
Auslieferung Deutschland / Österreich / Schweiz: siehe Impressumsseite